To Dick & Willy

Welcome to my "crazy"
world of "show-biz"

Best Wishes,

Vincent

10/20/82

"SHOW-BUSINESS" IS TWO WORDS

or... What to do while waiting
for your options to be ...dropped!

"Show-Business" Is Two Words

by
Bob Vincent

MAIN TRACK PUBLICATIONS

12435 VENTURA COURT • STUDIO CITY, CALIFORNIA 91604

Library of Congress Catalog Number TXu10-020
© 1979 by Main Track Publications
Studio City, Callifornia
ISBN Number 0-933866-00-3
Published in 1979
Printed in the United States of America.

The Determining Sound of The Group, 91
Salary Split, 96
Types of Lounge Groups, 100
Canned "Disco" Dance Music, 103
Pacing of Shows and Dance Sets, 106
Comedy Material, 108
Rehearsals, 109
Costumes, 111
Pictures & Publicity (Groups), 112
Relationship With Agent, 114
Personal Managers (Groups), 120
Traveling Wives & Families, 121
Relationship With the Owner, 125
Meet The Customers, 128
New Material-Trade Magazines, 130
Recording The Group, 131
Audience Reaction, 133
Showy-Dance Music, 134
Keeping Your Personnel Intact, 136
CHAPTER 7 — Las Vegas — Reno —
                   Lake Tahoe — Atlantic City 138
The Forty's & Fifty's, 140
Diminishing Supply of Stars, 142
Country & Western "Cross-Overs," 144
What Changed The Lounge Business, 145
Good Old Days!, 147
Note to Owners & Operators, 149
CHAPTER 8 — Agents & Personal Managers 150
The Difference Between Agents & Personal Managers, 152
Jack Benny-Irving Fein, 154
Two Types of Agents, 157
Qualifications of an Agent, 158
What It Takes To Be A Good Agent, 162
Major Riddle, 166
CHAPTER 9 — Hotel and Club Owners & Managers 170
Owners & Architects, 173

Knowledge of Show-Business, 174
Buying Of Entertainment, 176
Know What Policy You Want, 177
Who's Going To Buy The Entertainment?, 178
Contracts, 179
Playing Semi-Name Acts, 182
Attitude Towards Entertainers, 183
Advertising & Publicity, 190
Expanding Lounge Entertainment Policy, 192
Separating Food & Beverage Departments, 193
Beverage and Entertainment Directors, 194
CHAPTER 10 — Architects & Interior Designers 196
Acoustics, 198
Uncontrollable & Controllable Sound, 200
Establish Entertainment Policy, 201
Physical Layout of Room, 202
Stage Type & Size, 203
Sound Equipment, 204
Sound & Spotlighting, 205
Sound & Spotlighting Schematic, 207, 208
Artist Domination of Audience, 209
CHAPTER 11 — Fairs & Expositions 212
First 50 Years, 214
Contemporary Artists, 216
Who Buys The Entertainment?, 216
Artists Material For Fairs, 220
Western Washington Fair, 220
Revamp Sound & Lighting, 222
Sound & Lighting Schematic, 223-227
Klondike Days-Edmonton, Canada, 228
Central Washington Fair, 230
Free Acts, 232
CHAPTER 12 — Musicians Unions 234
Big Band Days, 236
Early Administrative Problems—A.F. of M., 237

Advent of Lounge Groups, 238
Taxation Problems, 239
National Association of Orchestra Leaders, 240
Allied Musicians Union, 240
Right To Work States, 241
Taft-Hartley Act — Landrum-Griffin Act, 241
National Labor Relations Board, 242
Excessively High Minimum Scales, 243
Advent of "Rock & Roll," 244
Early Attitude Towards "Rock & Roll," — A.F. of M., 246
Goodwill Gestures Towards Members — A.F. of M., 248
Civil Laws-Regulation, 249
International Theatrical Agencies Association, 249
Recommendations for A.F. of M., 250
Summary, 251
CHAPTER 13 — International Theatrical Agencies Association   252
Founding Fathers, 255
First Officers, 255
Major Irritations, 255
Meetings With A.F. of M., 257
Article 25 — A.F. of M., 258
Code of Ethics Adopted, 259
Canadian Agencies, 259
Canadian-American Tax Problems, 260
New Agreement with A.F. of M., 261
Agents As Independent Brokers, 262
CHAPTER 14 — Heads or Tales 264
Ed Sullivan — Frank Sinatra, Jr., 266
"Gary Moore T.V. Show" and "I've Got A Secret," 268
Jayne Mansfield — "I've Got A Secret," 270
Judy Garland — Leighton Noble, 272
Lena Horne, 274
Julius J. (Bookie) Levin — "Super Agent," 275
CHAPTER 15 — Author's Hopes For The Future 282
INDEX 288

Preface

There's no doubt that sex between two consenting adults can be exhilarating, but intercourse between a performer and an audience, including three or four climaxes, is *just* as satisfying an experience to a hungry performer, and the exhilaration and headiness is just as satisfying to the audience.

The purpose in writing this book is to explain the ways a performer can achieve these "climaxes." If you do not bring each audience to a climax at least once or twice during each show, you have only "diddled" them, and left them with an unsatisfied feeling. As a result, you have not fulfilled the *real reason* you were on stage.

I relate the satisfying of the audience to sexual intercourse, because both relationships must be tender, very thorough, and totally satisfying to both parties. To achieve this, you must be in a "one-on-one" relationship with each member of the audience from the moment you walk on stage, until you leave. If you want to be a successful performer you should not only read this book, but commit it to memory, and make it your daily bible. I can assure you that without a consistent personal contact with your audience, you will never become a true solid performer. That doesn't mean you won't reach stardom in some form or other, because there are many artists who get a hit record, and have a momentary degree of success. I've seen many of them come and go in my 35 years in this wonderful, crazy business. The only way to continue your stardom is *also* to become a consistently solid performer.

On the surface, the world of entertainment appears to be simple and just a lot of fun. Underneath all of this fun, and the thing that makes it work, is the marriage of a lot of tangible and intangible elements, so that the performer who delivers "the word," is able to transmit the intangible "feeling" and "meaning" of the word to his audience without any distortion of his intent. In this manner the audience will have the proper emotional "reaction" to his "action." This is basically what entertainment, — mass motivation — is all about.

In this book, I will attempt to illustrate the basic methods

1

whereby performers can more readily, with consistency, make the connection with the audience. I will break down both the "show" and the 'business" aspects of this word. You will more clearly understand why this is *not one word,* and why it is absolutely necessary that you know both sides of the coin, in order for you to become successful in this most fascinating form of communication.

I will not only cover the artistic and business end of showbiz, but I will also cover such contributing factors as acoustics, sound, lighting, architectural and interior design, stage size and location, and how to deal with club owners, hotel managers, entertainment directors, and musicians unions.

Besides night clubs, I also cover the various areas of "live" entertainment such as fairs and expositions, concerts, gambling casinos, night clubs, and the cocktail lounges.

Throughout this book you will hear me repeat one word over and over again — *honesty.* This is the most important ingredient you *must* have in order to establish a one-on-one relationship with your audience.

—Bob Vincent

About the Author

Bob Vincent, born Vincent Cernuto, has paid his dues in "show-business." As a youth he sang constantly, and had a great love of music. By the time he was a sixteen-year-old, in high school in Detroit, Michigan he was singing with the Western High School dance band. During these years, 1935 and 1936, he also played fourth tenor sax in the band.

During his senior year in high school, he auditioned for a local radio show in Detroit, called "The Happy Hour Club." He became a regular on the show, along with such other future stars as Amos Jacobs (later known as Danny Thomas) Johnny Desmond, Art Mooney, Danny O'Neal, Bob Chester and a few others. Besides singing on the radio show two or three times weekly, some of the members of the show were hired (for $15.00 per weekend) to perform in the local neighborhood theatres around Detroit.

Danny Thomas was often the emcee while Bob Vincent, and a girl singer named Rosemarie Mandella, now Mrs. Danny Thomas, made up the show. They were accompanied by piano, drums, and violin. These appearances caused Bob Vincent to realize, for the first time, that he had a natural ability to get in a one-on-one relationship with the audience.

Following graduation from high school, Bob entered Wayne State University in Detroit, and became a member of a college radio show called "Saddle Shoes and Swing." This was in 1937, the jazz era. While in his first year in college, he entered an amateur singing contest at the Grand Terrace Ballroom with Lorry Clark's Orchestra and won a two-week paid engagement with the band. This engagement crystallized his love for music and show business, and he quit college to devote all his time to playing and singing. The next few years, Bob Vincent sang and played with every band in Detroit and finally formed his own orchestra. But just as he began to get a considerable amount of local notoriety the Second World War began.

After many physical examinations for the army, which he failed because of very poor eyesight, he went to Flint, Michigan, and was hired by A-C Spark Plug Inc., to work as a stock

3

chaser for the war effort. Still, he couldn't stop playing and singing, so he formed a big dance band and played weekends around Flint. He explained to his superintendent that the day the war was over, he would quit. Sure enough, when that day arrived, he left Flint, Michigan and headed for the big city — New York.

Within one month Bob Vincent landed a job playing at Glen Island Casino in New Rochelle, New York, with Shorty Sherock and his Orchestra. The band played at Glen Island for a whole summer season, during which time they broadcasted coast to coast over all the networks — CBS, NBC, Mutual, and some short wave broadcasts to South America. Bob Vincent's voice and name was becoming known all over the country.

Bob decided to leave the band to spend more time in New

Al Trace and the Silly Symphonists

Bob Vincent

York City after a year with Shorty. He got a job singing with a small band called, "Al Trace and the Silly Symphonists." This was a small dance band of nine men and a girl singer who, incidentally, was Toni Arden. Bob, not only sang, but this was the first experience he had in getting laughs. The band did a lot of comedy bits, *ala* Spike Jones, and during this stay in the Dixie Hotel in New York the band had a hit record called "Mairzy Doats."

Following the record hit, Al Trace was booked into the

5

Blackhawk Restaurant in Chicago for a long engagement. Just before leaving New York for Chicago, the band with Bob Vincent doing the singing, recorded a tune called "You Call Everybody Darlin'." Over a million records were sold on this song in 1947.

In quick succession came many important engagements: The Chicago Theatre, Loews State Theatre in New York City, many appearances on the NBC Paul Whiteman network radio show, many records on Columbia, Decca, Manor, Regency, and over one hundred Langworth transcriptions.

Now that Bob Vincent was established, he decided to leave Al Trace and try to make his way as a solo singer. After about three years of clubs, hotels, more records, and unfortunately, no more hits, Bob decided to settle down. He took a job as an agent with Mutual Entertainment Agency Inc., of Chicago, specializing in talent development. It was during this next 10 years that Bob booked and helped to develop many young musicians and entertainers, two of which were Wayne Newton, and Kaye Stevens.

In 1962, because of the considerable amount of business that Mutual Entertainment Agency was doing in Reno and Lake Tahoe, Nevada, Bob came to the attention of Bill Harrah and was offered the position of Entertainment Director for the entire Harrah's operation.

For the next three years, Bob Vincent had the opportunity to develop his ability as a producer and stager of every superstar in the business. In the South Shore Room at Lake Tahoe, Bob presented such stars as Harry Belafonte, Judy Garland, Andy Griffith, Sammy Davis, Jr., Danny Thomas, Barbra Streisand, Lawrence Welk, Dean Martin, Red Skelton, Jack Benny, George Burns, Bill Cosby, Rich Little, Mills Brothers, Phyllis Diller, Liberace, Ed Sullivan, Phil Harris, Jack Soo, Donald O'Connor, Kay Starr, Teresa Brewer, Nat King Cole, Carol Channing, Robert Goulet, Wayne Newton, Bobby Darin, Jim Nabors, Don Knotts, Jerry Lewis, Louis Prima, Earl Grant, Sandler & Young, Andy Williams, The Osmonds, Harry James, Tennessee Ernie Ford, and Tony Martin-Cyd Charisse.

In addition to staging the above artists, Bob Vincent also presented, and coordinated, several television shows on the South Shore Room stage; including the "Garry Moore Show," featuring Carol Burnett and Allen King, the "Tennessee Ernie Ford" show, and "I've Got A Secret."

In addition to presenting superstars during his three-year tenure, Bob also produced, with various choreographers, such as Dorothy Dorbin, Barry Ashton, and Moro-Landis, a production line of 16 girls. A new number had to be produced every two to three weeks.

As you can visualize, with all of this vast experience, Bob had the opportunity to observe how all of the great stars performed their magic over the audience. This really completed his education.

In 1965, Bob Vincent resigned his position with Harrah's, to manage Wayne Newton and several other young artists. After a year of personal management, during which time he helped launch Wayne Newton on his present successful career, he formed an agency called Mus-Art Corporation of America, and Main Track Productions, Inc. The next 12 years saw these two companies join the most successful, independent companies in the entertainment industry.

As a result of Bob's vast knowledge and acquaintanceships in the entertainment industry, he was the moving force behind the formation of a national association called the "International Theatrical Agencies Association" (I.T.A.A.), which unanimously elected him its first president. In 1978, Bob was elected President Emeritus for life.

Bob Vincent decided to share his experience by writing this book so that all of the vast knowledge he has gathered in the last 35 years might help the superstars of tomorrow.

If you are in the business, you owe it to yourself to study this book. If you're not in show business, you'll enjoy reading about the crazy, wonderful, art form called "entertainment."

—Margaret Cernuto

one
What It Takes
To Be A Performer

What It Takes To Be A Performer

I can't promise to make you a star, but by studying this book, I can give you the tools with which you can become a star *performer*. If you have a certain amount of natural talent, and if you will make a total commitment to being "honest" with your audience, this book holds the missing ingredients. It will also save you at least five years of wasted time, running up "blind" alleys!

Throughout this chapter you will see the word "honest" repeated many times. It's the most important method of transmitting any message to your audience, regardless of whether you are a singer, actor, comic, or politician.

There's a fine line between giving a plastic, well-rehearsed performance to a sea of "faceless" people and an honest, one-on-one, personal relationship between you, and each witness to your performance.

Honesty is most difficult when you are standing before hundreds of people. From childhood most of us are told by our parents, "Don't act like that or people won't like you!" By the time you become a young adult your honest feelings have been stifled so much that you find it difficult to know exactly who you are, and how to express that "real" you. All of these personal "hang-ups" have to be broken down and eradicated before you can become a *complete* performer.

If you will examine all of the stars in show-business today, you will find that there is an predominance of Italians and Jews. If you know anything about the upbringing of children in these two ethnic groups, you can readily see why there are so many of these people in showbiz. By nature, most of their parents are openly expressive, and their children generally are allowed to express themselves honestly. This opportunity to talk, sing, laugh, etc. gives these children a head start toward being performers. This does not mean that you must be Italian or Jewish to become a performer, but it obviously helps if you have been brought up in this kind of atmosphere.

If you do not have this freedom of expression within yourself, I am hopeful, by explaining the importance of being honestly expressive, that this book will assist you in getting rid of your personal inhibitions.

When I was Entertainment Director at Harrah's Club at Lake Tahoe, Nevada, I had the golden opportunity of studying the methods of delivery by stars like Judy Garland, Wayne Newton, Dinah Shore, Jack Benny, Danny Thomas, Harry Belafonte, Sammy Davis, Jr., and practically every other star you can think of. We played them all in the three years I produced and staged all of the headliners at Harrah's.

All of these people had their own identity and personal delivery, but they all used pretty much the same formula, and all of them were "honest" with their audience. They almost totally forgot themselves and the only thing they were conscious of, was the words of the song, the story or joke they were telling, the dance they were dancing, or the instrument they were playing.

The amateur performer tends to show how clever he or she is, and gives what I call a plastic, contrived performance. The mechanics are there, but the honest commitment to the audience is missing.

Judy Garland

I was fortunate to witness several Judy Garland performances and when that "little lady" came on stage, you knew that she had dedicated all of her heart and soul to the audience. The air was full of electricity, and every fiber of Judy's emotional being was transmitted to each and every member of the audience. This was the epitome of the honest exposure of "self" I've mentioned previously in this chapter. Judy gave all she had to give, every moment she was on stage.

Our contract with her was limited to one show per night, instead of the usual two, because by the time Judy finished her one hour and twenty minutes on stage, she had nothing left to give. She had opened her skin and showed the audience her heart, her lungs, her intestines, and all of her other vital organs!! She gave you a 100 percent total emotional experience!

Speaking of Judy, it reminds me of a true story that occurred the last night Judy played for us at Harrah's Club. The story

11

illustrates how pathetic Judy's life had become at this point of her career.

At this time, Judy was undependable because of her drug problem. From past experience it was even doubtful that we would get a consistent one show a night out of her. We did, however, recognize that Judy would be a great drawing card for us, and also that it would give us considerable prestige. We agreed to play her on a one-show basis. This was contrary to any other artist we had ever played at Harrah's Club.

When Judy arrived for her engagement, I got a phone call from her doctor in New York giving me the prescriptions for uppers and downers which were necessary to keep Judy alive and performing, and I was told that the dosage would have to be kept within strict limitations, because it was getting to a point where Judy was taking a dangerous amount of uppers and downers.

In an effort to make things as comfortable as possible for Judy, it was necessary for me to see her each evening about six o'clock, and assist her in waking up, so that I could ask whether or not she felt capable of doing the evening performance, which took place at approximately 9:00 p.m.

Because of Judy's medical problem, it was necessary for her to take downers to sleep, and even then Judy never really got to sleep until about 8:00 a.m. She would sleep all day and take a pill to assist in waking up, so she would be in pretty good condition by 7:30 in the evening. In order to further assist Judy, and make her feel more comfortable, we kept a nurse and security guards available, so she would have someone to talk to, and play cards with during the early morning hours when she couldn't sleep.

Upon seeing her at 6 p.m., if I learned she could make it, I would call the *Maitre d'* at the South Shore Room and tell him it was okay to let the customers in for the show.

This method still left us in a pretty tense situation every evening, because people came from hundreds of miles away in order to see Judy Garland, and if she didn't do a show, it was a great disappointment.

Opening night was a tremendous event, with more flowers than I've ever seen before in my life. Judy was so high-geared about this opening night that she was about 15 minutes late for

Bill Harrah   Judy Garland

her curtain call. By the time she made her entrance there was a *gasp* from the throats of all the 900 people who came to her. It probably was the most thrilling reaction I've every experienced in show business. Judy of course, electrified the audience for one hour and 20 minutes.

The next day we went through the same routine and Judy did another great show, this time a little less nervous. On the third day, I went down to see how she felt and she didn't feel up to doing a show, so we cancelled that night. Naturally, the people who were waiting to see her were disappointed.

On the fourth day I went down to see how Judy felt and she

13

said that she felt fine, so I called the South Shore Room and had the *Maitre d'* allow the people to come in. I noticed the limousine pull into the rear entrance at about 8:00 p.m., so I felt that everything was secure, because I could see Judy sitting in the back seat with her maid.

At 8:45 I received a frantic phone call from the room attendant in the dressing room area, explaining that Judy Garland had had a stroke, and was paralyzed. Naturally, the first thing I did was to call a doctor, and then went down to the dressing room area.

Judy was lying on the cot in the dressing room and appeared to be unable to get up, but she was talking clearly. Just about that time, Dr. Peter Irving appeared and examined Judy. After his examination, Dr. Irving called me outside in the hall and explained to me that Judy had not had a stroke, but she was firmly convinced that she had, and he felt it was impossible to force her to do a show. Naturally, we had about 900 people upstairs waiting for her appearance.

I explained my problem to Dr. Irving, and asked him if he would be kind enough to come upstairs and come out on stage with me, and make an announcement to the 900 people in the audience that she was physically unable to appear!

Dr. Irving and I went on stage, and Leighton Noble, our band leader, played a fanfare as we walked out to make the announcement. Naturally there was a large roar of discontent, and many of the people hollered out such remarks as, "How many barrels of booze did she drink last night?" and "I want my money back!" It got to the point where I thought there may be a lynching, and I was going to be the "lynchee." So I said to the audience, "Would you please let me have Dr. Peter Irving explain her physical condition to you." So with this, I forced Dr. Irving to take the microphone, and he continued my explanation by confirming that Judy was physically unable to appear.

With this, there was another big groan and a lot of mumbling from the "natives." I stepped to the microphone and said, "Ladies and gentlemen, because of your disappointment, Bill Harrah feels that we should pick up all your checks." Now with this, there was applause and a large cheer went up, and I immediately had the curtain brought down.

Next day, I received a telephone call from Bill Harrah and

he said, "Who gave you the authority to comp the house last night?" I said, "Bill, it seemed like the only way to go in order to keep nine hundred people fairly happy with us." He said, "Well, without realizing it, you did the right thing, because we had the largest gross revenue gambling take in the history of Harrah's Club last night!" This was because all of these 900 people still had money in their pockets, and they went into the casino one hour and 20 minutes earlier than usual. "It was a good thought," said Harrah "but before you ever do it again, please call me." I said, "I will, if I get a chance to get to a telephone before I get lynched!"

The following day we cancelled the balance of Judy's engagement, and replaced her with Mickey Rooney, and Bobby Van. Two days later, it was noted in a San Francisco newspaper gossip column, that Judy and her current husband, Sid Luft, were seen having dinner together in a well known restaurant.

Obviously, Judy had recovered from her stroke!

EGO KILLS MORE PEOPLE THAN CANCER

two

One On One - Forget Thyself

One On One -
Forget Thyself

The title of this chapter, in addition to being in a one-on-one relationship with the audience, suggests that you "forget thyself." In order to truly be involved deeply with the audience, you must not be concious of "self" and only be totally committed to the "word."

Many young performers give what I call "plastic performances," because it's as if they have brought a full-sized mirror on stage with them, and are continually looking in the mirror at themselves. There's nothing more devastating to your act than to give the audience the impression that your only purpose of being on stage is to show them how clever you are, and that they are lucky that you showed up to entertain them.

You must remember that the minute you appear in view on stage, several hundred eyes and ears are examining you, *very carefully*. All of your assets and liabilities become apparent immediately. If you're an egotist it shows!! If you have no depth of emotion it shows!! and if your sole purpose for being on stage is to make money and only please yourself, and not the audience, that shows too.

For this reason, it's much safer for you to leave awareness of yourself in the dressing room, and only bring on stage your own, or someone else's lyrics, music, direction, and dialogue. Ideally, you should be a nice, sincere, humble, personality who loves the audience honestly. Then, with good lyrics, music, direction, and dialogue, you've really become a professional performer, **in the highest degree possible!**

Being unaware of yourself may sound easy, but it isn't. Due to our early insecurities in life, we tend to keep checking our clothes, our hair, our make-up, our manner of walking, our over-weight or under-weight, etc. From our initial awareness of the opposite sex, we are continually looking at our reflection in store windows, mirrors, and any other shiney, reflective surface. Being insecure, we need to reassure ourselves that we are still desirable to others.

As a performer, you need to be absolutely sure of yourself when you walk on stage, in order to give the audience the feeling of total security. For this reason, you need to completely forget about yourself, and make that total commitment to every sound that emanates from your lips, and every gesture that comes from your body. This total commitment will connect your spirit with that intangible element, which will keep you and the audience in total harmony through out the entire show.

This unawareness of self is the same as the businessman who, as a solid citizen, and a pillar of his community, becomes involved in a community circus fund-raising event, by dressing up as a clown, complete with a wig, putty nose, and funny costume. While he is in the costume and make up, he can perform the damnedest stunts and do things he would never do, if his friends could recognize him. For the moment, he has completely forgotten himself and all of his normal inhibitions, and he can allow his emotions and natural instincts to take over.

When you are on stage, pretend that you do not exist, and you are only a spirit on stage with no real identity. You'd be amazed how much freer you will become and how much greater your impact on the audience will be.

Bill Cosby

The first time I played Bill Cosby at Harrah's, even though this was his first major engagement, Bill had that unawareness of himself, and he had this one-on-one contact with each and every person in the audience.

Bill was comparatively unknown when I first saw him at a small club in San Francisco, and I thought he would be ideal as an opening act for one of our star headline girl singers, so I made a deal with Bill's manager for him to come into Harrah's Club as an opening comic. When Bill arrived the day of rehearsal, I asked him what special instructions he wanted to give to my lighting crew, and he said that all we had to do was to light the curtain with a big circle at the edge, and he would stick his head out, look at the audience once, then pull his head back in, then, stick it out again and stare at the audience, and then pull his head back in, and the third time he would stick his head out he would keep on walking, and to follow him to the center of the stage and put up the pop-up microphone, and leave the rest to him. Now, this is a brand new comic who, to my knowledge, had never appeared on any major stage prior to this engagement. Bill further explained that he needed a regular soda fountain, wood-backed chair to sit on.

We got him his chair, and then came the first show. We hadn't really seen Bill Cosby do his act. We told him how much time we wanted and he said, "it's no problem, just let me see a clock."

There's a clock built right into the stage of Harrah's Club, so he could see how much time he was doing.

Bill Cosby's name was announced and we put the spotlight on the edge of the curtain, and sure enough, Bill stuck his head out and stared at the audience with his big eyes and pulled his head back in, and there was kind of a laugh. He stuck his head out again and stared at the audience for maybe two or three seconds this time, and there was a bigger laugh. He pulled his head back in. The third time he stuck his head out for about three seconds, he just kept walking.

He was walking so slowly it had to take him a good fifteen to twenty seconds to get to the center of the stage, and another three or four seconds to turn the chair around and put the back toward the audience, and then another three or four seconds to sit down on the chair. We pulled up the pop-up mike out of the apron to the height he wanted, and it was probably a total of 25 seconds before he started to talk! That's an awful lot of dead air on stage. Particularly when you have a brand new comic who you don't really know. If you've ever been on a stage where you've had to outstare the audience for that amount of time, it takes an experienced pro to do that successfully.

At no time did anybody get the feeling that Bill Cosby didn't know what he was doing. At no time did you ever get the feeling that he was insecure about all of the dead silence, and at no time did you ever get the feeling that he wasn't absolutely certain that his show was going to be a thorough success.

Artistic Charisma

For three years, I stood in the South Shore Room of Harrah's Club and watched all the greats make their entrances onto

Bill Cosby

that massive stage, and without exception I, and the audience, both felt that intangible "magic" come across the footlights. You knew, without a doubt, that you were going to have a pleasant emotional experience. You knew that the artist knew exactly what he was doing at all times, and you were in "good hands."

You also knew there was something "special" about this person on stage. I call it charisma. It's something you can't define exactly, just a quality some people have — an aura they carry with them, no matter where they are.

How many times have you been in a gathering of people

21

and for some unknown reason all eyes suddenly turned toward the door, as a particular person entered the room? They weren't better dressed than anyone else. They weren't necessarily better looking than anyone else, but there was definitely something "special" about this person.

Having spent 45 years working with and being around entertainers, I have come to the conclusion that the getting-on-stage every night, and giving of your emotional "self" to the audience constantly, expands your personal "aura", so there is definitely a difference between the confidence that a performer has in public, and people in more staid professions. I'm sure you have seen it in the typical salesman, who, in a sense is in showbiz without getting on stage.

The degree of charisma that one acquires, I firmly believe, is in direct relationship to the amount of sincere interest you project in your daily contacts with everyone you touch, whether it's on stage, or in your personal life.

The more interest you show in pleasing others, the more charisma you develop, and by the same token, the greater performer you become.

Sandler and Young

To illustrate how performers with charisma will dominate a stage, even though they are surrounded by a multitude of other performers (some in the nude) I have this example: while I was at Harrah's Club I had to make a trip to Las Vegas for a meeting with a headliner, and during my free time I went to see the new "Casino de Paris" show at the Dunes Hotel. It happened that a friend's wife was dancing in the show, and he wanted me to see her special dance number. All the time that this large cast — 85 nudes and two boy production singers — were on stage, I couldn't help but watch the two boy singers, whose names were Tony Sandler and Ralph Young. They were production singers, and even with all of the nudes on stage, my attention was still drawn to these two people. I said to Matt Gregory, whose wife was in the production, "If you would arrange to put these two boys together in an act, I will buy them for Harrah's Club and put them in the lounge. They have great chemistry for each

other, and such great feeling on stage, and are such profes-
sionals, I know they would make a great lounge act. And who
knows? One day they might become big headliners."

"Well, okay," said Matt. "I'll talk to Tony and Ralph and
let you know."

About a month went by and I came back to Las Vegas and
ran into this same friend of mine. "Whatever happened to those
two boys that were singing at the Dunes?" I asked.

"Well, it happens that we have signed them to our personal
management company, and they are out at my partner Key
Howard's house, running through some tunes for this act that
you've been talking about."

We drove out, and I heard Sandler & Young do what
ultimately became one of their hit records, a tune called "Side
by Side." Tony Sandler, who is French, sang it in French and
Ralph Young, who is American, sang it in English. I thought it
was very well done, so I said to Matt Gregory, "Draw up a contract and I will sign it right now for six weeks at $2,500.00 per
week, with an option of $3,500.00 for another six weeks."

"Are you serious?"

"Yes, even though they haven't completed their material
yet, I know that the chemistry of these two will work, so draw
up the contract and I'll sign it."

Needless to say, he drew up the contract and I signed it.
They opened at Harrah's Club in the lounge, and it wasn't too
much longer before they became headliners all over the country!

The Ten Commandments
of Show-Business

As I mentioned in the beginning of this book, in 1962 I was
hired as Entertainment Director by Harrah's Club, and as such,
was responsible for all entertainment utilized in both Reno and
Lake Tahoe. I started in April of 1962 and resigned in January of
1965. During this time, I can thank Bill Harrah and the rest of
his staff for the greatest training and experience a man could
ever get in show business. I not only learned many things about
the entertainment business, but I was thoroughly trained in the

23

necessity of taking care of details. The experience was invaluable.

Being at Harrah's for almost three years gave me an opportunity to study the methods that were used by all the super stars, and the lounge acts in bringing the audience to a "climax." Each artist used his own style to achieve this, but as I studied their methods, I found that there were certain basic fundamentals that they all used to satisfy the audience.

I am going to list these basic fundamentals that all performers *must* have in order to really be successful. They are as follows:

1. **Honesty.** You must be what you really are, without assuming other people's mannerisms, gestures, body movements, etc. In other words, you've got to reveal the **real you** to the audience at all times.

2. **Establish your credibility immediately!** The audience must get an immediate feeling that you have "done your homework." You must put them at ease by giving them the assurance that you know where you are going at all times, and that you are not nervous, or insecure about your material, your voice, technique on your instrument, or whatever else you are trying to do to entertain them. You must immediately put your audience at ease with the knowledge that they are going to be taken care of for the next hour or so, and that they are **going to get their money's worth.**

3. **Sincere love for the audience.** If your attitude on stage is that you are attempting to show them how "clever" **you** are, or how handsome or beautiful you are, and that **they** are lucky you showed up, this is a fatal mistake. You must be honest in your love for the audience, love of your profession; and your **only** purpose for being on stage is to give them a thoroughly moving, emotional experience, that will make them **feel good all over.**

4. **Once on stage you must totally forget your identity.** You cannot be concerned with you "ego — self," in order to give the audience the emotional experience they need to "climax." In other words, once you are on stage, you should not be concerned about how your hair looks, how your suit or dress fits, how you are holding your hands while you are singing, etc. You should be unconcerned about your physical self and be in-

volved in a "spiritual, intangible" connection with the audience, on a one-on-one basis. Each sincere emotion you feel while performing should relate directly with each and every person in the room.

For an extreme example, let's suppose you had a knife in your hand and you **plunged** that knife into your heart in full view of each person in the audience. Everyone in the audience would feel the blade of that knife *in their* own hearts, as if it were happening *to them personally.* This is what you must do to them with **every** word you say; **every** note you sing; and **every** joke you tell.

5. **The audience must be taken through a variety of emotional experiences in order to be completely satisfied.** In other words, you must pace your show so that it does many things to them. Too much comedy is not good. Too many fast songs are no good and too many slow songs are no good. Too much dialogue is no good! The attention span of an audience is very limited. Therefore, if you give them too much of any one thing for too long, you will lose the audience. You must have instinctive good taste in feeling your audience, and knowing when you have reached that certain point where a change is due. Young, inexperienced performers haven't developed this fine instinct, and as a result, they keep "losing" their audiences. A real pro rarely loses an audience once he gets them. In most cases, the real pro gets his audience in the first minute he or she is on stage and they keep the audience until the curtain drops.

6. **Establish your image, and keep it.** Each performer, whether he or she realizes it, has a certain image in the minds of the public — whether it's Lawrence Welk with his clean, "square type" image or Dean Martin with his drunken looseness of demeanor or Frank Sinatra with his sensual, sexy life style, or Carol Burnett with her wholesome love of family, God, and country, or Steve Martin with his "craziness."

Whatever your image is, **you must never destroy it.** You must not show the public that you have "feet of clay!" The mass public does not like to have their idols changed in any way. Any departure from the person they bought in their minds, whether it's good or bad, could be **fatal** to your career. Make certain you have a good public relations firm handling your publicity. Be sure **they** realize what your image is and are ready to protect it.

7. **Keep your act fresh.** There is nothing worse for an artist, than to get bored **with his own material.** It doesn't matter how good an act you have, after you have done the same show for some time, you will find the original "thrill" is gone, and **you** are no longer involved with the same excitment **you** had when it was **brand new. Your boredom is transmitted to your audience** and as a result, you will find you cannot hold their attention. You become what I call a "plastic performer." It's absolutely imperative that you keep refreshing your act with new material, new songs, new gimmicks, new arrangements, etc. as quickly as you realize that the "old thrill is gone!" You can't fake "enthusiasm" when you don't **"honestly"** feel it.

8. **You must stay "on top" of the changing trends in show business.** Many artists have died fighting the change in the public's tastes, or not keeping up with the changing trends. You must stay abreast with what's happening. You must constantly read trade magazines, watch the variety television shows, see the latest movies and pay particular attention to anything that pertains to your act. In other words, you **cannot** assume that because you were a success yesterday, you will enjoy this **same success tomorrow.** The public is very fickle, and as quickly as they accept you, they will **drop you,** if you don't **stay in tune with them.** In show business, you must keep working on your act, whatever it is, and keep it fresh for both yourself and the audience.

9. **Maintain a warm, "arm's length" friendship with all of the talent buyers and hotel owners you work for.** I've seen many artists kill the audience on stage, and then fall apart in the owner's office between shows. Sometimes the performer gets the impression that because he's successful on stage, he can take advantage of this temporary success and "run all over" the man who is paying him, by making unreasonable requests, and using abusive language, etc. You must remember, success is a "two-way street." You meet the same people going up, and if you have been a jerk while you were hot, when you begin to "slide", they all will help speed your demise! Remember, nothing is guaranteed **forever** in our business.

10. **Show business is TWO words, SHOW and BUSINESS!!** If you are the least bit bright, and if you are smart

enough to know that your success is really temporary, you will hire, and listen to, a competent business manager, and also a smart showbiz attorney. They are invaluable to you. They may be expensive, but at the peak of your earning power, much of their service fees can be written off. Even though you have hired a good business manager, don't turn all of your earnings over to him without any attention to what he is doing in your behalf. In other words, keep in touch with your account on a regular basis, so you know at all times what he is doing for you, with your excess income.

Fortunately, there are not too many unscrupulous business managers, and/or attorneys, but there are several cases where a star thought his money was being taken care of and it was, but it somehow, legally or "illegally," ended up in the business manager's and/or attorney's pocket.

Fortunately for me, for the last 14 years, I've had a great attorney, and a good friend, in the person of Howard Thaler, whose office is in Beverly Hills, California. Howard has guided me through my business dealings for all of those years, and I feel fortunate in having his counsel through my many trials and tribulations.

It's only good business that you stay abreast of your hired advisors. The *good managers* can be very helpful to you, but you must remember that your success and your high earnings could come to an abrupt ending. Never spend everything you are making, assuming the money will roll in forever. Take my word for it, it won't. Save for a rainy day.

Through the years, I've learned many other things, such as the importance of taking care of little details. Nothing should ever be taken for granted, no matter what business you're in. There should be preventative maintenance at all times.

In a sense, this is what an artist is doing when he constantly adds new material to his act. It's the artist's form of preventative maintenance.

EGO KILLS MORE PEOPLE THAN CANCER

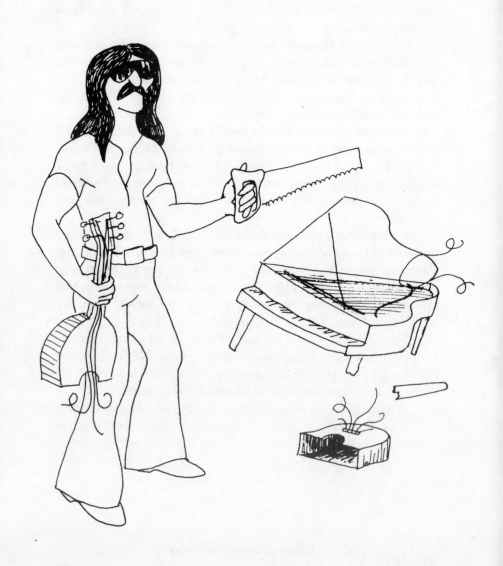

three

Learn The Tools
Of Your Trade

Learn The Tools Of Your Trade

The toughest part of being a performer is not when you are performing in front of an audience, but the endless hours spent in preparing your skills, and putting together your material. As a young performer, you are much like a quarterback on a football team. You must have at your fingertips a multitude of plays, because there is no way you can anticipate what style of opposition you are going to run into on any given Saturday.

As a performer, you cannot anticipate the mood of the audience prior to your walking on stage, and for this reason, you must not only be prepared with a variety of material, but you also must be in "tune" with the audience at all times, so you will "call the right play" at the right time. There is no way you will ever be able to peg every audience, every night, so you can do the exact same show every performance. You must have the ability to improvise.

Don't fall into the habit of writing out your show format prior to your entrance and sticking to it verbatim. Leave yourself some latitude to improvise and alter your original format, if you sense the mood of the audience calls for a change. There's no way you can predict what the audience wants until you get into your act; no more than a quarterback can write out the exact order of plays he will use in next Saturday's football game. He has a general outline of plays in mind, but he also calls what are known as "audibles" when he senses that the next play he originally had in mind is wrong. This is what you, as a performer, have to do in order for you to stay "in tune" with your audience. The ability to do this successfully makes the difference between an amateur or a professional.

Any performer who accepts money in exchange for services rendered must dedicate his performance and his material to what pleases the customer who is indirectly paying his salary. This is the law of entertainment and there can be no successful deviation from this law. Many young performers make the tragic mistake of thinking they can make a good living, and become a success by doing material that pleases *them*, without too much thought as to whether or not the audience is pleased at the same time. If you are fortunate enough to have the same emotional needs as the mass of humanity, and your style and material satisfies both you and the audience, you are indeed lucky. If you differ from the masses in your appreciation and understanding of what motivates the man on the street, you had better seek some advice from someone else who does have that feel, and take their advice, or get out of the business. If you don't satisfy 90 percent of all of the people in the audience, you are committing professional suicide.

Phil Harris Show

There are times when you can't see the forest for the trees. It happened to me at Harrah's Club when we played Phil Harris, with a complete package show which Phil was obligated to bring with him.

This story illustrates the point perfectly, and is something from which all artists might learn a lesson.

Phil was to originally supply a Dixieland band, an Afro-Cuban dance team, with two boys and a very pretty girl, plus himself doing the rest of the show. As time went on, Phil told me he had heard about a girl singer who was great, and felt she would be ideal for his show at Harrah's Club. Phil wanted to know if I thought it would be advisable to add the girl singer. I explained to Phil that we had a maximum of one hour and twenty minutes per show, and if he felt that he could squeeze a girl singer in, and still come up with a good show in an hour and twenty minutes, it was fine with me. So, he hired her.

Another week went by and Phil said he heard about a little Japanese girl who played kettle drums while suspended from a bamboo pole, and that he thought she would be another excellent addition to his show.

"Well, Phil," I said "We're getting to a point now where I think it's going to be difficult for you to do your own act, plus all of the other acts and still stay within an hour and twenty minutes."

"Don't worry about it. I will cut my show and I'll cut the

Dixieland band's numbers down. We'll move it along quickly and squeeze it all in an hour and twenty minutes."

"As long as you understand the problem, that's fine, do whatever you want, but remember our maximum time limitation!"

On the day of rehearsal, we had all of these acts: Phil Harris, the Dixieland band with six guys, the Afro-Cuban dance team, a girl singer, and a little Japanese girl drummer. The girl singer had a high-pitched, squeaky voice. It was one of her first jobs. She looked very amateurish. The little Japanese girl drummer was cute and had a good act, but it took up 10 minutes of time. We tried to put this mixture of artists together in an hour and twenty minutes. It was impossible.

I could see that Phil was rushing all of his lines, the Dixie band was playing faster than normal and the dance team was dancing quicker and faster. I told Phil, "It appears to me that we will end up with about an hour and thirty minutes, to an hour and thirty-five minutes, even rushing everything. We're going to end up with an unsuccessful show."

"Well, don't worry about it," he said, "after the first show we'll make a few cuts and we'll correct everything."

During the first show, Bill Harrah and I sat in our customary spot in the back of the South Shore Room making notes about the show. It was obvious to me, and to Bill Harrah, that Phil Harris was really running to squeeze every bit of talent he could into his own act, which threw his pacing off. Phil Harris normally works very casually, and under the circumstances, with the pressures involved, Phil was talking 100 miles an hour, and the show just didn't gel. Also, it turned out that we had an hour and 35 minutes of entertainment by the time the curtain closed.

Bill Harrah explained to me that every minute that we are over, the casino would lose a large amount of gambling revenue, and after all, that is how we pay for the show.

"I warned Phil Harris," I said to him, "before he came in for rehearsal that the original show he had was adequate all of the additional acts were unnecessary! I advised Phil that we only had an hour and twenty minutes maximum and he assured me that he would get it all done in that amount of time." Well, as we could both see, it was impossible.

Phil Harris   Bob Vincent

Bill Harrah made a very wise statement which I will never forget. He said to me, "What would you do if you had the right to do whatever you wanted to with the show, in order to make it a good show?"

"Well, first of all, we don't need the girl singer who doesn't sing well. We also don't need the little Japanese drummer."

"If you paid them off right now you could go back to a casual, relaxed show, right?"

"Right."

"Well then, why don't you pay them off? Pay the girl singer and the girl drummer off right now because, after all, if we keep them for three weeks, we have to pay them anyway, and for three weeks we would have a bad show. If we pay them off now, we will have three weeks of a good show, and there is no loss of money!"

I went downstairs to the dressing room and explained this to Phil. He was agreeable, because at that point, he was frustrated, knowing that the show was bad. I paid off the girl singer and the little Japanese drummer. We had an excellent show for the three weeks of Phil Harris' engagement.

Phil had learned the "tools of his trade." The only trouble with this show was that he had gathered "too many tools!"

The point of this story for all entertainers is, if you know you have a "cancer in your act, — cut it out!"

Keeping Your Material Current—and Topical.

How many times have you gone to see a performer and thoroughly enjoyed his performance, and after an absence of a few months, or years, saw him again only to discover that he is still telling the same "old" stories and jokes, or singing the same songs.

Two things happen when a performer doesn't change his act constantly. First of all, his jokes and stories become commonplace, because people tend to repeat stories and jokes to each other. Secondly, and just as important, you, as the teller of the story or joke, become bored with the repetition of the material and you lose the original enthuisiasm you had for it when it was brand new.

In order to keep your songs and stories "fresh," you must constantly deliver this material from the conscious part of your brain. As soon as you start delivering this material from your subconscious brain, you will lose your audience. Many singers, who become bored with a song from too much repetition, sing "I love you" to the audience subconsciously, while at the same time, the conscious part of the brain is thinking about such things as getting the car fixed, picking up his laundry, etc. You can see how difficult it would be for the audience to believe him.

Much of your material can be taken from the front page of the newspaper. Many humorous stories can come out of a non-humorous item in the paper. Also, if you use a news story from

Andy Griffith   Dick Linke

the local paper, it becomes really personal and complimentary
to the local customers who come to see you.

An example of this happened to me once when I went to see
Andy Griffith perform on a fair date in Ontario, Canada. I
originally went to see Andy's act so I would be better prepared
to stage his forthcoming appearance at Harrah's Club.

I arrived at the fair grounds in time for Andy's first matinee
performance. I sat in the grandstand and got the local's viewpoint of Andy's material and delivery. Andy laid the biggest
bomb during this show, that's ever been laid in the history of
show biz!

Andy was obviously rusty and he hadn't prepared himself
for the British-speaking audience that lives in Ontario, Canada.
As a result, he made many mistakes.

After the matinee show, I went backstage and as soon as
Andy realized that I had seen his first performance he loudly

35

proclaimed that he would not play the Harrah's Club engagement at all because he couldn't afford to ruin his reputation by dying there too. I assured Andy that with the help of Dick Linke, his personal manager, we could correct all of his current problems in Ontario and, furthermore, I could guarantee that he would have a successful show at Harrah's.

I told Andy that the biggest mistake he was making was that the Ontario people didn't understand a word he was saying because of his accent. The first thing we had to do was to slow his speech down so that these people, accustomed to the "King's" English, would be able to understand what he was saying.

The second suggestion I made to him was even more important. I said he was talking about America this, and America that, which doesn't go over too well with a Canadian audience. I added that the first thing we had to do was to pick up a local newspaper, and take some of the topical stories off the front page for use in the opening part of his next show.

We bought a local newspaper, and right on the front page there was a big dispute between the lady mayor of Ontario and the city council, regarding the repair of pot holes in the roads. We wrote a small chunk of comedy material regarding the lady mayor and her battle with the council, and in addition to this, we picked two or three other local items off the front page of the paper and wrote some minor humorous anecdotes about these local news items.

I further explained to Andy that he should brag about the fact that Canada is our good neighbor and we've been friends for years and years, and that if he wasn't such a confirmed North Carolina hillbilly, he would prefer to be a Canadian. Andy listened carefully, and he did exactly what I had suggested.

That evening he went out and killed the audience; got a standing ovation, and everybody loved him. From that point on, Andy Griffith knew that I could construct a show for him that would be a winner at Harrah's Club.

Needless to say, we built a stong show for him which was to take place at Harrah's about six months later. It included Jim Nabors and Don Knotts as his co-headliners, and the show was one of the most successful shows we had ever played. In fact, it was so fresh and new that the same customers came back to Harrah's two and three times to see it.

There are several points to make in this story. One is that no matter how bad an act is, it can be corrected with outside direction from someone who is knowledgeable, and who can see it from the viewpoint of the audience. The other moral to the story is that the artist must take outside direction because sometimes it's impossible for the artist to see all of the flaws and mistakes that are obvious to the customers.

Picking The Proper Keys

Before having an arrangement written on a new tune, it is most important that you pick the right key for the song, including any modulations you intend to use in the arrangement. Too many inexperienced singers pick the key in the mid-afternoon when they have just gotten out of bed, and before they have given their throats a chance to warm up. Much to their sorrow and discomfort, after the arrangement is written, they discover that the whole chart is from one, to one-and-one-half tones too low for maximum impact.

I highly recommend that you pick the key, either at the end of an afternoon rehearsal, or after the last show at night. At these times, your throat is warm, and psychologically your whole body is tuned up. These conditions will help you arrive at the ideal key for the song. It's a known fact among professional singers that in the evening you can sing a song at least one tone higher than you can in the morning or afternoon. Bear in mind, once you pick the wrong key and the arrangement is written, you're stuck with it! Unless, of course, you decide to have it re-written and re-copied at great expense.

It is also important to remember that each song usually has one or two climaxes written into it, and at the point of these climaxes, you should be singing at the top of your range in order to give it the excitement the passage needs for proper impact.

Speaking of getting your voice warmed up before performing, it's also important to get your mind and body warmed up just before the show. I recommend that you get to the club at least forty minutes before your first performance, so you can get yourself "psyched" up to the energy level necessary for you to generate the excitement in yourself, and transmit this same excitement to your audience. There's no way you can convince your audience that you're an exciting performer, if you're not honestly excited yourself! Be sure you are in the right frame of mind and body before you walk on stage.

The Proper Accompanist

A great pianist is not always a great accompanist. To be a great accompanist, one must not only be a great pianist, but he or she must have a beautifully sensitive "subordinate" soul. You must be an extension of the singer's emotional feelings, with the ability to immediately sense when the singer needs "full" support and when he wants you to be sensitively "silent".

In many ways it is far more difficult to find a great accompanist, than a great pianist, because this keyboard artist must be almost totally devoid of "ego." It is a known fact that a professional singer will not "read" a song exactly the same way every night, and for this important reason, the accompanist cannot allow himself to lapse into unconsciously playing the same arrangement. He must at all times be consciously aware that the singer may deviate from his "norm" on any given night and any loss of one-on-one contact between he and the singer might destroy what should have been an ideal performance.

Breathing From the Diaphragm

If you are a singer, speaker, comic, or a musician playing a wind instrument, you must learn how to breathe properly. It is important that you learn how to breathe deeply from your "diaphragm." I realize that many performers who are successful have never studied this form of breathing, but in the interest of your becoming a true performer, I must impress upon you how vital this form of breathing will be to your future career. It will save you countless sore throats, and your energy level will remain constant on stage for hours.

TOOLS OF YOUR TRADE

The principal reason for diaphragm breathing is to be certain that both of your lungs have taken in their full capacity of air, each time you take a breath. When you breathe from the diaphragm, you must make certain that the bottom part of your lungs are both full of air, which in so doing, will push out your stomach area, rather than raise your chest. This method of breathing must be practiced and actually should become a habit, whether you are performing or just breathing to stay alive.

The primary purpose of this form of deep breathing is to give you the ability to sing, or play long phrases without strain. There is nothing worse for your throat than to be forced to make a sustained sound, when you are out of breath! That's where 90 percent of all sore throats come from.

If you find it difficult to learn to breathe in this manner, picture a dog lying on the floor after a hard chase, and remember how he breathes when he's very winded. This is exactly the right way to breathe. Also, if you've ever watched a little baby breathe when it's lying on it's back, you will again see proper breathing from the diaphragm.

Put your hand on your stomach area and take full breaths, which push your hand *out* on the *intake of air*. On the expelling of air, your hand recedes into your stomach area towards your backbone, this is diaphragm breathing.

You should practice this for at least two hours a day until it becomes habitual, and until this is the only way you will breathe either on or off stage.

To Audition Or Not To Audition (and if so, how??)

Naturally, this subject only concerns the unknown new performer. In order for you to have some continuity of engagements, it may be necessary to audition for a prospective buyer.

The best way, of course, is to invite the buyer to see you perform on the job where you are presently working, but sometimes this is not possible. The question then becomes, shall I audition for the new potential buyer in his own club? Based on the assumption that you do not as yet have an agent (we will cover this in a later chapter), I recommend that you swallow your pride and do the audition in his club, under certain conditions.

Most club owners or managers do not realize what it takes for an act to audition under strange conditions, meaning that you're not acquainted with the strange sound system, a strange piano, different acoustics, and no audience. (Auditions are usually held in the afternoon, without customers.) Add to this the natural nervousness of a young act trying to make a good impression on a "cold-eyed," unsmiling club owner. It's a little frightening.

Having been in the position of being a buyer of entertainment, I know for a fact what my attitude was during an audition. First of all, I dislike to audition acts in the afternoon. Secondly, I usually was busy and had only allocated about twenty minutes, in my mind, for the audition. I was apprehensive about the act wanting to "pour" about an hour of his talent at me, which would make me late for my next appointment. Granted, they had given up their valuable time to audition for me, but I didn't need an hour show to make my decision. Usually, in their anxiety to get this job, they "oversold" me. This overly long audition sometimes hurt their chances of getting the job.

Before you audition, I suggest you gear your act to a maximum of 20 minutes, and before you start the audition, I would tell your potential buyer that you are only going to do 20 minutes. Also, tell him you will do more, but only if he asks for it. You can see where this statement will make a favorable impression on him even before you start.

The day before the audition, put together a 20-minute combination of the best of your whole act, even if you have to radically alter your normal one-hour show. It will pay off in the long run.

You must realize that chances are he either will buy you or won't buy you in the **first five minutes**. This is why I recommend that you do your strong opening "chunk" we designed according to the chapter entitled "Formulating Your Show."

Please do not "cop-out" about the strange sound system, and piano, sore throat, etc. There's nothing worse than a potential buyer being subjected to excuses before or after the audition. Either you did it or you didn't do it! A "real talent" can audition in his underwear, in a phone booth, and still get the job!!

No Room For Mediocrity

With our advanced communications systems today, (television, movies, records, video tapes, etc.), the general public has become more discriminating than ever about what they will spend their money for to be entertained. They will no longer accept mediocrity in performance.

This book was written to give you the guidelines to develop and bring out the best you have to offer. In order to reach the top of our business, you must first realize factually where you are at the moment, and how much real talent and dedication you have in order to estimate where you will end up in show business.

There are many performers working steadily and making a decent living, who I'm sure realize that they probably will never see their name in lights on Broadway. That's fine, as long as they realize their real abilities and make the best of it. There's nothing wrong with being contented to design good, substantial tract homes as against being the architect on the tallest building in the world.

However, if you know in your heart that you have unlimited abilities, and are willing to dedicate your entire life to the development of your potential, there is plenty of room at the top for another superstar. In fact, there is a desperate need for new names and new faces. (See chapter on Las Vegas, Reno, Tahoe, and Atlantic City).

Professional Pictures

One of the least considered, and most important contributions to your career is a good portfolio of pictures and publicity material. Most young artists generally do not start out with a lot of money, and they have a misconception that they should wait until they can afford to go to one of the big theatrical photographic studios, before they get good pictures. At the inception of their careers, when they are the least known, they make the fatal mistake of starting out with *very bad*, or worst of all, *no* pictures!

First of all, it is desirable, but not absolutely necessary, that you go to a major photographer for your pictures. If you can afford it, and you live near an established photographer . . . great. If you don't, please remember that there is a photographic camera store in every city in the country. Behind the counter of this store is a dedicated young camera salesman, who knows all about cameras. Chances are he owns hundreds of dollars worth of cameras and equipment himself.

If you are short of money and need pictures of yourself or your group, you should go to the best camera store in town and find a bright young salesman who would like to make some side money. Offer him some money to bring his camera and equipment out to some outdoor locations, to shoot at least two rolls of black & white, and one roll of color. The pictures should be in various natural poses, in various types of costumes. If you have picked the right man, with the right equipment, and the right location, you probably will end up with at least four good black & white poses, and at least two good color shots. All your camera man has to make certain of is; one, he shoots you in focus; two, he doesn't pick up a "busy" background which will up-stage you; and three, he shoots you in a *"vertical"* position in his camera. Bear in mind that these shots will have to be enlarged to 8"x 10" and most of all lobby displays and marquee boards are *vertical*, and *not horizontal!* For this reason, make sure he turns his camera in a vertical position when he's shooting.

Once the pictures are taken and enlarged to 8"x 10", all you have to do is put your imagination to work and create an interesting bio, or publicity story, on yourself, or your group. If you will go one step further and create a "hard-cover" folder to contain your pictures, bios, and press releases, you now have the ammunition necessary to allow your agent to go to work for you. This is very important in the beginning of your showbiz career, so don't sluff it.

Before taking pictures of yourself, it's necessary for you to buy costumes. The type of costume should be determined by an honest appraisal by yourself, or your personal manager, or agent, as to the type of image you are trying to establish. Your costume should be in keeping with "what you are" and should fit your personality.

Fortunately, in today's contemporary market, there are hundreds of clothing stores geared to the "today look", and chances are you can buy your costumes right off the rack. As a performer, I recommend that you never go on stage for two or three shows a night, wearing the same costume twice. You should change for *every* set!

Obscene Material

I'm not a prude, as you can guess by now. However, I sincerely believe that you do not have to resort to crude gestures, or obscene language to be entertaining. I'm aware that there are certain comics who are stars, and whose act is built around obscenity. Also, you will find that they work the majority of their professional lives in Nevada, where people expect and accept this kind of material. You generally won't find these people on television, and when you do, they usually do not come off well, because they naturally cannot do their "normal" material.

If you don't have this type of personality, and can't use foul language on stage without getting embarrassed, don't do it! I personally do not feel that this kind of material is desirable if you have all of the other things going for you.

John Davidson's
Singers Summer Workshop

Thanks to John Davidson, there is now a "Singers Summer Workshop." It started in the summer of 1978 and is located in Avalon, on Catalina Island, off the coast of Los Angeles, California.

John Davidson is a phenomenon in show business. It's a tribute to his entertaining ability that he has gotten as big as he is in the business without a hit record. He is the living proof that

43

an artist can make it big in entertainment based on talent alone.

Needless to say, John had some good "breaks" in his climb to stardom. He was able to gain much popularity through television, and movies, but the point I'm trying to make is that John was "ready" when the break came.

Now, because of his sincere interest in showing other young artists how to do likewise, Davidson has opened a school for singers called, the "Singers Summer Workshop."

John happened to mention his idea for the school on a television talk show, and the large response by mail to this brief mention of the school prompted John to put the plan into action. He immediately arranged to lease a private school on Catalina, hired a staff of musicians and vocal coaches, and the "Singers Summer Workshop" became a reality.

During the summer of 1978, Davidson personally selected

John Davidson's "Singers Summer Workshop"

John Davidson

100 "potential" singing stars out of approximately 20,000 applicants. These fortunate young artists all converged on Catalina in two different sessions of fifty applicants each. The first session was from July 3 through 30, and the second session took place from July 31 through August 27. By limiting each

session to a maximum of 50 singers, John felt that he and his instructors could give each of the students more personalized attention.

Davidson made it perfectly clear to all of the applicants that the purpose of the workshop was to give them proven, practical direction in perfecting their performing techniques. However, there was no guarantee that the school would get them work because of their attendance. The cost of each four-week session was placed at $800.00 per student, with Davidson picking up the difference between the income and the overhead. I feel certain that this tuition will have to be increased in the future.

During each four-week period, each student was obligated to put together a 45-minute "act," with the help of Davidson and his staff. Besides teaching them how to sing and put their act together, they were also advised about their "visual" defects: weight problems, hair styles, clothes styles, etc. Davidson also arranged for guest lectures from such seasoned artists as Andy Williams, Kenny Rogers, Jack Jones, and Ed McMahon. On Saturday and Sunday, the students went into Avalon, the island's only town, where they performed in one of five shows, for the estimated 15,000 weekend tourists.

Davidson's hopes and dreams appear to be coming true. The tremendous response from thousands of potential singers and performers to his workshop guarantees its success. As you can tell from reading "Show-Business Is *Two* Words," Davidson and I agree. It's time that something concrete is done to develop new stars of tomorrow. Let's hope that Davidson's enthusiasm for this project will become contagious, and spread into other parts of the entertainment world.

Barbra Streisand — Liberace

In this chapter, "Learn the Tools of Your Trade," there's a lesson to be learned about planning your show so that it fits your particular audience. You must realize where your appeal lies, and what type customer you appeal to. You can't possibly be "all things to all people."

Frank Sinatra has an appeal to certain type people, whereas

Liberace

Lawrence Welk's appeal is to a different type. Dean Martin appeals to a different type than Liberace, and so on.

In other words, there are enough types of possible customers available to every type performer. So, after you have analyzed what type performer you are, you should stay with your "bag," and not try to mix oil and water.

A clear example of this happened at Harrah's during a show that Liberace brought to us back in 1963. He had discovered a young girl singer that he was so impressed with, that he had added her to his show as a opening act.

Liberace has given many young performers their first big break in show business, and he continues to do so. In this case, his enthusiasm for her great talent got the better of his good judgment, and the mixture was almost disastrous. The young singer's name was Barbra Streisand.

I am sure that all of you readers realize that Liberace's primary appeal is to an adult audience, mostly women, who are from 40 to 75 years of age. In the beginning of Lee's career, it was more true than today. Over the years Liberace has developed such a fine reputation for being a great performer, that the age of his fans has increased in the younger adult category. In regards to my story, I am referring to the days when Lee's appeal was primarily to an older, more reserved customer.

Can you imagine what a shock, it must have been to Liberace's audience in Harrah's Club when Barbra Streisand, who in 1963 was almost totally unknown, walked out on our stage as an opening act, and started to sing some strange arrangements which were unrelated to his audience?

It became immediately obvious to me, and all of the staff of Harrah's, that this young singer had a great voice, but she definitely would not be successful as Lee's opening act. Something had to be done.

I had a meeting with Lee and suggested that he open the show himself, and at an appropriate spot, introduce Barbra as *his* discovery to set her up with his loyal fans, so that she would avoid the instant resistance from his people, as she had in the opening show.

Lee agreed with my suggestion and we redid our format. It

worked out much better and Barbra felt very relieved that it had been changed.

The point of this story, of course, is that you new performers must find out where your image lies, and be consistent in your material and your presentation, so that you don't make the mistake of deserting the fans you appeal to. Don't destroy yourself in an effort to appeal to everybody. After all, there are millions of possible fans available to you. Once you find your niche, and you're comfortable with it, stay in it.!

EGO KILLS MORE PEOPLE THAN CANCER

four

How To Format Your Act

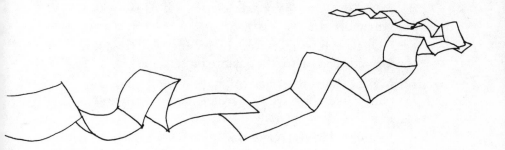

How To Format Your Act

For the moment, let's think back to your purpose of being on stage. The audience must be satisfied, or you have failed. It's just common sense that in order for you to make your job easier, you must create a good impression on the audience immediately, because you are actually being auditioned by them each and every show. You can't assume that because you killed them on the last show, that you are going to be a guaranteed success thereafter. I'm sure you've heard performers say, "Boy, was that a lousy audience!" In truth, it wasn't a lousy audience. They did a lousy show. Please remember, "there are no bad songs, only bad singers."

Knowing that your first impression is going to be lasting, and that you must immediately convince your audience they are going to get their money's worth, it is wise that your opening number, or "chunk" as I call it, must do a multitude of things for you. It must:

a. Establish your humility and sincerity.

b. Establish your credibility as a singer, dancer, musician, comic, etc.

c. Establish your intelligence in putting together a clever opener, which is relative to the tastes of your audience.

d. Establish your personal identity so they will remember you.

e. Give them bits and pieces of what they will be seeing and hearing, for the balance of the show.

f. Make them realize that you have a good sense of pacing, so they won't become bored with too much similarity of material.

g. Establish that you have class!

In other words, your opening chunk should almost be like an overture. It should start out with an exciting intro and first song, and without playing or singing full choruses of any one song, the opener should continue on with a direct seque out of one song into another, and so on, with changes of tempo and changes of keys. Of course, the end of the opening chunk should build to an exciting climax, with an obvious, clearly designed finish, so there is no doubt in the audience's mind that they should "get ready to applaud!"

After the opening chunk, without saying a word, you should go into your second song, which should have a totally different "feel" than the opening, should still be a medium fast tempo, and also have a good climactic ending.

After the second song, you should have created a desire in the audience's mind to want to get to know you better. Now is the time to talk to them to say, "Hello, I'm John Jones and I'm here to show you a good time." Here's where you should have something humorous to say — not a joke necessarily — but something to establish you as a human being, with human frailities, the same as your audience.

This talk should not take more than 30 seconds, before you set up your third song, which should be something of a comedy or novelty nature. Here's where you play the "bagpipes," make a doll out of balloons while you're singing a love song to it, do a tap dance on six-foot stilts, or something else just as crazy. By this time your audition should be over and they should love you. (Incidentally, this is also the spot where the owner of the club goes into his office to call your agent in order to find out how soon he can have you back.)

Time now for your fourth song. You have just finished with your "getting to know you" spot, with talk, humor and something unusually interesting. Now's the time to get back to work with something musically serious and high tensed. You're all through being humorous and charming. Here you come with sweat and energy. This song should be the current, hot, up-tempo hit contemporary song of the day.

It should have continuous energy and excitement with possibly a change of key on the last chorus, and also possibly a double tag ending! In any event, it should finish big, high, and hard.

The reason for the fourth song being high and hard is to set up what we call the "soft spot," or fifth song. After all of this volume of sound, the audience should be ready to ease back in their seats and let you make love to them. There comes a time, at least once in every show, where you must show your sensitivity.

This should be done with a complete departure from anything that has preceded it. The song naturally should be a hit ballad of the day but, most importantly, the instrumental background should have a totally different "feel" and "sound."

Let's assume you have been using the full orchestra complete with brass, saxes, rhythm, percussion, etc. In the soft spot you need to come "way down" by keeping much of the orchestra or combo silent. Here's where you use an accoustical guitar, a celeste, a Fender Rhodes piano, a string machine or an acoustical piano.

The effect you want to achieve at this moment is complete hypnosis of your audience. If this spot is handled properly, there shouldn't be a sound in the house. The only thing you should be able to hear is your voice and your accompanist. That's all! When this happens, there's nothing more beautiful, or emotionally satisfying.

Coming out of the soft spot, which incidentally, should not last for more than a minute to a minute-and-a-half, we must once again "wake up" our audience, and take them out of their hypnotic trance. The sixth spot should naturally be a medium fast tempo, and should once again be something humorous, but not funny (unless of course you are a singing comic). With this sixth spot, you are beginning to "go for home!" You are now starting to build your gradual climax.

This gradual climax to the end will be spread over the sixth, seventh, and eighth songs. Each of these songs should be complete in themselves. However, they should be carefully picked so that each of them get a little more intense, until you get to the eighth song, which is where you give it all you've got, both visually and audibly.

The ending on the eighth song needs to be filled with every trick that you and your arranger can devise, with the thought that you should get an *"honest" standing ovation!*

If you have done your homework properly, if you have put all of the above ingredients in proper order, if you have been honest and sincere, if you sincerely love the audience, if you have developed your charisma, and have revealed it throughout the entire show, chances are you will get that standing ovation.

If the applause is thunderous, and they won't let you get off the stage without one more song, I recommend you grab a stool and let them down easy with one chorus of a pretty soft ballad. End of show.

Please remember that it would be fatal to try to top yourself. After your big eighth climactic number, don't try to do another one. The ballad, sitting on the stool is exactly what the finish needs, and when you exit this time, stay off. You've had it, and so have they. Leave them wanting.

The formula for a successful show, as I have just described, has worked for every performer since the beginning of show business. The exact application of each performer's method of applying the formula, has to be left up to the individual. I am merely giving you the basics. The end result must always be the same. The audience must love you, respect you, and experience at least two or three "climaxes" in an hour. That's the only way you can develop a successful career on a sustaining basis, and most of all, that's the *only* way you can increase your money. No agent can consistently sell you for more than you are worth. Your salary is only determined by the net dollars you put into the operator's pocket.

Please remember I am trying to convey to you the methods whereby you can become a great performer, **without a hit record.** Should you develop into a great performer, and then come up with a hit record or a major television show, or movie, you are really in "fat city."

If you are working in a self-contained group, it is vitally imperative that you have a "quarter back" who can "rap" with the audience. Naturally, if you are doing a single, you must learn to be a good "rapper." By rapping I don't mean that you should write out speeches and memorize them to be repeated in the same word-for-word, plastic manner every night, and every show. This is the kiss of death.

In comparing your emceeing to a quarterback on a football team, can you imagine what would happen to the team if the quarterback wrote out a list of consecutive plays the night before the game, and called the plays exactly as he wrote them out regardless of what the opponents defense was doing?

Don't assume that you will have the same kind of audience each show. It never happens.

I know several artists who have a set act, with the same order of tunes, and the same "pat" conversation between each song. The only way that they can continue in the business is if they have a *new* audience each time they walk on stage.

If you can work as an act in a main room in Las Vegas, you might get away with a "pat" act. There's still one big danger under these circumstances. After a time, you get **bored with your own act.** This is when you lose your one-on-one contact with the audience! Most all of the big superstars who work to a new audience every show, vary their material just so that this fatal separation from the audience doesn't happen.

Lawrence Welk

Speaking of enjoying your show, there's no one who enjoys his show more than Lawrence Welk. Lawrence also knows that there are "golden moments" that happen when you least expect them. Lawrence has done his show to a live audience for so long, that he keeps an "improvisational looseness" in his format in order to take advantage of certain unrehearsed things that might accidentally happen, which gives his show a certain honest, "down home" charm.

One of these golden moments happened during Lawrence Welk's engagement at Harrah's Club, and it involved your author. This incident illustrates the advantage of not "locking" yourself into a strict, unbendable format, whereby you might lose a great opportunity to move your audience.

Each June or July, Lawrence Welk took a hiatus from his television activities, and played a three-week engagement at Harrah's Club at Lake Tahoe. Lawrence and I got along famously and we played golf almost every day. At no time did I ever reveal that I was once a singer, performer and a saxophone player.

The second appearance that Lawrence made for us was a show that had a patriotic payoff at the end, complete with a large 40-foot flag behind a scrim, rear-lit, with a fan blowing the flag, and the chorus singing "God Bless America" and "America The Beautiful." The applause was coming up at the wrong time and destroying this ending. It became a problem. While we were doing our first and second shows, I couldn't quite figure out

Lawrence Walk   Bob Vincent

how to adjust the closing routine so the applause would come at the end.

While on a plane trip from Reno to Las Vegas I got an idea as to how to change the ending. I called Lawrence as soon as I got to the hotel in Las Vegas. From the telephone booth, I sang a little bit of "God Bless America" and "America the Beautiful" to Lawrence, in order to illustrate the right time to put the light on, and the right time to reveal the flag.

Lawrence got the impression that I was a pretty good singer and said to me, "Look, young fellow, why don't you sing with my band when you come back."

When I got back to Lake Tahoe the ending was solved, and it came to be one of the most beautiful shows we ever did.

On Lawrence Welk's closing night, I happened to be sitting at the front table with Danny Thomas and his wife Rosemarie. They had joined us because Danny was going to follow Lawrence Welk as our next attraction. In Lawrence's speech to the audience at the end of the first show on closing night, he

57

happened to look down and saw me sitting there at the front table. He said to the audience, "Ladies and gentlemen, here's our Entertainment Director, our boss, sitting right down here at the table, and we want to thank him for all the wonderful times we've had during the last three weeks, and all the money he paid me losing at golf. Incidentally, he sings a pretty good song. How would you like to hear him sing?"

With this, naturally, the audience applauded, and Lawrence looked out at me sitting at the front table and said, "Well, young fellow, you want to come up here and sing a song?"

I kind of smiled and said, "Yes, Lawrence, I'd love to."

Instead of walking all the way through the house over to the side stairs, I merely stepped onto my chair, onto the table and stepped right up onto the stage. Now Lawrence was really puzzled, because he hadn't felt that I would be that willing, or maybe he didn't think I was even going to come up.

Now we're standing there on stage looking at each other, and Lawrence tried to figure out what I'd do next. Since I'd spent 30 years of my life singing and performing, I walked over to the pianist and whispered in his ear the name of the tune I wanted to sing, and the keys, and a brief format of what I was going to do.

All the time I was doing this with the pianist, Lawrence was standing there with a kind of amused, half embarrassed look on his face. The audience, of course, didn't know exactly what was going to happen. There was 15 or 20 seconds of dead air while I was talking to the pianist.

After I had my quick talk-over, I walked back to Lawrence and asked him if I could borrow some of the boys out of the band. I called down the musicians I wanted from the small Dixieland band, and they all stood behind me. I then said, "Okay, Lawrence, just stand back and I'm going to sing the song."

Lawrence kept standing in front of me with his baton ready to conduct. I said, "No, Lawrence, just stand back and everything is going to be fine. I'll do the tune and you just stand there and watch me."

I sang an arrangement that I'd done for years on an old song called "Cecelia." The boys in the band were pretty hep. I

Lawrence Welk Orchestra and T.V. Performers

gave them hand signals on the change of key, and change of tempo on the end, which culminated climactically.

Lawrence was thrilled to think that I took complete charge. He said over the mike, "I've got to have this young man sing this same arrangement on my television show."

Of course, the response was very favorable and that was the end of the show.

About a month later, while in Los Angeles, Sam Lutz, Lawrence Welk's manager, telephoned and informed me that Lawrence wanted me to tape my segment of the show. I went to the studio and taped "Cecelia," just as we had done it on stage at Harrah's Club.

I can't tell you what a thrill it was for me to have appeared on the Welk show. My mother loved it!

EGO KILLS MORE PEOPLE THAN CANCER

five

What It Takes To Become A Star

What It Takes To Become A Star

Going back to the early 1900's, before radio, before talking pictures, and naturally, before television, there was a thing called "vaudeville." Acts such as singers, jugglers, animal acts, and every possible show you can think of, traveled what was called the "vaudeville circuits," which were housed in theatres all over the country. The circuit theatres were graded according to their size, money spent, and prestige. For example, there was the Gus Sun Time and the Akerman & Harris Circuit. These were the lowest circuits going, and where the new, young artists got their start. From these two circuits you graduated to the Keith Circuit and the Orpheum Circuit, depending on whether you were working the East Coast, or the West Coast. Once you made the step up to these theatres there was an increase in salary, larger theatres, and again, more prestige.

When you played through the circuits for several years and in so doing "honed" your act down, you finally got a crack at the Hammerstein Theatre in New York, or in later years, The Palace!

At this point of your career, the new gramaphone record companies became interested in you, or you were being sought after by Flo Ziegfield, Lou Walters, Oscar Hammerstein, or one of the other Broadway show impresarios. It wasn't long until talking pictures came into being and, of course, this huge mass media made many instantaneous superstars, and also *un-made* some old ones!

Things are completely different now.

Hit Records

Everyone knows that the quickest way to become a star is to get a "hit" record. You may not realize that there are from 300 to 400 records released all over the country **per week**, and there are only about 50 new records introduced on each radio station **per week!** You can readily see where many records never get heard over the air, and for this reason, many potential hit records never even get a chance to "get up to bat."

The only reason I am telling you this is to make you realize that it would be wise for you to develop your "skill," and become a great performer, because it may be a long, long time before that hit record comes along. While you're waiting and working on that hit record, at least you'll be eating.

As a rule, the record companies are no longer signing unknown singers to long-term contracts. In the past 10 years, the record companies have reduced their creative departments drastically, and have resorted to buying the finished product from either the artist, or an independent producer, who has spent his own money on making either a great demo, or a complete master, which the record company either passes up or buys. If they buy the master or demo, *then* they sign the artist, and at that point take on the responsibility of financing further record sessions. This method greatly reduces their initial investment and risk, and has proven to be much more successful for all concerned.

Original Song Material

As you can see by the above, it now becomes important for you as an artist, to develop your composition skills to the best of your ability, as well as your voice. Many artists such as Jim Webb, Neil Sedaka, Carole King, Barry Manilow, James Taylor, Paul Williams, etc., initially submitted their original songs to the record companies for other singers to record, and subsequently, they were recorded themselves, because of their great compositions. Eventually some of them became star recording artists.

The record companies are primarily interested in great writers and producers, because if the song is very strong, they can always find a singer to deliver it. Great original writers are much harder to find than great singers. Keep this uppermost in your mind and start composing. You might find out you are as good a writer as you are a singer.

I recommend that all performers buy and study every hit record that applies to your particular style. Study it thoroughly.

If you expose yourself to enough of the hits, I firmly believe that your brain, and your ear will begin to tell you what the "market" sound is, and will give you at least a general idea of what the mass record buyer is looking for.

I believe if you will think for a moment about all of the current hit songs and records, you will realize that the writer and artist are telling honest straight stories in the language of the present generation. There is very, very seldom a "Moon" and "June" tune that becomes a hit. The new generation, who are the primary buyers of records, will not settle for phoney, plastic, hypocritical lyrics any more. They also are not impressed by the perfect "round voweled" baritone singer. They want an honest message, and they don't particularly care how much voice training you've had!

Fortunately, the adult ears have become accustomed to the "rock" sounds. Also, fortunately, the "rock" sounds have become more sophisticated, which make them more palatable. The beginning of "rock and roll" was a combination of three or four chord changes, with loud "fuzzed" out guitars, and a heavy "lead-footed" drummer. As this kind of music progressed, so did the quality and musicianship. Today, such groups as *Chicago, Abba, Eagles, The Bee Gees,* etc., have combined the great musicians, singers, and arrangers of all time, in a fine big band contemporary sound. We are no longer faced with the "three-chord" players.

At this point, bear in mind that you should strive for your own identification. There are no two people exactly alike. Yet, we all have an opportunity for acceptance. There is nothing that will kill you quicker than being an exact copy of a currently established star. Nobody wants to buy an imitation of what they already have.

One of the big dangers in our business is mediocrity. In the beginning of your career, when you realize that you aren't too well equipped, you work hard because you know that you must get some measure of success just to hold onto a job. After you have some measure of success, when you have just enough skills to get by, you reach the most dangerous part of your entire showbiz career. At this point many artists wither and die.

Because you are fairly successful, and because you are being paid fairly regularly, you have a tendency to relax and "dog

John Davidson   Bob Vincent

it." I am warning you that this is the crucial moment. It is vitally important that you recognize the danger signs, and keep on working on your act and your skills, so that you can get over the "hump" of mediocrity.

The development of your ability as a performer is a "daily" constant search. There is no such thing as "that's good enough." Many, many established stars have made the mistake of thinking that their popularity would last forever. They didn't continue to progress and stay up with the times, and for that reason, they are no longer in demand.

In our business, there is no such word as "forever," or "never!" How many times have you heard someone say, "He'll never make it!" Or, "He'll last forever!" The people who said those things have had to eat their words, what with the ever-changing tastes of the masses. Everything is possible! Remember Tiny Tim and Mrs. Miller?

Naturally, there are other possible ways of becoming successful. John Davidson became a star almost exclusively out of television. To my knowledge, John's never had a big hit record. Shaun Cassidy also became a star out of television, and since has gone into the record business. David Soul (Starsky & Hutch) came out of television, and has since had a hit record. Of course, we can't forget Carol Burnett and Johnny Carson. These "television-made" stars are rare exceptions, and are in the minority when you figure how many became stars because of song writing, and recordings.

New Material

In order for you to be a great performer, it is necessary that you maintain a "fresh" act at all times. I don't care how great an act you start out with, if you don't constantly add new material, and new songs to it, what started out to be great, has got to slowly become uninteresting. It isn't that the original material becomes less effective, it's only that you, yourself, become "bored" with it. I don't care how good a story is, or how great a song is, the more you tell the story, or sing the song, the less effective it becomes in terms of *moving you*. As a result, when your own act doesn't move you, it naturally no longer moves your audience.

I'm certain that you can think back to the times, when you added a new brand new piece of material to your act, how exciting it was the first time you did it for an audience. When it no longer works for you, it isn't because it is no longer good, it's just that you no longer deliver it with your original enthusiasm. It again comes down to honesty. You can't be honest with material you no longer believe in. If this happens to you, it's time to add some new material. This is a constant need so you should never rest on your laurels. Keep looking and adding new material to your act constantly. It may be more work for you to keep up this search, but you'll be far more successful on stage.

Each show that you do should be considered as a new separate entity and a new challenge. Just because you killed them on your last show, doesn't mean you will kill them on your next show. You must remember that each time you step on stage in front of an audience, there is always a certain amount of auditioning going on. You have to re-prove yourself to the audience, even though some of the same people are still there from the last show. You must remember that they have spent additional money for food and beverage, and they again must get their money's worth from you.

I'm going to pose a hypothetical example for you which will illustrate the point. If you were told, (and you thoroughly believed), that the job you were on was the **only job left in the world for you,** and that you had to please each audience thoroughly or be taken outside and shot! What kind of a show would you do?

The trouble with many performers is that they don't make total commitments to every show, because they assume that if they don't do well on this job, there will always be another one. If you *truly believed* that the job you are on is the *only* job in the world for you, your whole attitude would change. Believe me when I tell you you do not have an alternative. **This is your only job!** Take good care of it, or it could be your last.

Importance of a Publicist

As soon as an artist becomes financially able to afford a publicist, or a public relations firm, to handle the making of his career "image," I highly recommend he do so immediately. This should happen before he buys a new Mercedes Benz, a new home, a new pair of shoes, or a new fur coat for his wife.

Particularly in the beginning of his career, it is vitally important that his name appears in all of the show-business trades, and the Los Angeles, and New York City newspaper gossip columns. There are about one hundred buyers of talent in Los Angeles and New York, who control all of the "star-making" vehicles, who read the "trades" every day. Granted they are smart enough to know that most of the names that they read about in these trade magazines are "planted" in the columns by a publicist, but they admire and respect the fact that you, as a "progressive" thinking artist, had the brains to know that this is important to your future. This foresight on your part, plus the money you are spending, shows that you have faith in your talents!

As I have mentioned elsewhere in this book, once you

establish an "image," it's important you keep it! No matter what you may do to slightly damage that image, a good publicist can keep your image intact.

Should you hire a publicity firm to handle you, it is of course very important that you feed them every possible bit of information that you can think of that might be newsworthy. Your publicist can only "fabricate" so much news about you. It's important that you give him as much information about your daily activities and the future "possibilities" as you can. Being almost in daily contact with him also keeps you uppermost in his mind. Don't forget you're not his only client.

Not only do publicists get your name in print, but they are very close to many of the television variety and talk shows, such as: Johnny Carson, Phil Donahue, Dinah Shore, Merv Griffin, Mike Douglas, Tom Snyder, etc., and they could be very instrumental in assisting your management in placing you on one or more of these shows. These shows are very important to your career.

There are other daytime shows in the major cities that are also important to you. If you have any kind of "heat" at all with a record, a small part in a movie or television series, your publicist will make it appear as if you had already arrived.

Granted, it will cost you quite a bit of money. You may think you can't afford it, but you really can't afford to be without it. Some public relations firms will take a gamble with you. If they are sold on your talents, and your financial possibilities, they will start you at a lower fee than normal, in the hopes that they can ride all the way to the top with you.

If you are unable to hire a publicist, it is still possible for you to do certain things for yourself, until such time as you can afford to hire a publicity firm to "pump up" your name value.

As an example of what can be done, let me relate an incident that happened at the time I was managing Wayne Newton.

Following the first hit record Wayne had on "Danke Schoen," and just about the time "Red Roses For A Blue Lady" was released by Capitol Records, we secured an engagement to play for one week at the Deauville Hotel in Miami Beach. Our deal was $5,000 per week, plus room and board. The only problem was that it was the week before Easter which included the

George Burns   Wayne Newton

beginning of Passover and Good Friday! How's that for good timing . . . . in Miami Beach, yet!!

One of the main reasons we took this tough week was that we wanted to prove to Morris Lansburg, the owner of the Deauville, that we could do business for him, and most importantly, Mr. Lansburg also owned the Flamingo Hotel in Las Vegas, which we wanted badly!

Because of the importance of this engagement, Wayne and I decided that I should go to Miami two weeks before our opening, and spend the entire $5,000 on additional advertising and publicity. We were able to get Jack Benny and Bobby Darin to do some "voice overs" behind six television spots, and twenty-three radio commercials. We also decided to double the normal Deauville ads.

When I arrived in Miami, I rented a car and made a visit to practically every disc jockey within 75 miles of Miami, paying for radio spots, and pleading with them to play "Red Roses For A Blue Lady." I also invited them as our guests for opening night. Additionally, we decided to hire an airplane to drag a sign over the beaches and the horse and dog tracks. I also was able to convince several record stores in Miami to put displays of Wayne's record albums in their windows.

In order to get the most for our limited money, I had concentrated all of the above advertising and publicity events to start on Monday, four days before opening, which fell on Thursday of Holy Week.

A few days before the Monday advertising campaign was to take place, I received a call from Mr. Fried, the General Manager of the Deauville Hotel, asking me to come to see him.

As I walked in he said, "Mr. Vincent, we have no reservations for your Mr. Newton and I'm afraid that it's going to be embarassing for your client to sing to an empty house!" I said, "Mr. Fried, if you're asking me to cancel our engagement, the answer is no, and furthermore, we *will* do business for you!

I should explain to you readers that Mr. Fried was not aware that we had already spent our $5,000 for all of this extra advertising and publicity. Furthermore, he was not aware of what else I was doing, and that in a few days, all of this activity was going to happen.

Mr. Fried continued, "Well, we've signed the contract, and

we will live up to it. Mr. Lansburg and I are going to a meeting in Boston and I will leave you a phone number should you change your mind and decide to cancel."

I took the phone number, but I assured him that I would not be calling him.

Monday came and all of the publicity events began to happen. The plane was flying ... the ads came out ... the T.V. spots began ... the disc jockeys began to play our record of "Red Roses For A Blue Lady." Also ... I forgot to tell you that our first guest shot on the Ed Sullivan T.V. Show happened on Sunday, the day before all of our publicity started.

On Monday night, I was standing near the reservation desk and the phone was ringing off the hook! The reservations clerk was mumbling to herself, "I can't understand it! Yesterday we had no reservations for Wayne Newton, and now we have 300 reservations for the dinner show opening night and about 200 for the second show!"

"Great" I said, "maybe the message will get to Boston!"

The next afternoon I checked with the reservation desk and found out that the dinner show was almost sold out for opening night, and reservations were rapidly coming in for the rest of the week.

By the time Wayne and the rest of our people came in on Wednesday afternoon, our reservations for the entire engagement looked pretty good!

Incidentally, I hadn't said anything to Wayne regarding the cancellation request by Mr. Fried, because I didn't want to upset him! Now that I knew we were in good shape with reservations, I told him the entire story.

On opening night, and upon arriving at the dressing room, we discovered that there were none of the usual accouterments; no soft drinks, no liquor, no flowers, no fruit ... nothing!

Wayne went on stage opening show and killed them! Naturally, he got his usual standing ovation on the end, and the waiters and waitresses couldn't believe the business we were doing! The cocktail show was also almost full, plus Wayne got the same reaction from the audience!

The next night, Good Friday, was a duplication of opening night, only better! There was, however, one significant change. When we came to the dressing room for the first show, the room was filled with flowers, fruit, liquor, and soft drinks! Apparently, the message got to Boston!

Reservations for Saturday, Sunday, and the balance of the week were almost capacity. Wayne and the rest of our company decided to relax at the pool Saturday afternoon and get some sun.

After about an hour of lying around, I happened to look towards the entrance to the pool area and who should enter, almost on a dead run, — Mr. Lansburg, Mr. Fried, and two other officials of the hotel. As they approached, I leaned over to Wayne and said, "Here comes the kiss!"

Suddenly, we were surrounded by Mr. Lansburg and company. Of course, they were most complimentary of the amount of business we were doing, etc.

Mr. Fried was practically standing over me as I lay on the lounge chair and, as he was bowing over my head, I looked up at him and said, "I suppose you would like to forget our last conversation!"

He said, "Of course, I was only joking!"

"That little joke will cost you $10,000 per week at the Flamingo in Las Vegas!"

While they were all in such a good mood, we made our deal to play the Flamingo Hotel and for our first Las Vegas appearance in a main room we got $10,000 a week!

The point of the story is, when you've got a product that you know without a doubt is saleable, you've got to "shout" about it! There comes a time in everyone's professional life when you have to "put your money where your mouth is!"

In any event, as soon as any performer gets the least little "spark" lit under his career, the next man he should talk to is his publicist. He's the only "fortune teller" you can believe in!

In "Show-Business Is *Two* Words," I can give you all of the basic formulas in order for you to successfully entertain your audience. There are some recording artists who have achieved success through a "quick" hit record, before they had an opportunity to prepare themselves as seasoned performers. Many of them have faded out of show business because of this lack of professional savvy. Please remember that the public may pay to see you ONCE because of your sudden stardom, but if you don't entertain them that first time, you'll never see them again!

The ideal way to become successful with longevity, is to prepare yourself as a performer, and at the same time, seek that elusive hit record by writing and recording. Remember, the record companies are looking for that new creative artist, just as hard as you are looking for them.

Wayne Newton

Speaking of preparing yourself as a performer, Wayne Newton was probably the most "prepared" star there was at the point of his first hit record. I would like to tell you a true story about Wayne, which points out his early determination to become a star!

Before Wayne Newton was a star, he had a lounge group called "The Newton Brothers." It was made up of Wayne, his brother Jerry, and their road manager, Tommy Amato. "The Newton Brothers" were appearing at Harvey's Resort Hotel at Lake Tahoe, which is located right across the street from Harrah's Club. Previous to my taking the job as Entertainment Director at Harrah's, I had been Wayne and Jerry's agent with an agency out of Chicago, called Mutual Entertainment Agency. I had handled the Newton Brothers lounge act for about three years when they were playing nothing but lounges, so I was quite familiar with the act.

A few months after I had accepted the position of Entertainment Director, the "Newton Brothers" played a two week engagement at Harvey's Resort Hotel, Lake Tahoe.

During the second week of their engagement, Tommy Amato came to see me in my office at Harrah's, and asked me if it wasn't possible to put them somewhere in my lounges for a couple of weeks, because they were short of money.

I explained to Tommy that the only spot I had open was two weeks in the Reno lounge, and was on the worst shift that we had, starting at noon and ending about 4:30 p.m. I told him that if he still wanted it, I would be glad to put them in starting the next day, and would give them $2,500 per week. That was agreeable with Wayne, and he confirmed it. The Newton Brothers opened in the Reno lounge the next day at noon.

It so happened that three days after they opened in Reno,

we had an entertainment meeting in the conference room, which was located above the Reno lounge. Bill Harrah had a fetish about never being late for anything, and it happened that we were all in the conference room waiting for Bill when he showed up about five minutes late.

As he came through the door, he said to me, "Who is that lounge act working down in the lounge right now?"

I thought for a moment. "That's the Newton Brothers. I had two weeks open, so I put them in just to fill the two-week hole."

"The reason I am late," he explained, "is that I had to walk completely around the building to another stairway in order to get up to the conference room. The casino and the lounge are so full, I couldn't walk down the aisle. As soon as this meeting is over, I want you to make them an offer for two years — twenty weeks minimum per year — at thirty-five-hundred-dollars per week. Let me know what they say."

I was thrilled for two reasons: one, they were doing a great job for me in the lounge, and two, I was pleased because it might be the beginning of a big future for them. They had knocked around lounges for years and years, and I figured that this may be their big reward.

As soon as the meeting was over, I went to the phone and called Tommy Amato to tell him the good news. "Bill Harrah saw you this afternoon and authorized me to offer you forty weeks over the next two years at thirty-five-hundred-dollars per week!", I said.

"Well, I should be thrilled with it, but I'll tell you what happened," Tommy replied. "Last night, Wayne and Jerry and I made a firm decision that we would never work another lounge again for the rest of our lives! We're tired of working lounges. We feel we deserve better treatment, and we feel we're ready for the main rooms. We've decided that we will not work another lounge again. However, we would be willing to accept fifteen-hundred-dollars-per-week in the South Shore Room, if you could play us as an opening act for one of your stars."

I couldn't believe it! I explained to him that it's rare that any lounge act can work in the main room, what with having to move all of their equipment on and off stage, and besides, they would only get 15 minutes, if I could work it out.

Wayne Newton

So I told Tommy, "Why don't you and Wayne take the forty weeks at thirty-five-hundred-dollars-a-week for the next two years. Maybe by that time, we could figure some way that you can play the South Shore Room."

But he was steadfast. "Nope. We made a firm decision last night and we will not deviate from it. We will not work anywhere but the Main room. If you can't give us fifteen-hundred dollars in the South Shore Room, we'll pass the lounge at thirty-five hundred dollars for forty weeks."

I explained this to Bill Harrah and he chuckled to himself and thought that maybe a little more money might change their minds. "Look," said Bill, "call them back, tell them I've changed the offer and I'll give them forty weeks over the next two years — twenty weeks each year — at a minimum of five-thousand-dollars-per-week."

With that, I thought to myself, they can't possibly turn this offer down because I knew they were broke. I also knew that their chances of getting main room work was pretty slim. I proceeded to call Tommy Amato again.

"Look," explained Tommy "we realize the offer is fantastic. We've never had an offer like that before and we may regret it, but **we will not work another lounge, period!** We definitely are going to work main rooms or we are going to quit this business. We will play the South Shore Room for as low as fifteen-hundred-dollars-a-week, if you can work out some kind of arrangement for us."

Of course I told him that that was impossible, and I thought he was being very foolish, but I couldn't sway their decision so I hung up.

Bill Harrah chuckled again and said to me, "Well, offer him seventy-five-hundred-dollars-a-week for 40 weeks for the next two years, and I think maybe that will get them to change their minds."

I called Tommy and asked him to come up to my office because I had to discuss something with him, that was too important to discuss over the phone. I sat him down and said, "Look, as a friend, don't let me make you this offer and turn it down again, because you're going to break my heart. It'll probably be the biggest offer you'll ever get in your life. Bill Harrah just authorized me to offer you seventy-five-hundred-dollars-per-week for forty weeks, over the next two years. Now you can't turn that offer down."

"Look, we are adamant about it. We know Wayne's going to be a star one day, and we know that if we keep working lounges for the rest of our lives, we will never make the main rooms. We definitely are not going to take any lounge for any price. Please tell Mr. Harrah that we appreciate the offer, and please don't go to ten-thousand-dollars-a-week because it'll be the same story. We will not work another lounge again — ever! Also, please ask him if there isn't some way he can play us in the main room at fifteen-hundred-dollars-a-week."

I explained to Tommy that it was impossible. I thought the

boys were being very foolish, and that they probably had closed the door to any further offers.

I called Bill Harrah again. Needless to say, Bill was amazed and slightly amused. "Well," he said, "looks like we're up against a stone wall. We better forget about making any further offers."

At that time, the Newton Brothers were being handled by G.A.C., which was the forerunner of the current agency, I.C.M. Bobby Burns was their personal sponsor. It happened that Jack Benny was going to play a concert date in Sydney, Australia, and the only main room that Bobby Burns could find to play the Newton Brothers was at the Hilton Hotel in Sydney, during the same time that Jack Benny was going to do his concert. Bobby Burns asked Irving Fein, Jack's personal manager, and Jack Benny to see the Newton Brothers, and pay particular attention to Wayne, who he felt was a big talent.

Everybody returned to America. I got a phone call from Tommy Amato upon his return. He said, "Guess what! We're going to play the South Shore Room, after all! Jack Benny came in to see us in Sydney, and loved our act, particularly Wayne, and has made us a deal to work as part of his act when he plays Harrah's Club."

"That's great! you deserve it."

"Guess what else? Guess what Jack Benny is paying us!"

"I'm afraid to ask." I said.

"Fifteen-hundred-dollars-a-week!"

That's the true story of how Wayne Newton got to the South Shore Room, which started him on his way to stardom.

Jack Benny

Speaking of Jack Benny, I would like to relate what we went through in order to get Jack Benny, plus his good friend, George Burns to play at Harrah's Club.

When I was hired by Bill Harrah, he asked me to concentrate on firming up engagements with both Benny and Burns. Apparently, my predecessor had tried unsuccessfully to get them, and Bill was determined that I continue the pursuit.

One day it occurred to me that if I were able to get a firm

George Burns

engagement with one of them, I would stand a good chance of getting the other. I knew that Jack and George were good friends, and if we could secure an engagement with either one, the other would probably come to Harrah's for the opening, This would give me an opportunity to meet the other star and show him our fine theatre and also the excellent treatment we gave to our headliners.

It happened that George Burns and Carol Channing had played a date together in Las Vegas and their engagement was very successful. I decided to make an offer to both George and

Jack Benny

Carol to play for us with the same show.

After many weeks of negotiations with the agencies who represented Burns and Channing, I was able to secure an engagement.

Sure enough about four weeks before the George Burns and Carol Channing date, I received a call from Irving Fein, Jack Benny's personal manager. Irving mentioned that Mr. and Mrs. Benny were interested in coming to Tahoe to see George and Carol's opening, and was wondering if we would take care of the details, such as transportation from the airport in Reno to

Lake Tahoe, housing, etc. I assured him that we were beautifully equipped to take care of Mr. and Mrs. Benny, and Mr. and Mrs. Burns (Gracie Allen), and please feel free to come up a couple of days before the show opened.

Naturally, we were pleased that our plans had worked out so well. Not only were we fortunate in getting a great show with Burns and Channing, but we also would have a good chance of interesting Jack Benny in playing for us. We made plans to house them in our North Lodge, where we had several suites for our stars. Each suite had a living room, a sitting room, a large master bedroom, and a private bath.

We assigned one of these suites to George Burns and Gracie Allen, another suite, which was right next to it, to Jack Benny and Mary Livingston, and, of course, another suite to Carol Channing and her husband.

The day of their arrival came and Bill Harrah had assigned one of the biggest Rolls Royces that we owned to pick up everybody at the airport, and bring them to Lake Tahoe. Of course, the Rolls Royce was stocked with a selection of liqueurs in the back seat, plus there was a built in television set.

Our drivers picked up the stars at the airport in Reno and drove them up to Lake Tahoe, which is a distance of about fifty miles. Of course, at the North Lodge in the suites, we had fixed some beautiful bouquets of flowers and baskets of fruit. Everything we could possible think of was taken care of in order to make the suites look appealing. Upon their arrival, I introduced myself to Mr. and Mrs. Benny; Mr. and Mrs. Burns; and Mr. and Mrs. Lowe (Channing). We then showed them to their suites.

We were gathered in Jack and Mary's suite and Mary Livingston had to go to the restroom. As we were sitting there talking, and they were being very complimentary about the exquisite accommodations, Mary Livingston came out of the restroom and proclaimed rather loudly to Jack Benny, "You know Jack, you could never play here! I know how you hate to take showers, and they don't have a bathtub in their suites here!!"

Naturally, my heart did flip flops. I was completely wiped out by the fact that this one little incident might kill our whole scheme to get Jack Benny to work for us.

As soon as possible, when Jack Benny, Carol Channing, and George Burns and everyone else in the party had gone over to rehearsal in the South Shore Room, I called Bill Harrah quickly and told him of the unfortunate incident about the bathtub. Bill, in his usual manner of approaching matters directly, said to me, "How long can you keep them out of the suites?"

"Well, I think they'll be in rehearsal in the South Shore Room for about three hours."

"Fine, in three hours you will have a restroom with a tub in it in Jack Benny's suite."

With that, I left and went over to the South Shore Room so I could delay the rehearsals for as long as possible. A bevy of carpenters, painters, and plumbers went to work on the suite, and tore out the stall shower, set in a bathtub-shower combination, retiled, replastered, and repainted the restroom in three hours!

From time to time, I would slip out of the South Shore Room to see how they were coming. It was amazing how many people Bill Harrah had sent to get the job done in such a short time.

When Jack Benny, and Mary and George Burns and Gracie came back to the North Lodge, Mary went into the restroom and said to Jack, "Jack, you must play here! Anybody who would go to this much trouble to please you, must be nice people, and I think you owe them an engagement."

Right there on the spot, I made a deal with Jack Benny to appear for us at our next open date, when he was available. That's the true story of how we got Jack Benny to play for Harrah's.

Tony Martin — Cyd Charisse

I've mentioned Bill Harrah's name so much throughout the book that I would like to relate a story that involved Bill, and Cyd Charisse and Tony Martin, when the latter two were appearing at Harrah's. This story will give you some idea of the wealth and power of this giant of the gaming industry.

It so happened that Bill Harrah liked to entertain each star, and their entourage, at least once during their engagement. It

Cyd Charisse   Tony Martin

usually was an early cocktail dinner party at the Villa Harrah, located on the water's edge at Lake Tahoe.

Villa Harrah was built at the cost of one-million-five-hundred-thousand dollars, and contained thirteen-thousand square feet of living space. In it was a banquet hall that could seat 100 for dinner. Needless to say, it was the most luxurious home I've ever seen and even the stars were impressed with it's elegance.

Prior to the dinner, it was my custom to give the stars and their company of musicians, and back-up singers and dancers a tour of this magnificent show place.

Near the end of our tour of the Villa, I took them into the lower kitchen and from the kitchen we went outside through the pantry door which leads up a set of brick stairs to the outdoor Olympic size pool.

It was April and there was no snow on the ground. As we came up the outside stairs to the pool, we had to make a turn in the stairs, and in the shade next to a concrete railing was a small pile of snow which hadn't melted, because it was constantly shaded by the stairwell.

Cyd happened to look over the railing and saw this small pile of snow. Mind you, there was no snow on the ground anywhere except this snow hidden in the stairwell.

Cyd exclaimed to Tony, "Look Tony, there's snow on the ground next to the railing! I wonder why it hasn't melted?"

Tony walked over to Cyd's side of the stairs and looked at the snow, and slowly looked back at Cyd and said — "He didn't want it to!!"

Getting back to "How To Become A Star," there is no set formula. If you have born talent . . . if you have dedicated yourself diligently, if you have maintained a good, clean business relationship with all of your associates . . . if you have been "honest" with the audience each and every time you've stepped on stage; and most of all . . . if the "man upstairs" has tossed you the "brass ring," and you had the good sense to treat it with respect, . . . you might become the next Super-Star.

six

The Performing Musician

The Performing Musician

With the demise of the big bands in the forties, there came into being what is commonly called the "cocktail lounge group." They originally were made up of members of the big bands, who realized that the glory of the bands such as Benny Goodman, Tommy Dorsey, Glen Miller, etc., was a thing of the past, and in order for them to make a living it was necessary to form small groups of three, four, or five musicians, which would be inexpensive enough to play in the little bars/cocktail lounges. In the beginning, they merely sang some of the currently popular songs, and played for dancing.

Naturally, as they began to become more successful, they started to rehearse more "show" material, so that they would be in bigger demand and make more money. Soon they discovered that the bass man was kind of a "funny" guy, so they began to write comedy material for him and thus, was born the "performing musician." As the popularity and the demand for these musical "show" groups spread all over the country, the musicians who originally were big band players became extroverted, singing, "comic-performing" musicians. Not only did they do live comedy, they also began a craze called "record pantomime."

Speaking of record-pantomime, one of the earliest artists to use this form of entertainment was Roy Davis, who introduced his record antics at the Paramount Theatre in New York City in 1940. Other artists who began in show business in this manner were Dick and Jerry Van Dyke, and Jerry Lewis.

From about 1945 up to the present, the largest segment of "full-time" employed entertainers were involved in making their livelihood in the cocktail lounges of America. I would estimate that there are over 100,000 entertaining, performing musicians currently employed in Show-Business, working in lounges today.

Beginning of the "Lounge Business"

In the early days of the cocktail lounge groups, there were a handful of agents around the country who specialized in

86

Louis Prima, Keely Smith and Sam Butera and The Witnesses

developing, and booking small musical combos. Some of the most noteable agents in this field at that time were, Joe Glazer (Louis Armstrong), Julius J. (Bookie) Levin, Jolly Joyce, Allan Ruppert, Fred Costa, Art Raye, "Mac" McConkey, Milo Stelt, Eddie Hall, Penny Mayo, Bill Rothe, Jack Belmont, Noel Kramer, Dick Shelton, Roy Cooper, Augie Morin, Bill Burton, Fred Petty, Dick Stevens, Arne Prager, Stan Zucker, and a few other "pioneers" I may have forgotten.

These gentlemen saw the handwriting on the wall when the big bands began to fade, and they started to develop the cocktail lounge groups as we know them today.

Some of the early, well known lounge acts that had various degrees of success were the Mary Kaye Trio, Redd Foxx, Don Rickles, Louis Prima, Keely Smith, Sam Butera and the Witnesses, The Characters, Shecky Greene, Joe Maize and the Chordsmen, Kay Martin and her Bodyguards, The Matys Brothers, The Lancers, Eddie Peddie and the "Zany-Acks," The Metro-Tones, The Novelites, Freddy Bell and Roberta Lynn,

Kim Sisters, the "Goofers," Kings Four, Danny Bridge and The Tunesmen, Gaylord & Holiday, The Beachcombers, Kirby Stone Four, Stan Nelson Trio, Earl Grant, The Vagabonds, The Treniers, Steve Gibson and the Red Caps, Bill Haley and the Comets, and a few others I may have inadvertently overlooked.

Today there are some fine lounge acts who might become stars, if they could just get enough exposure in the gaming areas. Even though they may not be known nationally, the following artists are great entertainers: Sidro's Armada with Beverly Brown, Keri Crossman and "Seventh Heaven," The Chasers Fore, Kathy and Judy Bryte, Glen Bailey & Circus, Terry Allen, Command Performance, Opus VI, The Zaras, Frankie Carr, Glen Smith, Rick and Neal, Billy Kay, "The Mob," "The Checkmates," Freddy Bell, Main Street Singers, The Muglestons, Bobby Mercer Road Show, Lewis and Clark Expedition, D.D. Smith, Tori Lysdahl, Terry Stokes, Julie Miller, Roberta Lynn, Marlene Ricci, Don Campeau, Dae Han Sisters, and Jerry Sun Show.

If the operators in Nevada and New Jersey, will open their lounges up to the casinos, like they used to in Vegas, and give the lounge artists a chance for regular exposure, I'm positive that we would develop some new stars of tomorrow, out of these fine performers.

Lounge Business — Launching Pad

Since the advent of the cocktail lounge groups, many of our past and current stars cut their eye teeth in this area of the business. Such stars as Bobby Darin, Shecky Greene, The Smothers Brother, Rowan & Martin, Wayne Newton, Paul Anka, Redd Foxx, Don Rickles, Ann Margaret, Frank Sinatra Jr., Bill Cosby, Liberace, Glenn Campbell, The Captain & Tenile, Nat King Cole, Oscar Peterson, Jerry Van Dyke, Dizzie Gillespie, Simon and Garfunkle, and most of the super star groups such as, Chicago, the Beach Boys, the Eagles, Led Zepplin, Heart, the Rolling Stones, Commodores, Natalie Cole, Pablo Cruise, the Beatles, War, the Spinners, Ray Charles, the Temptations, George Benson, and the O'Jays. Most of the country western singers and groups such as Willie Nelson, Mel Tillis, Roy Clark, Johnny Cash, Kenny Rogers, Dolly Parton, Waylon

Jack Ross — Dick Lane Sextette

Jennings, the Statler Brothers, Conway Twitty and Loretta Lynn, also began on the cocktail circuit.

If the truth were known, practically every name star at one time or another, made their living in the lounge business. Today, this area of show business is about the only place left for the new stars of tomorrow to learn how to perform. There is no more vaudeville, no more big bands, no more small night clubs with house bands — just the cocktail lounges.

When the lounge business was young, most of these rooms were badly equipped. They had bad sound reproduction, little or no spot lighting, and they had terrible acoustics. The stages were generally up behind the bar, and the noise from the bartenders blenders, dropping beer bottles down the chute to the basement was unbelievable.

Today, conditions have changed radically. Now some of the cocktail lounges in hotels, motels, and free-standing clubs have installed good sound equipment, good lighting, fair acoustics in most cases (though they still have a long way to go in this department!). The bandstands are no longer behind the bar. No longer is the cocktail lounge considered to be some lowly, dark crevice where a performer makes his living, without admitting it.

Hotels — Motor Inns

The Hotels and Motor Inns of America have begun to realize that in order for them to be a "full-service" facility, they have to build bigger and better equipped lounges. The large chain hotels and inns such as Holiday Inns, Ramada Inns, Rodeway Inns, Sheraton Inns, Hilton Inns, and Marriott Hotels have all increased the quality of these entertainment areas, and much to their delight, have discovered an increase in beverage sales after 8:00 p.m.

The purpose of this chapter is to give you the benefit of my 35 years of experience in the lounge field. For the last 25 years, I have booked, managed, and produced hundreds of musical lounge groups, and I'm proud to say that many of these people have become well known in the business. One of the reasons for writing this book is to eliminate the necessity of my telling new prospective stars the same things over and over again. I'm also hopeful that the information and advice I'm about to give you will make your climb to stardom a little quicker, and a whole lot easier.

A group's success is largely dependent on how long they stay together, so it is vitally important that you examine the "character," and the personal side of each man or woman

The Vagabonds

selected to become a member of the organization, before hiring them. This factor is just as important as their playing and singing ability.

THE DETERMINING SOUND OF THE GROUP

Several million dollars are spent daily for records and albums, which should tell you that the sound of your group has to duplicate, as closely as possible the "total sound" of the hit records of the day. The record industry actually dictates what instrumentation you need to include in the group sound. Not only the playing ability and instrumentation, but also quality and style of the singers.

Before you even think of hiring sidemen for your group, please remember that they will have to live in close proximity for many, many weeks or years, so be careful about hiring people that have any mental or social problems. What good is hiring a great guitar player, rehearsing him for hours, costuming him, loaning him money, and then find out he's a "flake." Now comes the problem of replacing him, and the whole process starts all over again.

Also, stay away from hiring a sideman who has a wife and two or three kids, particularly of school age. No matter what he says about how his wife understands that he'll have to travel, or "Don't worry, they'll travel with me on the road." Sooner or later, he'll get a phone call in the middle of the night and his wife will be crying and pleading with him to come home. The next day, he'll give his notice.

I'm not advocating that you do not hire sidemen with wives and no children, or wives with a small baby. As soon as the kids become of school age, you'll have a problem. (I will cover "Traveling Wives and Family" in another chapter.)

This advice is given to you only to insure your chances of success with a minimum of problems. Take heed!

With this in mind, here is what you should be looking for in forming your group: A guitarist who sings. His playing ability should cover not only the "funk" sounds of the disco-rock records, but, ideally, he (or she) should be able to play "pop" guitar in the vein of the guitar "greats" of the forties. This is necessary, if you intend to climb out of the rut of just being a rock and roll dance band. If this individual can also "rap" well with the customers, he could possibly become your "mike man." With his type of instrument, he has the physical ability to front the group. Since the advent of rock and roll, the dominant sound of the majority of hit records has been guitar. Going back to Bill Haley and the Comets, Elvis Presley, Chubby Checker, Bo Diddley, and many others, every kid in the block owned a guitar. Naturally, with advent of the guitar amplifier, this instrument really came into its own.

The next instrument necessary in today's sound is the

The Kings Four

"multi-keyboard" man. Notice I didn't say organist. It used to be that all you needed was an organist, but again with the sounds of the record industry becoming more varied and sophisticated, it is necessary that you find a keyboard man who plays and owns, (or will buy) an organ, Leslie speaker, moog synthesizer, string machine of some type, Fender Rhodes piano, and God knows what other keyboards that are becoming popular. In other words, he has to be able to give you all of the keyboard sounds that it probably took two or three men to record, in the studio. This man also has to have some financial backing just to afford to buy this equipment. In addition to buying the equipment, he has to buy a sufficiently large van to haul all of it from job to job. (You club owners might keep these costs in mind when you make such statments as, "I can't see why they have to get so much money.")

The keyboard man, in most cases, is the musical leader of most groups due to the background of musical education he has had to go through in order to play all of this equipment. In addition to his playing ability, he should also be able to sing, if not solo at least harmony parts. Because he is physically buried behind his multi-keyboards, I do not recommend that he become the "rapper" of the group. He's too far removed from the vision of the customers.

The bass man is the next addition to the group. Naturally, he should be playing an amplified bass, rather than the old upright bass. Also, because he is mobile with his instrument, he could possibly be your "rapper" and solo male singer. He and the guitar man could possibly split the front emcee chores between them. The bass man must be in complete accord, musically, with the drummer. They actually have to work together, as if they were one person. They must feel the same funk together, and actually the bass notes and rhythm patterns provide the drummer with an augmented "bass drum" beat, so that it gives the drummer more latitude to play creative, melodic drums. That's why these two people *must* be compatible.

Now we come to the glue that holds the whole rhythm section together, the drummer. His basic job is to quickly establish the groove and hold it. Generally most drummers in today's music beat off all tempos and somehow manage to instinctively establish the right tempo and groove 99 percent of the time. If the tempo is wrong, if the groove doesn't "settle in" immediately, the whole tune is played in "hard labor."

In addition to setting the tempos and holding the groove, he has to be born with good instinctive taste. He has to know immediately *what* to play *when*, and what *not* to play. He not only holds the rhythm section together, but has to kick the group into an inspired performance. This doesn't necessarily mean playing loud, but playing accompaniment to what is happening with all of the other members of the group. If he just "pounds" with a tasteless rock beat, without feeling what is hap-

The Characters

pening with the rest of the band, it's no good. He must be sensitive, listen to everyone else, and play accordingly.

The addition of two or three horns are necessary in today's
musical sounds. Of course, if part of your rhythm section can
double on a horn, it saves hiring other people. I've seen some
groups with a keyboard man who doubles horn, a bass man or a
guitar man who doubles horn, which give a quartet the sound of
six men! This doubling ability is a big asset to any group, and of
course, saves you from splitting up the money. If you have
some horn doubles, it might be necessary to only add one horn
man. He naturally should be a singer and again, because of his
mobility, he could possibly be your emcee and solo singer.

The frosting on the cake is the addition of a girl singer. I
know that many male groups do not want to get involved in hiring a girl in the group because of the possible emotional hassles
it could cause. Again, it's important that any girl you hire is
thoroughly screened as to her character, and her ability to get
along with the guys. I've seen many girls who fit into the group
as if they were another guy and there were no problems. It all
depends on the girl and, of course, on the boys' attitudes toward

95

her. If all of the guys will remember that this is a business, and not just an easy way to make a living and get lucky every night, it's entirely possible that the addition of a girl player, or singer would cause no problems.

From the customers' standpoint, a girl is a big asset. I'm not saying that having a girl in the group is absolutely necessary, but it will help make your group more easily acceptable to the customers and, of course, to the owners. Here again, if you have a "great" all-male group, a girl may not be necessary. If you don't have a great group, you had better reconsider adding a girl.

In most cases, I don't advocate adding two girl singers because you are just doubling your jeopardy. They could cause internal jealousies, plus an unhappy competitive feeling between the girls. Also, if you have two front girls, it becomes necessary to have them choreographed and costumed identically. All of this adds additional expense to your overhead.

If the records of tomorrow become even more sophisticated, I'm afraid the bandstands of tomorrow will have to be huge, just to hold all of the instruments. In any event, the sounds of today are much more pleasing to the ear than the early days of rock and roll. I believe the quality of the present record sounds have done much to bring together the musical tastes of both the new and old generations. There is no longer the deep resentment by the older generation towards the loud music of the young contemporary artists.

Salary Split

In the beginning of every group, the salaries received are usually so minimal that the groups usually split up their weekly salary in equal portions. The question of splitting the money becomes a problem as soon as the value of the group exceeds the minimum scale, and there begins to be discomfort with the equal split formula by some of the members.

There are many different ways of solving this financial problem, and each solution is dependent upon the original set up of the group.

In one type of group there is a definite leader. He's usually

The Treniers

more mature, more experienced, and a strong personality. He usually hires sidemen who are told in front that he is the boss, so to speak, and they are hired as musicians and singers who are expected to do exactly as he dictates. They have no management responsibility at all, and are expected to play and sing, and be on time for the job and rehearsals.

The money paid to these sidemen is usually a flat salary, which is negotiated with the leader. The sideman sometimes gets his salary, plus so much a mile for his automobile. But, he is solely responsible for his own personal expenses. If the leader gets *gratis* rooms with the contract, it usually includes the sidemen. If the leader does not get *gratis* rooms, he makes an arrangement with each sideman to pay them a higher salary. However, they are obligated to pay for their own housing out of it. The leader, in this case, takes the gains, or losses, without discussing the contract prices with the sidemen, and he usually pays all other business expenses.

This type of financial arrangement can work out successfully, *if* the leader is very talented! . . . very forceful in his business dealings! . . . and convinces his "employees" that they are "going somewhere" with their futures! . . . and that they will not have too many weeks out of work! It is the leader's job to motivate his sidemen to work for him in a happy, optimistic atmosphere! If he can do all of these things, chances are his sidemen will stay with him.

The more common set-up is a cooperative group, who work together as partners. They sometimes have an appointed leader, who handles the business of the group, and in exchange for this extra responsibility he is compensated some extra money. Under this set-up all of the partners see the contracts and, as such, they equally ride the gains and losses together.

They usually pay all of the business expenses off the top such as, agency commission, personal manager commission (if they have one), transportation, housing, payments on their equipment (except for their own instruments), and miscellaneous business expenses. After this overhead is covered, the rest of the weekly salaries are split equally.

This kind of partnership is usually simpler to handle, and the fact that they all see the contracts gives them the feeling of participation in the success or failure of the group.

Under the partnership arrangement, I have sometimes witnessed a "semi-partnership" where there may be one or two more talented, more experienced members, who are carrying more of the load than the others.

In this case, I have seen groups pay all expenses off the top and then pay the members on different percentages of the net salaries. For example, two of the members of a sextette would each get 20 percent of the net; and the other four partners would

Shecky Greene

each get 15 percent. These percentages are negotiable, depending on each group.

The ideal set-up must be designed so that all of the members feel that they are getting a fair shake, so that there is a happy, unified working relationship.

In this partnership arrangement, all major decision should be decided by a majority vote of the members, with each member getting *one vote*, no matter what percentage of salary he is receiving.

Incidentally, regarding the payment of income taxes to the

99

Internal Revenue Service the leader is the employer, in the "leadership" set-up and, as such, he pays the state and federal employer taxes on the salaries paid to his sidemen.

In the case of a partnership, each partner is responsible for his portion of the state and federal taxes, and in fact, I recommend that they have an attorney, and an accountant draw up a formal agreement which they all sign, establishing their business arrangements.

The above two working plans cover 90 percent of all groups, with some minor variations of both methods. Whatever method you use, make certain that none of the members carry any grievances to the stage with them, so that you can go to work each night, happy with each other.

TYPES OF LOUNGE GROUPS

In describing the above lounge groups, I have only written about the typical Las Vegas lounge act. For your information, there are other types of lounges which are somewhat different in sound, style, instrumentation, and clientele.

Take for example the lounges which fostered such stars as; the Smothers Brothers, Kingston Trio, Seals and Crofts, Carole King, James Taylor, Simon and Garfunkel, Bob Dylan, and many others. They were commonly called coffee houses. They generally were small intimate rooms catering to a more college-oriented clientele. Their instrumentation was generally limited to acoustical guitars, upright basses, and possibly acoustical pianos. Loud sounds were not advisable and the lyric content was "folkish" or sophisticated comedy. Everything the coffee house performers did was done to stimulate an intellectual acceptance by the audience.

Another type is the jazz lounge. These too were originally small intimate rooms, usually located along side streets in New York City (52nd Street), Chicago (Rush Street), Los Angeles (Sunset Blvd.), Kansas City, and New Orleans. These lounges fostered such greats as Art Tatum, Oscar Peterson, Nat Cole (Nat Cole Trio), Errol Garner, and the recent crop of jazz greats like George Benson, Herb Ellis, Chic Corea, Chuck Mangione, Herbie Hancock, and many many others.

There is a definite indication that the demand for jazz

Gaylord & Holiday

records is growing and the jazz names are drawing larger crowds in their concerts. For many years, it appeared that jazz might disappear from the musical scene, but recently there has been a resurgence of this fine art form.

Much of the increase in the popularity of jazz can be attributed to the college graduates who had been exposed to big-band jazz during their college days. Every university of any size has at least one or two big jazz orchestras, which come out of their music departments. In some of the more musically oriented colleges and universities, such as North Texas State University in Denton, Texas; Berklee School of Music in Boston; Eastman School of Music in Rochester; and several others. There are anywhere from five to nine big jazz bands in rehearsal every day.

Naturally, all of these jazz bands give several concerts during the year and they are well attended by the college students. With the graduation of all these young adults, and their getting

Danny Bridge and the Tunesmen

into the job markets, it should naturally create a bigger demand for this form of music in the concert halls. Who knows? This could be the beginning of the return of the big bands.

Another form of jazz is the dixieland band. In most major cities, there was at least one "dixie" club. Years ago it was, "Eddie Condons" and "Nicks" in New York City, "Jazz Limited" and the "Blue Note" in Chicago, and the "Radio Room" in Hollywood. The names included "Wild Bill Davidson," Bob

Crosby's "Bob Cats," Jack Teagarden, Wingy Minone, Louis Armstrong, Pete Fountain, Louis Prima, Roy Laberto, Dukes of Dixieland, Al Hirt, Bob Scobey, Sidney Bichet, Pee Wee Russell, and many others.

This form of jazz has diminished in recent years but it left its mark in all forms of our music today. This music was originally born in the negro songs of the cotton fields. It also came out of Bourbon Street in New Orleans, and the riverboats that steamed up and down the Mississippi. Dixieland can truly be called the "music of America."

Now that I have identified all of the various forms of lounge groups, I feel that it is most vital for someone in your group to become involved with the audience on a one-on-one relationship each and every time you start playing. You must have someone who fronts your group, and honestly loves the audience.

If you are just good musicians and good singers, but you have no natural desire to please the customers, you will find little or no success.

Canned "Disco" Dance Music —

How Long Will It Last?
Where Did It Come From?

About five years ago there were subtle signs that the music business was going through another change. Young adults were demanding more dance music and less floor shows. They were also demanding that the live bands play the same tunes that they were buying on records by the millions. Not only did they demand the same tunes, but they wanted to dance and listen to these songs played *exactly* as they had heard them on the records.

Around 1974 in the cocktail lounge field, all of the better paid lounge groups were looking toward Las Vegas as their ultimate goal and, as such, they were concentrating their main attentions on putting together "dynamite" show material, and whatever time was left in their rehearsals they spent in learning a few new dance numbers. They were not overly concerned about their dance sets, and as a result their dance music was just passable. Their concentration was show ... show ... show!

What they weren't totally aware of was the fact that the young adult market was looking for good "funky" dance music, and could care less about their floor shows.

Also, what the "show" groups didn't fully realize was that Las Vegas had less and less need for "show" groups, because they had closed up many of their lounges making them into Keno and Bingo parlours, or changed them into theatres where they featured nude revues.

I can remember warning my own lounge groups about the change from floor shows to good dance music and, in the beginning, many of my show groups refused to pay attention to the warning, and continued striving for better shows, in anticipation of a date in Las Vegas, which was becoming increasingly non-existent!

It was obvious now, five years later, that my warning was valid, because there are very few floor show lounges in existence. If they are using shows, they are only using one show per night, and the rest of the night is made up of good, disco, top 40, dance music.

Where did the canned, disco music come from and why? It came about basically for two reasons.

First, the "live" lounge groups refused to concentrate on good, authentic, "right off the record" dance music.

Second, it became advisable for the operators to install twin-turntables and some special lighting effects, plus a $350 disc-jockey with a line of chatter to play the disco hits.

Today, there are an increasing number of canned music dance clubs being converted from "live" music, plus there are many totally new canned disco-dance palaces being built.

True, the lounge groups now realize that the dance trend is here to stay for at least a couple of years, and they have made the transition to playing good "off the record" dance music, but the damage has already been done. Millions of dollars have already been spent by the operators for "disco" recording and lighting equipment.

In spite of the above there is still hope for live bands. Many of the larger disco-dance palaces are using both "canned" music *and* a "live" band alternating with each other. If there is enough size and seating capacity, this is the most profitable policy.

Tommy Amato   Wayne Newton   Jerry Newton

Also, it is a known fact that the excess volume of sound, plus all of the psychedelic lighting effects are not palatable to most people over 30 years of age. Where are the rest of the people over the "disco" age going for their fun and relaxation? Naturally, to the hotels, motels, and clubs featuring good food and a little less nerve-wracking, but still contemporary "live" dance music.

It is a known fact that the majority of the loud disco dance clubs have to charge a cover at the door, because the "dance crowd," on the whole are not big spenders for food and beverages. They spend most of the night "crusing" and dancing.

This means that the over 30 crowd who patronize the "non-disco" places of entertainment are more likely to spend more money per person for a pleasant evening of live entertainment and dancing.

It is my personal observation that the loud, canned disco craze, which was given great impetus by the movie, "Saturday Night Fever," will last for a couple of more years, before there will be another change. What that will be, nobody knows.

My advice to all of the musicians and performers who hope to make a good living in entertainment, is for them to be constantly aware of whatever changing trends our business will go through in the future, and make the changes with the trend. Don't fight these changes! Many have tried and are now in other lines of business . . . not entertainment!

WHAT IS TAKES TO BE A PERFORMER
(See Chapter 1 Page 8)

ONE ONE ONE — FORGET THYSELF
(See Chapter 2 Page 16)

LEARN THE TOOLS OF YOUR TRADE
(See Chapter 3 Page 28)

HOW TO FORMAT YOUR ACT
(See Chapter 4 Page 50)

WHAT IT TAKES TO BECOME A STAR
(See Chapter 5 Page 60)

All performing musicians should carefully study the above Chapters, which were written for "single" artists, but also apply to "lounge groups."

PACING OF LOUNGE GROUPS SHOWS AND DANCE SETS

I have seen some groups that have written out beforehand the exact running order of all the songs they are going to play for the complete evening. They make no deviations at all, regardless of the audience reaction, audience lack of acceptance, audience departure from the club, or anything else adverse. Under this system, it is easier for them to remember what's coming next in the order of songs and "bits," so they figure that's the way it should be done.

In other words, they are working under the assumption that *all* audiences have the same desires and needs, that *all* audiences will feel the same way every night, at exactly the same time. Under this set-up, you are giving a plastic, contrived performance which you have memorized.

You must remember that unlike a main room or lounge in Nevada, where you get a new customer practically every time you return to the stage, the lounges around the rest of the country, have the same people at least two or three times each week. If you don't bring back these same people at least two times each week, you're really in trouble.

If you will just take a moment and think about it, you will remember how effective your shows were the first night, and then as you did the same shows in the same order, to some of the same people, how your effectiveness diminished.

Besides boring your audience, and the help, with this repetitious program, you have got to be bored with it yourself. After awhile, you begin performing from your sub-conscious mind, and at that point, you have lost that one-on-one contact with the audience that I covered in detail in Chapter 2.

Naturally, it would be impossible to use a whole new format each show, each night. I recommend that you have a general outline of your show or dance set in mind, but if the mood of the audience changes for some unknown reason, you can improvise your material to suit the desires of the audience. Leave yourself room to improvise.

In a real sense, your emcee, or the one who is calling your plays, is much like a quarterback on a football team.

All quarterbacks have a series of plays that are available to them, just the same as you have a supply of songs and bits accessible to you. Under a given circumstance, he has the latitude to call what are known as audibles from the line of scrimmage, even though he may just have given his teammates a different play in the huddle. He read the opponents' moves as soon as he started to call the signals and changed the play entirely.

This is what you, as a signal caller for your group, have to do each time you get on the stage. You must be in tune with the needs of the customers at all times. You must realize that no two audiences are alike, on any given night, or any given set.

Another big asset in mixing your format, every night, is that the other members of the group cannot mentally go to sleep. If you are using a set format that they can rely on, they tend to let their minds wander to other things while they're playing and singing. They could be singing, "I love you, my darling," and at the same time be thinking in their conscious mind about getting their car fixed, or taking their laundry to the cleaners, or a number of other unrelated thoughts that have nothing to do with the words they are singing.

If this is happening, all of the honesty of the words disappear. The audience doesn't believe what you are saying or singing, and you can't blame them because *you* don't believe it either.

Another big reason that you should not format your shows and dance sets exactly the same each night, is the fact that you will lose the waitresses and bartenders. Remember, they must listen to you every night, and although they are not there to be entertained, they too have feelings, and get bored with the repetition. If you ever lose the waitresses' and bartenders' enthusiasm for your act, chances are they will help you lose the customers.

Comedy Material

There must be a basic honesty in the delivery of humorous material. Comedy is a very difficult, and a very delicate part of the entertaining arts, and there's nothing worse than a forced comic, or a forced performer. For this reason, when you're picking the members of your group, try to find at least one performer who has that innate instinct of natural delivery of humorous material, that comes off as a *natural* part of his being. When you find this individual, you will be able to come up with a good variety show when you start putting your material together. Each member of your group *must only* be asked to perform what he can perform with *honesty* and *proficiency*. *The worst thing in the world is to try to make a comic out of a straight man, or a comic out of a serious, introverted musician who has no feel for it!*

If you have that guiding light in front who has that natural

Dick Catan and the Beachcombers

comedic ability, then the accompanying musicians can build a frame around the picture, so to speak, in their group vocals, in their doubling on various instruments, in their musicianship, and in their contagious feel of the beat that is necessary to build into each show.

It's impossible, and it's *inadvisable* to have comedy for a full hour consecutively. A show must be well paced and must have all kinds of ingredients. The basic ingredient should be good music, (with a good beat), well played, good intonation, and with humor and instrumental novelties sprinkled throughout the show, in order to give it a change of pace.

REHEARSALS

Because you are dealing with several people with different personalities in a group, it is necessary to establish a regular weekly rehearsal schedule that everyone can keep. In this manner, the members can schedule other personal events around the rehearsal schedule.

Rehearsal should be on a regular basis, i.e., every Tuesday, Thursday, and Saturday, with the exception of the Saturday when you close the last job, and have to pack for the trip. There should be no excuse for anyone missing, or being late for rehearsals. If necessary, institute a fine for anyone late or missing a rehearsal. Remember, it's not fair to all of the other members, if someone is negligent.

Sometimes, it's difficult or impossible to rehearse on the job, because of long lunch-hour service, or because the owner has a policy against it. If this happens, there is no reason to eliminate your regular rehearsals. There is a lot of planning you can do in your rooms such as, designing new "chunks" of show material, revising some of the material that you are presently using, listening to records of new songs, or comedy material that you can commit to memory, without the necessity of using the stage.

This time can also be used in organizing your business. I recommend that the non-performance duties of the group be distributed equally among the members of the band as follows:

1. Pictures and publicity.
2. Transportation (Keep the vans in order).
3. Upkeep of all electrical equipment.
4. All financial records (taxes - advances, etc.).
5. Business contacts with agents-owners, etc.
6. Gathering of information regarding new hit records, changing trends, etc.; the trade magazines — Billboard, Record World, Variety, etc.

Assign the above duties to those people who have the best aptitude for each job, and make certain that they realize that the *total* responsibility of handling their particular area is entirely theirs, and that you will not accept any "cop-outs," if the job is not done properly. They should be able to solicit help from someone else, but the final responsibility is solely theirs.

Also, if you cannot rehearse on the stage for some reason, there is no reason why you cannot take a guitar, and a snare drum up to the room, and rehearse the harmony parts to the songs you are learning for the future. In other words, there should be no reason for you **not** to get together on a regular basis to improve the act.

You would be amazed, if you knew how much the club owners are impressed by an act that rehearses regularly. When they see you in the lounge three or four times a week, they know that you are aggressively interested in your careers, and

Here and Now

in making him a profit. If you don't rehearse at all, it's the "kiss of death" in his eyes.

Costumes

I realize that by the time you buy all of your instruments, amplifiers, sound system, and enough trucks to haul it all, your financial resources are pretty thin, or non-existent. Now the subject of uniforms, or costumes comes up. With the advent of the rock bands, the superstars such as the Eagles, Pablo Cruise, Chicago, Earth, Wind & Fire, Rod Stewart, etc., all tend to dress without any conformity. In fact the people in the audience, at their concerts, are often times better dressed than the artists!

That's fine for them because they've already arrived. With their record and concert success, they can afford to dress any way they want. For unknown groups trying to make it up the ladder without any records at all, the picture is completely different.

I'm not proposing that you need to buy tuxedos, or that you all need to wear identically the same things! What I am saying is that you should buy, or have made, costumes that have a show-biz flare, and are in the same mode. There are a lot of mod shops all over the country where these clothes (costumes) can be bought, right off the rack.

It is necessary that you have at least two changes of costumes, so that you can keep them clean. Also, without costumes, your professional pictures are going to look pretty bad. Leaving it up to each member to pick out his own costume can be disasterous! Everybody has different tastes in clothes . . . and some people have no clothes sense whatsoever. It's best that all members go to pick out the stage clothes, so you can get a consensus.

In addition to the costume, everyone should be wearing the same color and kind of socks, and the same identical color and kind of shoes. I've seen some groups with good looking costumes, but with all different color socks, including white, and with the rattiest looking shoes you ever saw.

Pictures and Publicity (Groups)

You may or may not realize that your agent (assuming you have one) is forced to sell you, about 80 percent of the time, to buyers who have never seen the act. You can imagine what happens when the agent has painted such a glowing picture in the operator's mind of what a great group you have, and how good looking everybody is, and how beautiful your girl singer is, only to have the operator say, "They sound like what I'm looking for, *send me some pictures.*

All of a sudden the agent's heart starts beating twice as fast because he just got a mental picture of the awful pictures he has in his files, on this same "great" act. Needless to say, many a deal has been lost because the agent was forced to send bad pictures on an act that constantly complains because they are not-working steadily, or that he isn't getting them enough money.

If you don't have a great press kit, with at least three different black and white poses, and one good color pose, plus a bio of the group, you are doing yourself a big disservice. You are losing far more money per week, than what the pictures would cost!

I realize that money is usually short in the inception of any group, but if you don't want to waste all of your investment in instruments, transportation, costuming, etc., for God's sake, please realize that your agent cannot build a million dollar house with a ten cent saw.

When you are taking outdoor shots, please explain very carefully to the photographer, that you are only interested in getting a good picture of the members of the group, and not a picture full of trees, rocks, houses, horses, and a lot of other non-essential things.

Many photographers try to get artistic and before you know it, he's forgotten the real purpose of the shooting. When a busy picture is reduced to be put into an ad, or into a single column story about the group in the entertainment section of the newspaper, the group is lost entirely.

The only thing necessary in the picture is the entire group, standing or sitting in an informal, happy arrangement, without any uniform gestures. It should have the feeling of an informal picnic, with people who like each other, having fun. There is no need to get anything, or anyone else in the picture *except the group.* In this way when the picture is reduced for the ads, you can still see what the members look like!

During the picture session, the group should be able to change their costumes, so that not all of the pictures will look alike. This will show how successful you are and will make it easier for your agent to get the money you are worth. Because so many artists are now using color pictures, it's important that you have a supply of both black and white and color. For your information, it's not as expensive to repro color pictures as it used to be.

A good press kit, including the above variety of pictures, a bio on each member of the group, plus whatever press stories you have received, will go a long way toward insuring your success. Without it, you will make the job of handling your act difficult, if not impossible.

Relationship With Agent

In this chapter on the artist, I'm going to delve into the relationship between the lounge group and their agent or agency. Fortunately, I can give you the view from the group's standpoint as well as from the agent's standpoint because at one time I was the leader of a group and I know the feelings on both ends. I'm aware that most new combos feel that an agent is necessary but, he's someone **they wish they could live without.** The popular conception of an agent is that of a guy who sucks your blood for 10% or 15% and does **nothing for it! This could not be any farther from the truth.**

Since retiring from performing in 1951, I have been in the agency business right up to the present, with the exception of my three years at Harrah's Club, and one year that I spent managing Wayne Newton. In most cases when a group initially organizes for the first time, and they have a brand new attraction, it's practically impossible to find an agent who is willing to start with a group from the very beginning, and assist them in the formation of their act. This is understandable, because, as you will see later on in the paragraph covering "Agencies," it is virtually impossible for an agent to do the booking, and also tend to the artistic end of organization — rehearsals, personnel problems — because the margin of net profit in the agency business, particularly when you are handling unknown acts and selling *new* talent, is very slim. Because of this short net profit, it's practically impossible for an agency to get involved with an act, until after they have initially gotten themselves organized, and possibly were able to obtain their own first engagement. Naturally, most agents are looking for talent, but they are only able to sell the talent *after it's been organized,* and at least on a working engagement so that they can bring other customers in to see the act. In other words, an agency cannot sell a product that he hasn't seen or heard.

The usual formula for a new group is to: (1) get together their personnel, (2) get rehearsals organized and rehearsed to a point where they can cover a complete evening of entertainment with music and possibly some entertaining bits, (3) get themselves some sort of costume even if it's only one or two uniforms, (4) get some pictures taken, and (5) find that initial job, either by auditioning, or by previous connections.

Up to this point, there probably isn't an agent in the country who would be interested in booking your act, because the commodity is unknown, the quality is unknown, and in most cases, the personnel is unknown. Sometimes an agency will get involved at the inception of a group, primarily because one or two members of the group were in another successful group, and the agent, or agency were very interested in these members from a previous affiliation. However, if it's a brand new group, and if they are totally new members who have never been with an agency before, chances are you will have to get yourselves started, and obtain your own first job so that you can show the world what kind of commodity you have to sell.

If the act has anything to offer, chances are there will be several agents interested, and at this point it would be wise for the leader to call the various agencies and invite them out to their place of engagement.

Sometimes the artists have a little mistrust of the agencies, because they show little or no interest in the act before they were able to get this first engagement by themselves. However, this is a necessary policy of all agencies, and it's something that you're going to have to live with. From the point that you're onstage, and you begin to have some value; and you begin to get some notoriety, you will then find that practically all of the agencies, particularly involved in the lounge business, are going to become interested. Naturally, their interest will be tempered by how effective and how much entertainment ability your group has. There isn't an agent alive who isn't constantly looking for better acts, and particularly those acts with a new, bright future.

Now comes the question of should the artist sign an exclusive contract with an agency. In 99 percent of the cases, attractions would like to be able to stay clear of any signed affiliations and they would like to have *all* agents interested in handling the act and booking the engagements. This appears to be the ideal situation, on the surface, but there is a definite drawback to this relationship, and I will explain in detail what happens when you are nonexclusive.

First of all, there isn't an agent alive who will give his utmost 100 percent attention to an artist, or to a group that is not signed to him. It's only human nature for an agent not to get himself too involved with too much expenditure of time and money with an artist, or a group, where he has no protection. So for this reason, even though the agent tells you that he will give you his 100 percent interest and cooperation, it isn't good business, from his standpoint, because he probably already has signed many other acts, and his **first allegiance** must go to the acts that are already signed to him.

Another danger of not being exclusive to an agency, is the fact that in your submitting yourself to several agents there is no way of your knowing exactly what **prices** they are quoting to the various operators all around the country. Another drawback is the fact that when an operator is submitted the same act by two or three different agencies, the act loses some of its value. A constant submittal of this same act over and over again by too many agents gives the operator the opportunity to pit one agent against the other, in order to drive their price down. When an agency does not have the exclusive right to tell the operator that it's impossible to deliver this act for less than a certain figure, there is no protection for the artist.

If the agent doesn't have that kind of protection, he gets a feeling of insecurity when he submits the free-lance act, and for this reason, his ability to sell this act successfully is reduced considerably. If this condition exists for some time, his attention has got to be diverted to some other act who is willing to sign, or who has already signed with his agency. So, what appears to be desirable on the surface, really is not good for the artist.

I recommend that the artist reconsider, and sign with one agency. Before doing so, it is imperative that the artist check the track record of all of the agents who have professed an interest

Sidro's Armada

in his group. Find out which acts he handles, and where they're playing. I recommend that you make a phone call to several of the artists who are already being handled by this same agency, particularly those who have been handled by this agency for some time. Talk to the leaders of the other groups, and find out what kind of interest, what kind of attention, and what their personal feelings are toward the kind of job the agency is doing for them. Naturally, you are not going to get a 100 percent good report on any agency, but after four or five phone calls, to four or five different group leaders, it shouldn't be too difficult for you to decide which agency would be the best to handle your attraction.

There are several agencies that specialize in musical groups. This would be the best agency for you to get involved with, because they are specialists in this field.

In recent years, several of the major agencies have toyed with the idea of establishing a small band, or lounge division, as part of their agencies — principally for the development of new young talent, but as of the printing of this book none of them have made a full commitment to the lounge group business.

If I were an artist or the leader of a group, I would find myself a job, and stay on this job for a long enough period of time so that I could develop my act. Also, at the same time, I would give myself a chance to analyze which agency I would choose.

Bear in mind that when you sign an agency contract, there has to be two signatures on the contract — yours, plus the signature of the agent, or the head of the agency you are signing with. When he signs that contract, there is a two-way obligation for the agency to perform certain duties, and for the artist to perform certain duties. If the artists do everything right, and if the group is reasonably talented, there's no logical reason why you and the agent can't be successful together.

I would also check to make sure that the agency you sign with has the power to book your act nationally. Some agents are territorically strong in one city, or one area, and yet have very little, or no connections in the other areas of the country. In order for you, as an artist, to make a decent living, and have a chance for that big brass ring, it's absolutely imperative that you get a chance to work the best rooms that there are to be had in the *entire* country.

Ask these questions of the leaders who are already signed to a particular agency: the names of the rooms where they have played, what cities they were in, what kind of treatment did they get, and how much money did they make. If you ask enough questions of the other group leaders, I think you will get enough information, for you to determine which agency you should sign with.

Once you've decided to sign with an agency, it's wise that

Command Performance

you give the agency, and your particular agent, your full
cooperation. Give him the benefit of your confidence in regards
to the engagements that he proposes to you. You should assume
that he's doing everything in your best interest. Naturally, as
time goes by, if you find that things are not going well, and that
bookings are not in keeping with the quality you deserve, then I
think you should have a conversation with your agent and find
out why certain things haven't been done, and why certain jobs
haven't come about. There may be a logical answer. I'm not try-

ing to make excuses for your agent, but often what appears on the surface, is really not true in actuality. In any event, make the best of your marriage for as long as you're married, and do everything you can to keep that marriage in good, amiable condition.

Also, it is most important that you pay your commissions on time at the end of each week, **as promptly as you get paid!** The payment of commissions to the agency just further obligates the agency to perform in your behalf. If you **pay** your commissions on time, there is no excuse for them not to extend every possible effort and energy, to your benefit. If you **don't** pay your commissions, you hardly have any argument when it comes to criticizing their performance. Bear in mind that there is no other outside income to the agency except the commissions that come in from their artist. The cost of operation for the agency will run higher than you realize, so you can see there is very little sympathy for acts who do not pay promptly.

While we're on the subject of your relationship with your agency or your agent, it is most vitally important to your future that you keep track of any operator, or any person who comes to you while you're working, and expresses an interest in your act. If he tells you that he's an operator or that he owns a hotel or a nightclub, or he's a television producer, director, or he's with a record company, it is wise for you to get this party's name, address, and phone number, and **immediately** send that information to your agent. Also, it is wise to give this interested party your agent's name, address, and phone number, so that you can make certain that someone follows through with this possible lead.

There is always a chance that it is merely a customer who is trying to impress you with his importance, or he's trying to impress his girl friend. There is also that possibility that he could be for real, and by ignoring him, or by not taking down the information and sending it to your agent, you might have missed a golden opportunity.

Personal Manager (Groups)

Many young, inexperienced groups feel that they need a personal manager, in order to become stars. They like the fact that they can load all of the responsibilities of their business on someone else, so they can concentrate on their music. Their thinking in this regard is fine, except in most cases, they sign with the first "fast talker" who approaches them with a proposition, and live to regret it!

When you sign with a personal manager, aside from an agent, he doesn't really have to do anything except to prove that he had "advised and counseled" you! This is his total legal responsibility, in order to keep his contract with you in force. He doesn't have to book you and in fact, his personal management contract states that he is forbidden from booking you on any engagements. So, his primary functions are to assist you in your artistic endeavors, call your agent regarding your bookings, try to get a record company interested, and if possible, try to get you on television or in the movies. If he is creative, it is possible that he may be able to write you some special material, or possibly an original song for a record.

In other words he is, or should be, a "personal" assistant to you and the group. If all he does for you is call your agency, and relay the agent's message to you, then he's not what you are looking for in a manager.

I'm not implying that you should **never** sign with a personal manager. At a certain point of your career, he could be very valuable to you. I thoroughly recommend that in the event of a sudden hit record, or a major television show, you definitely should sign with a personal manager, or a personal management firm (see chapter 8). When money is no longer a problem, then is the time that you desperately need the advice of your manager. At that point, you won't have to look for a personal manager. He'll be looking for you.

Traveling Wives and Families

It's practically impossible for a husband and wife, with more than one small child who is no older than two or three years, to become a part of a traveling small band. By the time you have two small children and one is in school, it is necessary for the wife and the children to settle down in one location. If a man is married and has two children, his days of travel with a group are limited. He's naturally going to want to spend as much time as possible with his family. In an effort to maintain any kind of financial stability, a group must go wherever the best money is, and it's practically impossible to make a large amount of money, if a personal problem dictates that they stay in one place.

When I say road groups, I mean the commercial entertaining show groups. There are many rock groups who rarely play commercial dance lounges, because they refuse to play top 40 material. They do stay in the major record markets like Los Angeles, New York, Nashville, and Chicago, just so they can write and record their own original material. These are not the road groups I am referring to in this book. These rock groups have based their whole existence on records and concerts only. They are willing to make any sacrifice necessary, in order to get that hit record.

I find, in my experience, that the groups that really become proficient, are the ones who travel in the early part of their careers, and get away from the family duties. It also gets them away from their friends, calling and inviting them out to social events, from the golf courses, and from the other diversions that happen when they are playing in their home town.

Sometimes there is a problem between the members of the group because the wives get overly critical in expressing their own opinions regarding whether or not their husbands are getting as much publicity, whether they are getting as much time to do their solos, etc. The wives have a tendency to gossip among themselves about various aspects of the group.

If you're going to have your wives on the road with you, and if they are going to be traveling in conjunction with other wives, then every wife should realize that the group business should not be discussed by her. Her opinions are strictly her opinions, and if she wants to voice them to her husband at night privately, that's fine, but to voice opinions among other wives, or to voice opinions among other members of the group, is a very bad mistake. This can do nothing but create an unpleasant atmosphere in the group, and eventually can be the reason for the group splitting up, or of certain members leaving.

Wives have to keep in mind that it's tough enough to get

along under the circumstances of rehearsals, and having to prove themselves every night on each show. Their husbands are under enough pressure without having to come home at night and have his wife tell him how much she thinks he's being neglected and how much publicity he isn't getting. This only makes him uptight, and eventually he's going to have to leave the group or get fired, one of the two.

There's another problem that could arise in this area. Please bear in mind that the operators have to make a profit in order for your husbands to be a success, and you have to use great discretion in taking up tables. For example, never sit right in front of the bandstand, or at the choice tables when you're not spending any money.

It's wise not to come in to see the group on Fridays and Saturdays when you know the club is going to be filled, and it's also wise to use good common sense in not reserving tables every night, regardless of whether they are empty or full. It makes it uneasy for your husbands who, during intermission, should be spending some time talking to customers.

There's a good time and place to be there, and there's a good time to disappear. If you're going to be in the club taking up his time, and taking up his attention, the boss has got to resent it.

Also, as wives, be careful about taking advantage of any food discounts, or any comp food that might be part of the contract. It isn't wise, for you to eat steak and lobster-tail every night, when you wouldn't do it normally. Why take advantage of a good thing. Just eat what you would normally, and don't invite you girl friends in for dinner. Or if you happen to be traveling to a city where you have relatives, don't take advantage of the food discounts by bringing in extra people.

The food discounts were primarily meant for the working members of the group, and the wives are included in most cases because it only makes good sense. If you're going to take advantage of it, the first thing you know, the operator will cut off the food discounts, not only for the wives and children of the group, but also the group.

Just a final word to the wives of the working members of the group. Use good common sense and realize that whatever

123

you do, also reflects on the success, or failure of the group, particularly when you're living on the premises of a hotel, or motor inn where the group is working. Bear in mind that if you have children, the children should be kept under control. Also, if you have dogs be sure that you walk the dogs so they don't tear up the rooms, or dirty all over the floors, and walls, and chew up the furniture. *It is very unwise to carry any pets at all!* first of all, every motel owner has to resent them, and it really isn't fair to the pet. If you must have a pet on the road, please, no St. Bernards!

As I said before, whenever you get the free room situation, it's something that should not be taken advantage of because everything you do while on the premises of the building is under some kind of approval or disapproval by the housekeepers, the maids, the assistant manager, the bartenders, or whomever. So, if you really want your husbands to be successful, and if you don't want to put any further obstacles in his way, bear in mind that you are an integral part of this act and your behavior could affect him radically!

In traveling around the country, there are single musicians in the group, and some married whose wives are not traveling with them. It's bad business if the male members of the group get involved with the waitresses, the hostesses or the desk clerks around the hotel where they are working. I realize this is difficult in some cases, but you are better off if you are going to do any kind of socializing, to stay away from the help in the place where you're working.

There's an old saying, "imtimacy breeds contempt." Again, we're talking about the best way to become a success in this business, and that is to recognize all of the possible problems, and handle them intelligently.

While we're on the subject of being social, there are many groups out today with at least one or two, and possible three girls in the group. Now, everybody recognizes the danger of having a mixed group, from an emotional standpoint, so you're better off if you can establish a mutual agreement that the boys and girls in the group are strictly going to treat things as a business, and stay away from each other. Of course, that magic thing can happen, where two people fall in love and get married. That's a different story. But if you get social and intermingle in the group, there's bound to be petty jealousies and there will be internal problems.

Relationship With The Owner

It's a known fact that for years the club owners and managers, have had a rather low opinion of musicians, even though they knew that they were necessary to their beverage sales. Truthfully, they were somewhat justified in their feelings, because the majority of the groups, up until the 1970's, were kids who had never traveled very much. When they had housing on the premises in a Motor Inn or Hotel, they went "ape" with the service they were getting. As time has gone by, and as the Motor Inns and Hotels have gotten more sophisticated in their lounges, and as the groups have matured in their behavior, the relationship between the performers and the owners has improved considerably.

I believe whatever problems still exist, are only caused by a lack of understanding. Most club owners think that the act is overpaid and that they are only on the road to have a ball. Some owners feel the artists really aren't concerned whether they make a profit or not and that musicians play loud just for spite.

On the other hand, many performers think that the operator is making a fortune off their talents, that the only reason he has entertainment in his club at all is so he can fraternize with the girl singer, that he hasn't spent a nickel on advertising their appearance, and that he's an old fogie who doesn't like contemporary music.

Neither one of them fully realize what the real truth is. First of all, from the entertainer's standpoint, they are not being overpaid (at least not as unknown lounge acts). It costs the typical quintette of musicians and singers about $13,500 for their instruments and sound systems. Add to that at least two vans to haul it all, plus one automobile, and that's another $20,000

On top of that initial investment of $33,500, which has to be repaid to the bank, comes the following costs; transportation, food, rent at home (in some cases), insurance, repair of instruments and equipment, costumes, pictures, commission to

125

agents (and sometimes personal managers), dues or taxes to the A.F. of M., and whatever is left (if any) for some fun. If the club owners knew exactly what it costs in cold cash, let alone the physical exertion, they would understand the act's request for more money.

On the other side of the coin, the operator is stuck with paying the artists the contract price, whether or not he makes any money. He has a large investment in his building, with all other operating costs such as debt retirement, waitresses, bartenders, cost of liquor, insurance, taxes, etc.

Neither the operator, nor the artist has a bed of roses. Also, the artists are not exactly having a ball on the road. How would you like to pack up all of the instruments and equipment, every two or three weeks, and then travel 700 to 1000 miles in 14 to 20 hours without sleep, and open up in the next lounge bright and cheery?

Without explaining both the artists and the owners problems any further, I sincerely suggest that every artist, and every owner, have a heart to heart talk with each other, so that they will have a better understanding. This would go a long way toward creating a more friendly business relationship and indirectly, it would help create high gross beverage revenues for everyone's benefit.

Speaking of more money, I'm sure I speak for most owners when I say that they are looking for those "sure winners," in acts that are so good and loaded with fresh material and talent, that they would be forced to pay more money. All an operator wants to see is his gross go up. The smart operators know that they only get what they pay for, and there are no real bargains.

The consistently successful operators, if they have any seating capacity at all, want to buy the best acts available and will spend the top dollar for them. If, as an operator, you are limited by small seating capacity, and to a small budget, you must realize that you are really gambling on the quality of your attractions.

As an artist, your degree of talent, plus your dedication, rehearsals, costumes, charisma with customers, your class, and all of the other ingredients you should have, will determine your price. Your agent may determine your first price in a club where you've never appeared before, but *you* establish your own second price. If you make it for him, the owner is happy to pay. If he doesn't he's a poor business man.

Also, the owner is going to think a whole lot more favorably about your group if you don't show up opening day to set up during his busy lunch hour. If you can control it, try to arrive at the club at any time except lunch or dinner hour. You can certainly see that this would get you started off on the wrong foot. If you're in doubt about the next operator's physical set up, a phone call ahead would be a good investment in your future relationship.

When you arrive at the club, and you see that the club owner has spent a large amount of money on a house sound system, **please try his system out** before you use your own. If it doesn't suit your needs, then use your own sound "P.A." At least he will know that you tried his system and he won't feel quite as bad about the money he spent for it. Once in a while you will find a fine sound system already installed. If so, I suggest you use it, and be sure to tell the owner how good it is.

I don't have to explain to you how much theft there is today, especially of musical instruments, microphones, etc. To save you and the club owners a lot of grief, be sure to take all of your little instruments (trumpets, saxophones, guitars, basses, etc.,) up to your rooms at night. It's also a good idea to take the "mike heads" off the stands, and have the night manager lock them up, or take them to your room also. There's nothing worse than coming down to the lounge the next day and finding some of your equipment missing. It creates bad feelings between you and the owner because you feel that he has no security, and he feels that you're careless with your instruments and equipment. Don't take any chances.

And regarding your wives or family traveling with you, just one more word of advice. You must remember when you are playing in a motel or hotel, it is just as important that you (and your family) and all of the group look "reasonably well dressed during the day, as well as at night. That doesn't mean you have to wear suits and ties, during your off hours, but it will hurt your relationship with the owner if you are around his lobby and dining rooms in Levis, a torn shirt, and open toe sandals! Also, if you have a wife and kids on the road, see that they look presentable and that the kids are not a public nuisance.

Another tip which I personally found paid off for me years ago, is that when you check into a motel where you are appearing, tip the housekeeper and the maid who are taking care of your room *on the first day*. You will be surprised how many more towels, and other "goodies" you'll get from the maid, if you lay a couple of bucks on her. Start in the beginning, not when you're leaving. You know that you will be asking for special concessions such as more towels, being quiet outside your door, making up your room late in the afternoon, etc.

The token will also insure that the maid and housekeeper will not be turning in bad reports on your group's questionable behavior.

Another classic mistake made by inexperienced artists, and groups, is to make all kinds of demands — an extra room, cash a check, discount on food, free coffee and cokes — **before** the owner has had a chance to see and hear you opening night. Your chances of getting these extra concessions would be much greater, if you would wait until **after** opening night, when you are sure you are going to be a success. You'd be amazed how many more "goodies" you can get, when the owner knows that he's gonna have a "fat" week. Remember not to overdo your requests from the owner. I've seen acts do great on the stand, and then, because of some personal situation between a member of the group and the boss, they could never get a return engagement.

Should you at any time get into any major problems with the owner or the lounge manager, it is best that you don't try to handle it yourself. Call your agent or personal manager, if you have one, and let them handle the problem. It's best that you and the management stay on friendly terms, because you have to live with them daily. Let your agent handle whatever it is over the phone. In that way, it gets handled impersonally.

Meet the Customers

During your intermissions, it is important that you take advantage of this opportunity to get acquainted with the customers. I recommend that each member of the group go to a table and introduce himself to the people without being too forceful. Naturally, they will probably invite you to sit down and have a drink.

I suggest you sit down, but don't accept the drink, not because I think you're liable to drink too much. The reason for not taking a drink is so that you won't have to sit more than five minutes, and then you can leave and go to another table and do the same thing. If you accept the drink, you would have to sit at *one* table for the whole intermission.

If each member of your group does likewise, all five or six of you could possible cover 40 to 50 people in 20 minutes. You'd be surprised how much easier it is to entertain fifty people who you have just met, particularly if you remember their names, which allows you to do some kibitzing with them during your show or dance set. This makes your job of entertaining people ten times easier.

Bear in mind you are usually on the job for five hours per night, and it's wise for you to take advantage of everything you can to get acquainted with the people who are paying the bill. It's bad business for you to *only work when you're on stage.*

Another way to make your job easier and ingratiate yourself to the owner is for the emcee of the group to come to the club at least thirty minutes early so that he can quiz the maitre d' or the hostess about any special parties, weddings, birthdays, anniversaries, etc., scheduled for that evening. Find out the names of the people celebrating, or the president's name of the company having a party, and write them down. Also, try to get the maitre d' to introduce you to some of the guests. Again, when you are groping for clever things to say during the evening, you'll have several customers to work with, who you have already met. You've just made your job easier, and a lot of people happier, including the owner.

Let's, for the moment, suppose that the job you are on is the only job left in the world and if you lost that job, you were out of business. Also, let's imagine you were on a *night-to-night option basis.*

If you really believed this, what kind of energy, dedication, and sheer sweat do you think you would put into each set and each show? You know damn well that your attitude toward the job would be different than it is normally!

The trouble with most acts is that they think there is always another alternative, but what they don't realize is **there is no alternative to failure.** You must treat each job as if it's the **only job left,** and do everything you can to make it a success. Even if you hate the job, and don't want to return, it's your duty to give it your best shot. After all, you expect the owner to pay you in full anyway. In this manner, you'll make him and all of his employees big fans of yours. This is how you build your reputation, and insure your success.

New Material — Trade Magazines

In regard to deciding what new songs you should learn, there are several magazines that are published weekly and monthly, such as *Billboard, Cash Box, Rolling Stones, Record World, Variety, Country Music, Amusement Business,* and *Downbeat.* These magazines should be studied religiously. The people who publish these magazines go to a great deal of trouble, expense, and time, in accumulating the records and statistics of our business every day. If you're wise, and if you're really in the business to be a success, it is your duty to know what records are coming up on the charts, to know what comedy albums are being played, to know what forms of new rhythms are becoming popular.

The public, as we know, suddenly make decided changes in one direction or another, and it's your business to stay on top of all these new trends, and new changes. For this reason, I advise all my acts to buy the record magazines, and study the charts religiously. You must firmly realize that these collectors of statistics, regarding the entire music business, are very important to your career.

When you realize that there are millions and millions of dollars spent for records daily by people all over the country, in fact, all over the world, and these various magazines are collecting all of this information for you, you are not being very good businessmen if you do not stay on top of their information.

I suggest you tear out the Top 100 sheet, the Top Easy Listening sheet, the Top Country and Western sheet, the Top Rhythm and Blues sheet. Tear each of these pages out of these magazines and keep them on file, so you can watch the increased popularity of each record, as it climbs the charts.

There are records with so-called "bullets," which define a record that is really jumping in popularity at a rapid rate. Where it might come on the chart at 80 with a bullet; and next week it's maybe up to 50; then the following week to 40; or it might be all the way up to 30 or 20. The records with the red dot around the number means that they are selling very rapidly, all over the country.

About the time that record gets in the 40's or 30's, it would be wise for you to buy the record, or at least listen to it, to find out whether you could apply it to your group in some manner or another, so that by the time it gets into the top 10, or reaches the top record of the country, you will have learned it. If you wait until after the record has already been a big hit, and starts to fall off the charts, you are only going to get a couple of months use out of it. In most cases, the record or the tune will have become pretty trite by the time you get your arrangement written and memorized.

Also there are many humorous type tunes that come out on records that will give you a good supply of humor for your show. Comedy and humor is a difficult thing to come by for most people, because they do not think funny. It's difficult to incorporate comedy into a group, particularly when there is not a natural comedian in it. You can do humor, if you're not instinctively funny, providing the humor is part of the music, and has funny lyrics.

Recording The Group

As you have read throughout "Show-Business is *Two* Words," the fastest method of becoming a star is to get a "hit record." To the newcomer in show biz, this sounds rather simple to do.

To **make** a record is simple. With a small outlay of money and a friendly, helpful engineer in a small studio, a group of self-contained musicians-singers can make a two-sided single for approximately $350.00, if they are well rehearsed before they go into the studio. Chances are this record will turn out to be a "demo record," which the group could possible use to get some record company interested in recording them.

The record industry is so competitive, and the public's tastes are so changeable, that to get a hit record takes far more time, money, experience, and luck than meets the eye.

First of all, it's very seldom that the buying public will purchase an old standard tune, done up in a new dress. It happens occasionally, but not too often.

The public and the record companies are looking for creative writers who have a marketable feel for writing songs that will appeal to that typical fourteen or fifteen-year-old girl or boy record buyer. Most of the single records are being bought by these young adults. The story of the song has to relate to this market.

If you have creative writers in your group who can write for the market, the record companies will be far more interested in talking to you about a possible recording contract. If you do not have creative writers in your group, they will probably not be interested. They do not want the responsibility of finding good material for you. Also, they have found that much of their risk is reduced if they can hear your demos, on your original song material, done with a marketable sound before they become involved.

When a record company signs a contract with you, they obligate themselves to spend about $50,000 on the "possibility," and a very slim possibility, that they may have a new hot artist. What with production costs, promotion, merchandising, advertising, and all of the other expenses involved in launching a new artist, they are taking a big gamble. Coupled with this outlay of time, energy, and money, they know that there are about 300 to 400 records released each week by all record companies, and there are only about 40 new records introduced each week by each radio station around the country. Many of these radio stations subscribe to programming service companies. This means that many of them are introducing the same records each week. You can now see more readily what a huge gamble the record companies take when they say, "Okay, we'll sign a recording contract with you." Those "okays" are hard to come by.

In spite of the above, you must try to write original

material. You must make demos on your original songs with your own identifiable style. You must continue to haunt the record companies with these finished demos. This is practically the only way you are going to get out of the rut of playing funky dance music for the rest of your professional life. This is your only hope.

Bear in mind, the Beach Boys, the Eagles, Abba, Chicago, Pablo Cruise, the Beatles, Bee Gees, Elvis Presley, Olivia Newton John, Andy Gibb, Earth Wind and fire, Kenny Rogers, Johnny Cash, Loretta Lynn, and all of the other record stars felt the same way, and had to go through the same things. The day before they became stars they were unknown.

One more word of advice about your original song material. No matter how good the songs are, and no matter how good your arrangement of these tunes are, it is not a good policy for you to play your original songs for the customers who come to dance to your group. They come to hear the songs they have already bought that are hits and no matter how good your material is, they only want to dance to the hits.

If you want to slip in a song or two of yours at the end of the evening, when most of the people have departed, that's okay. I realize that you need to play these arrangements often enough to get the "feel" of the chart before making your "demo," but keep away from doing your tunes in the "shank" of the evening.

Audience Reaction

Over the years I've had many acts come to me and say, "How can you tell what is good show material, or what isn't?" Well, what they haven't done is listen to the audience.

There's only one real way to tell whether or not you're doing the right thing and that is to be sensitive to the applause and laughter, or the lack of it, from the people who come to see you. Often, acts get stubborn about doing things that they write, and they continue to do them even though there is no reaction from the audience. They fall in love with their own words or with their own ideas.

The audience is there to be used as guinea pigs for new material, for new jokes, and for new songs. If you don't get that

133

honest burst of applause, and you don't get that honest laughter, you're making a terrible mistake using it again.

No professional who is really seasoned would ever continue to throw a line, or to do a tune, that wasn't really well received. The young performers make the mistake of **not listening to the audience.** All they are interested in doing is listening to themselves, and as a result they miss the barometer that the audience is there to give them.

I highly recommend that every act tape their shows, and their music almost nightly, and then listen to the tape the next day in order to see where they get honest reaction. Hear where the laugh is coming! If it isn't coming, then the material either has to be changed, or it has to be dropped. If you've tested a piece of material, or tested a tune two or three times, and you're still not getting that good, honest enthusiastic response, there's something wrong with it.

Recently camera companies have perfected a video tape-camera, and video-recorder which I believe is a good means of criticizing your material. This gives you not only the sound of what you're doing, but also a visual look at what you're doing. This tape equipment can be purchased for about $3,000 to $3,500 including the camera, the recorder, and the monitor. If you can afford it, it's probably the wisest investment you can make in your own career. It's simple to operate, and one of the wives of the members in the group can easily video tape your shows almost nightly. This allows you to be able to analyze it the next day, in order to find out what you're doing that **looks** good or bad, and what you're doing that **sounds** good or bad.

I'm sure the investment for this kind of equipment would be well worth it, and would pay for itself in a very short time. If you can't afford the video equipment, then at least a portable tape recorder or a cassette recorder, would be advisable, so you can tape your shows, and listen for the sound of the laughter (or the lack of it!) and listen to the sound of applause, so that you can determine whether a piece of material is effective or not.

"Showy — Dance Music"

Remembering that there are millions of dollars spent yearly for the purchase of records, it is obvious that the buying public must be laying hard cash on the counter for some sounds that they love. If they are buying several million records of one kind, by one artist or group, what does that tell you? They must like the total sound of this record. It's not particularly just the lyrics, nor the melody, nor the arrangement. It's the *total* sound.

When the people come to see you perform, they want to dance to these tunes exactly in the same form, same sound, same tempo, same lyrics, same melody, same arrangement, as they heard on the record they bought. If you don't duplicate these record sounds, as closely as possible on your dance sets, they won't dance.

I realize that there are many musicians who feel that it is beneath them to copy other musicians' note for note. They have told me that they didn't spend all of their time, money, and energy in learning to play and sing, just to end up copying someone else.

In some respects, they have a valid point. It's true that it takes less talent to duplicate than to create. But first things first.

Before you can *create*, you must find out what the public is "buying," so that you can get **paid for what you create!** (Unless, of course, you are independently wealthy and don't have to make a living!) In order for you to thoroughly know what the public is buying, you need to become familiar with the market demands. You do this by playing the "hit" records, (in their original form) so that you will know what it takes for you to become a superstar, at which point you will **no longer** have to duplicate **other** artists' records. Simple, isn't it?

In other words, the sooner you find out what the "singles" record buyer (a 14 year old girl) is buying, the sooner you will know what to write for her, so that **you** can become the star artist, or group that every *other* new, young, unknown, group will have to duplicate, before **they** can become famous.

I've explained the above to you in minute detail only so that you won't have to get into any indecision with yourself, or each other, as to what you should do in order for you to get **out** of just being another dance band! I know what this frustration is and I too, would feel the same way! Getting out of being "just another dance band" lies within your own powers to change. Knowing now what it takes to alter your situation, get down to the serious work of studying what the public is buying . . . and

135

give them more of the same, only with your own style and imagination! Don't forget .... **the day before the "Eagles" wrote
and recorded their first hit record, they were just as unknown as
you are!!** Think about it!

Keeping Your Personnel Intact

It's necessary that your group stay intact so that cohesion
has a chance to take place. If you will remember, most of the
record groups have been together for years, and their records
reflect that tight togetherness. You get the feeling that they are
both musically and spiritually together. That's what it takes,
and you can't get that tightness unless the same members have
stuck together for some time, in spite of petty differences.

Once you have carefully selected the members of the group
(if you did it as I have indicated elsewhere in the book), there
should be no change unless it is **absolutely necessary.** Every
time you make a change in personnel, you take a giant step
backwards.

After you've gotten your first hit record, it's even more
vital that you keep the same personnel. When your fans start
buying your records en-masse, they begin to study you "in-
timately," and become aware of every member of the group —
your names, your likes and dislikes, your girl friends, wives,
etc. In other words, they build an image of all of you "together"
in their minds and they do not want that image changed at all.
Often, if there is a personnel change in the group, it hurts the
group's popularity, and sometimes destroys the group entirely.

Many musical groups do not realize that they are no different than any other business entity. The longer they stay
together, and develop their name value, through engagements
all over the country, record releases, publicity generated
through ads, television appearances, movies, magazine articles,
etc., the "market value" increases considerably. Their "company" could now be worth several thousand dollars, even
though they have yet to get their first hit record. That's hard for
an unknown group to realize.

Not only does their name have financial value, but, if they
would stop and realize how many *hours* they have put into
rehearsals, how many miles they have put on their vehicles, get-

ting from one job to another, how much sheer energy they have expanded in the building of this marketable value, they would not be so quick to fire one of the members.

If all of the members of a group, that have been together for any length of time at all, could understand that their company, or corporation, could be worth $500,000 in market value, and if they quit or get fired, they would lose their portion of this large amount of money, I'm certain there would be fewer changes in personnel!

Also, the unfortunate fact is, the reason they quit usually accompanies them to another group. They regretfully find out (too late) that no matter what group they join, nothing is perfect. Whenever two or more people work together, there is a certain amount of give and take necessary in order to get along, and keep the company together and growing in value.

In my experience, I find one predominant reason for groups breaking up. They do not believe that there is a **solid future** for the group in the make-up of the present personnel. Either the leader does not have sufficient talent and business acumen, or there are too many weak links in the chain.

In order for a group to stay together, they must thoroughly believe that they have a chance for stardom, and the subsequent big dollar. If, for some reason, they all do not believe this, you will find the most talented, ambitious members looking for other talented, ambitious groups to join.

If a unified, talented group of musicians and singers join forces, chances are they will stick together. They must respect each other as people. They must have an equal amount of talent. They must believe that it can happen, and they must believe in their leader.

Many of the superstar groups stuck together in this belief for as many as 10 years, before their first big break happened. You only read about their recent success. Nobody knows how many bad joints they worked in, and how many hungry nights they suffered through, in order to become "overnight" successes. Their true story is rarely ever known.

seven

Las Vegas /
Reno / Lake Tahoe /
Atlantic City

Las Vegas /
Reno / Lake Tahoe /
Atlantic City

The gambling casinos, and their theatres and lounges, have been considered for years the highest goal for all singers, comics, dancers, showgirls, and musicians. In the minds of all entertainers, when you have played where the "galloping dominoes roll," you have really arrived. This was true for the headliners, but unfortunately in recent years, is not true for the supporting acts, and the groups who play in the lounge.

Because of the high gambling profit, the hotels and casinos have always offered the highest dollar to performers who could fill, not only the seats in the theatre, but also the gaming area.

In the days before the advent of the large corporations, the casinos, particularly in Las Vegas, were run on a more casual "fun in the sun" basis, by the original owners who realized that they were in the "gaming" business primarily. The prices of rooms, food, and beverage were kept inexpensive, so as to attract the masses, who wanted to gamble. As such, the original owners knew that they were going to eventually make their big profit in the casino. In other words, the inexpensive rooms, food, beverage, etc., were merely to entice the masses into the gaming area.

Forty's & Fifty's

In the Forties, Fifties, and as late as the Sixties, the entertainment directors spent a considerable amount of money in their lounges, as well as paying a high tariff in the main theatre for the superstars. The format of entertainment was designed so that the superstars pulled the people into the hotel, and then following the main show, the lounges (which were originally open to the casino visually) would entice those same customers to linger near the casino area.

In the Forties and Fifties, because the lounges were visually open to the casinos, it was not necessary to always play names

The Mary Kaye Trio

in the lounge, and in many cases, because of sheer talent, some of the lounge acts eventually became stars. Stars such as, The Mary Kaye Trio, Kenny Rogers, Louis Prima and Keely Smith, with Sam Butera and the Witnesses, Roy Clark, Shecky Greene, Don Rickles, Redd Foxx, The Characters, Earl Grant, Wayne Newton, and many others originally were little known lounge acts.

In these early days the amount of time utilizing entertainment in most lounges was about 14 to 16 hours per day. For this reason there were many more entertainers and musicians employed by the casinos. In those early days, Las Vegas was a more free-swinging town, with a much more relaxed atmosphere. The people who gambled and lost in those days, felt that they at least had gotten their money's worth in spite of their losses. That whole picture has changed today.

With the advent of the large corporations, the hotels and casinos began to design all areas so that every department would make a profit. Room rates were higher, food was more expensive and the cost of drinks doubled. It became so expensive for a tourist coming to Nevada to pay the air fare, room rates, food and beverage costs, that the "poor" sucker had very little money left to gamble (which was why they came from Kankakee and Keokuck to Nevada in the first place.)

Gone also, was the relaxed "fun" atmosphere. No longer were there "open" lounges where you used to be able to "rub elbows" with Frank Sinatra, Dean Martin, Harry Belafonte, Sammy Davis Jr., etc., plus mingle with the dancers and showgirls from the production line. All that is gone with the "enclosing" of the lounges. They lost that "let's hang out" in the casino, and see who in the celebrity world is also "hangin' out."

If the owners of the hotels and casinos in Las Vegas would return to the Forties' and Fifties' concept of the "open," friendly lounge, I sincerely believe that a return to these fun rooms would be more profitable to them. As it is now, at about 4:00 a.m. you can shoot a cannon off in all the casinos on the "strip," and you might hit **three people.** If they would return to the semi-open lounges in the casino area, I believe many more people would hang around drinking and gambling and having fun until 4:00 or 5:00 a.m.

Diminishing Supply of Stars

One of the major problems facing Vegas, Reno, and Tahoe, plus Atlantic City, is the diminishing supply of superstars who can fill the main rooms, and the casinos with people who are big gamblers.

Stars in most instances today, are made as a result of hit records and, as we all know, most of the hit records are being made in the rock or contemporary field. We also know that these kind of instant stars are not, in most cases, the kind of attractions that will please a 50-to-60-year-old gambler, who can't stand the sound and type of music which fostered the hit record.

In addition to this, the new, current rock stars can almost make in one night in concert, what Las Vegas, Reno, and Tahoe offers for a seven-day week.

So, we have two basic problems with which Nevada and

now New Jersey are faced. The new stars who will draw from the contemporary record hits are not exactly what a mature audience want to see, and worse than that, if the talent buyers in these gaming areas wanted to buy these artists, they can't get them to work seven nights a week for a reasonable amount of money, compared with what they make in concert. Even if they would agree to pay them this exorbitant amount of money, I don't believe that these rock stars are ideal for the typical gambler's taste.

The only other media that is developing some new stars for the main theatres in Nevada, is television. Occasionally, a John Davidson, Johnny Carson, or an Andy Williams, will "pop out" of T.V. and become big attractions in the gambling areas. In most cases, however, T.V. stars are not good live performers. They haven't paid their dues in the live entertainment field, like such stars as, Bob Hope, Mitzi Gaynor, Debbie Reynolds, Red Skelton, Sammy Davis, Jr., Dinah Shore, George Burns, Jack Benny, Jerry Lewis, Frank Sinatra, Jimmy Durante, Dean Martin, Danny Thomas, etc. These people learned their craft in the live "vaudeville" circuits. In those days there were also a lot of little night clubs scattered throughout the country where an act could develop techniques, in order to establish a consistent one-on-one relationship with the audience.

The only real developing ground left are the lounges, where there are more artists making a full-time living in entertainment than all of the other forms of show business put together. They do not make more money per person, but there are more total people involved in this branch of the business.

Many of the current crop of stars such as Wayne Newton, Ann Margaret, Bill Cosby, Linda Carter, Bobby Vinton, Don Rickles, Shecky Greene, Roy Clark, Kenny Rogers, and many others, started in this field. This proves that the lounge business has potential for the development of new superstars, and if I were the owner of a casino in Las Vegas, Reno, Tahoe, and Atlantic City, I would be thinking seriously about developing my own stable of stars out of my new, great fun, "open" lounges. If this is not done, where else are they going to get new artists to fill their main theatres? How are the new commercial stars going to develop name value?

I suggest you take a page out of the sport scene. Where

would the baseball, basketball, and football teams be without their farm system, which they use to develop new players of tomorrow?

Country & Western "Crossovers"

The branch of our business that is starting to take over the theatres in the gaming areas, are the new type "Country-Western" stars. No longer can they be called Hillbillies.

Today there are no better entertainers anywhere, in any branch of our business, then Roy Clark, Dolly Parton, Mel Tillis, Johnny Cash, Charley Pride, Waylon Jennings, Willie Nelson, Buck Owens, Kenny Rogers, Loretta Lynn, Sonny James, Marty Robbins, Linda Ronstadt, Olivia-Newton-John, Crystal Gale, Ronnie Milsap, Anne Murray, Debbie Boone, Jerry Clower, Donna Fargo, Lynn Anderson, Tanya Tucker, Charlie Rich, and a new young singer that I feel certain is gonna' make it, Zella Lehr.

If you will examine this list of Country and Western artists carefully, not all of them are truly Country and Western. Some of them have to be considered what we call "Country Crossovers." It is a definite fact that the country artists are getting more sophisticated, and more of the pop record buyers, are buying the Country Crossover hits.

The so called "Country" artists, are putting more money and time in building a more varied act, and most of the above stars have already played the main rooms in Las Vegas, Reno, and Lake Tahoe with great success.

I will make a prediction that the gaming areas will be playing at least 50 percent Country and Western acts in their main theatres in the next few years.

The Country and Western agents such as Jim Halsey, Buddy Lee, Tandy Rice, Mike North and E.O. Stacey of I.C.M., Dave Doud and Sonny Neal of William Morris, Chardon, Shorty Lavender, Jimmy Jay, George Moffett, Billy Deaton, Lavender-Blake, Century II Productions, United Talent, Don Keirns, Keith Case, Charley Lamb, Dick Blake, and several others, are really sitting in the driver's seat for the future. I see

144

Roy Clark

nothing but great success for all of the Country and Western industry.

What Changed the Lounge Business

I tell a mythical story which sort explains what changed the
old, fun-filled "open" lounges, into the "closed" formal casino
lounge theatres. As the story goes, in the days of the open
lounges located near the casino area, two big Texas gamblers
came into the casino one night about 2:00 a.m., when the
lounge groups were really rocking, and as they were playing
craps, one Texas shooter said to the other, "Let's get the hell out

145

of here! I can't concentrate on these dice with all of that god-damn music blasting in my ears!!" With that, they picked up their chips and left.

The stick-man overheard the remark, and immediately told his pit boss that they had just lost a pair of $50,000 Texas shooters because of the loud music. The pit boss immediately went to the Casino boss and told him that they had just lost two $100,000 shooters because of the loud "rock n' rollers" and, of course, as the story goes, the Casino boss went to the hotel owner and said that they had just lost a half a million dollars in the casino, because of the *loud* rock n' rollers in the lounge.

There was an immediate reaction to all of this exaggeration and, as the story goes, the building contractors were called in, and the lounge was totally enclosed.

The new enclosed lounge-theatre reopened with deafening *silence!* At last, *peace* and *quiet!*

Sometime later, enter the same two Texas shooters returning to play a little craps. They played for a little while in this total silence, with none of the old excitment, and people milling around the lounge and casino, and in a short time, one Texas shooter turned to the other shooter and whispered, "Let's get the hell out of this place and go where's there's some action! This place is dying!" (End of story!)

There is a lot more truth than fiction in this mythical tale.

I say, let's put the "FUN BACK IN THE SUN!" Let's open up the lounges into the casinos, and keep the customers rolling and happy to stay up till 4:00 a.m., "having a ball," and co-incidentally dropping a few dollars on the crap table at the same time. Let's develop some more Wayne Newtons and Bobby Vintons out of these lounges. It'll be good for everybody, and will replenish our rapidly diminishing supply of commercial super-stars.

Up to this point, I have been primarily writing about Las Vegas. Their northern cousins in Reno, and Lake Tahoe, have kept more closely to the open lounge concept. Lee Frankovich at Harvey's Resort Hotel still has an open lounge, and many of our current stars spent many hours working at Harvey's. Doug Bushousen, Vice President at Harrah's in charge of entertainment, and his assistant in Reno, Russ Byloff, are still offering opportunities for new acts in both of the lounges in Reno, and

Lake Tahoe. The new Park Tahoe Hotel has a beautiful open lounge, as does Pat France, Entertainment Director at the Sahara Tahoe. Al Bello and Charley Mapes have open lounges in both the Mapes Hotel, and The Money Tree in Reno; and Bill DeAngelis at the M.G.M. Grand Hotel in Reno also has an open lounge.

Several other lounges in Reno such as, The Gold Dust East and West, The Eldorado Hotel, The Riverside Hotel, Harold's Club, The Shy Clown, The Holiday Inn, The Holiday Hotel, Fitzgerald's Hotel, The Onslow Hotel, and the new Sahara Hotel in Reno all present potential stars of tomorrow in their lounges.

I don't mean to imply that Las Vegas is totally devoid of open lounges. Dick Lane, Entertainment Director of the Hilton Hotels, has an open lounge in both the Hilton International and the Flamingo. Jack Eglash at the Sahara has a "semi-open" lounge. Walter Kane, Entertainment Director of all of the Hughes Corporation hotels has small open lounges in the Desert Inn, Frontier Hotel, and the Sands. Mitch DeWood, Entertainment Director of the Aladdin Hotel has an open lounge and Major Riddle at the Silverbird is featuring new, potential lounge stars.

Good Old Days!

In spite of the lounges I have mentioned above, in the Fifties' and early Sixties', you could walk into any hotel in Las Vegas, Reno or Tahoe, on any given night, and see such stars as Louis Prima, Keely Smith, Sam Butera and the Witnesses, alternating with Don Rickles at the Sahara, Shecky Greene and Count Basie at the Riveria, Harry James and his Orchestra, plus Billy Eckstein at the Flamingo, Wayne Newton and the Newton Brothers at the Fremont, the Mary Kaye Trio at the Last Frontier, Belle Barth and Rusty Warren at the Thunderbird Hotel, Roy Clark, and Kenny Rogers and the "First Edition" at the Golden Nugget in Vegas, Sonny King and Vito Musso at the Sands Celebrity Room, Hank Henry at the Silver Slipper, Rowen & Martin, and Gaylord and Holiday at Harvey's Resort Hotel at Lake Tahoe, Earl Grant, Jack Ross, Woody Herman

147

Sammy Davis Jr.

and his Orchestra at Harrah's Tahoe, Jimmy Wakely, the DeCastro Sisters, and Jerry Colonna at Harrah's Reno, Frank Sinatra, Jr. at the Frontier Hotel in Vegas, the Ritz Brothers, Xavier Cugat and Abbe Lane, plus the "Checkmates" at Caeser's Palace, Al Hirt at the Dunes, The DeCastro Sisters and Johnny "Scat" Davis featuring Cindy Layne at the Golden Hotel in Reno, Kay Martin, the Jo Ann Jordan Quintet, plus the Al Bello Revue at the Mapes Hotel in Reno, and Buddy Grecco at the Cal Neva Lodge at Lake Tahoe.

As you can see by the above, at one time there were more

148

stars playing in Nevada than you can see on a clear night in the sky! What happened?

My hope is that by some means, the industry can recapture those magic nights when, as a customer, you were afraid to go to bed before 6:00 a.m. for fear you might miss something.

For self-preservation, I feel that the owners and operators of the gaming industry need to do some soul searching in an effort to come up with some magic formula that will give all of the unknown hidden talents of the world an opportunity to be seen and heard to their best advantage, and to develop their name value.

(Note to the Owners and Operators)

Naturally, I am not aware of your profit picture currently, compared to what the profit picture was back in the Fifties' and early Sixties'. If it is true that the excess lounge sounds coming from the open lounges drove you to enclose these rooms, I'm certain that with today's acoustical and sound technology, there is a way to build your open lounges so that the visual effect is there, with just enough sound bleeding through to entice your customers to stay in *your* hotel, or better yet, to keep them from going to bed at 2:00 a.m.

I'm hopeful that this chapter in "Show Business Is **Two** Words," will start the powers thinking, and possibly someone will come up with an idea that will help regenerate our diminishing supply of great performers.

EGO KILLS MORE PEOPLE THAN CANCER

eight
Agents and
Personal Managers

eight
Agents and
Personal Managers

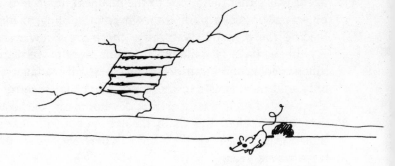

Agents and Personal Managers

"**Agent**" (A-jent, n) 1. A man or woman who represents a performer, or group of musicians. 2. A flesh peddler, a parasite, someone who sells you for a profit (his!!), someone who allows you to **keep 85% to 90%** of "your" money! 3. A necessary evil! A person in the agency business. **Agen-cy**. 4. The only business in the world where the "rats eat the cats!"

If you've never been an agent in show business, or if you've never had a good agent, you probably would believe the above definition, (not Webster's) of an agent. They have enjoyed (?) bad press since the beginning of entertainment. Take my word for it. 90% of what you read and hear about agents is not true.

Agents have long suffered the "slings and arrows" thrown from comics, actors, singers, etc. Most of the time the barbs were meant in jest, but unfortunately the listening public think that everything said about agents is true.

If you will look into the early beginnings of every current superstar (if they will admit it!), they will tell you that, in this period of their professional lives, there was some little agent who gave them a hand when they needed it badly. Unfortunately, when these artists became stars, chances are their first agent was either dead, out of the business, in an insane asylum, or was sitting in a park somewhere mumbling to himself, and feeding the pigeons. Naturally, there are a few exceptions.

In the days of vaudeville, agents were more respected and functioned as combination agents-personal managers. They not only sold their artists to the vaudeville chain theatres, but they also assisted their acts in artistic development. In those days, artists who worked the chain theatres got a full year's contract signed in advance, so they knew where they were going to be for a whole year.

The Difference Between Agents and Personal Managers

An agent, or agency, is usually licensed by the state as a placement agency. This is the same license that covers all other

152

job placement agencies. Agents are regulated as to the amount of commission they can charge their clients (up to 15 percent currently). They are also regulated as to the type of contracts they may use, and in fact, in California where I am licensed with my company, Mus-Art Corporation of America, copies of all our contracts are on file in Sacramento.

Agents are allowed to handle as many artists as they can reasonably handle successfully, with no other limitations as to the amount.

An agent's basic function is to "book" their artists, and generally, in the larger agencies such as William Morris, Premier Artists, Howard Rose, International Creative Management, Athena Artists, Agency for the Performing Arts, American Talent International, Jim Halsey Artists, Ltd., Regency Artists, Paragon, Monterey Artists, and a few others, the functions are almost totally limited to bookings, with very little direct contact with the artists. The reason for this is that most of the artists handled by these major agencies also employ Personal Managers.

Whereas agents generally "book" their artists, a personal manager is exactly what the name implies. Where an agent is not an employee of the artists, a personal manager is an employee of the artist. His job is to advise and counsel his client, in all things "personal" to the artist. Rather than the artist getting involved in calling his agent, in an effort to find out what bookings he has for the future, his personal manager is the direct contact with the agent.

In reality, a personal manager is an extension of his client. With his manager handling the multitude of details involving his business, and his career, the artist is left with more time to devote to the perfection of his act, staying in touch with his publicist, his fan clubs, etc.

Another function of a personal manager, if he has any artistic feel, is to critique his client's material, records, television appearances, movies, and all of his artistic endeavors.

In my three years at Harrah's Club, I unfortunately had an opportunity to witness the castration of a few fine personal managers by "self-made" (they thought!), self-directed, ego-maniacal superstars. In most cases, the personal manager was respected and listened to by the star, until such time as the star's career began to skyrocket.

Suddenly the latent ego of these individuals came to the fore, and the personal manager, who used to be respected, not only lost all of his intelligence and knowledge, but also allowed himself to be castrated by his former "friend" and client.

This is unfortunate when it happens because usually, because of the many demands on the time of the personal manager by his client, there was not time left to handle anyone else except this one artist. His star was his sole source of income, and for this reason, you can see why he took all of the grief.

There is some retribution in the above circumstance, because in most cases, this kind of egomaniac usually directs himself into oblivion. It's one of the unfortunate facts of show business, but I'm happy to say that, in my personal experience, these relationships are in the minority.

There are a few personal management firms who are made up of several personal managers, handling several clients each, under one "umbrella." This works out well in most cases, and also this allows them fewer sleepless nights in the event one of their clients becomes a "monster."

I sincerely recommend that every artist should hire a personal manager at the point of his career where his weekly income is just beginning to climb into the $3,000 per week range. Of course, he should carefully select this person, because he must not only be qualified from the business standpoint, but also he must be comfortable to "live" with. This relationship between artist and personal manager is like a marriage of two people, so it's important that you like each other personally, as well as respect each other professionally. The main function of a personal manager is, not knowing when to say "yes," but when to say "No!"

The union of these two people should be for "life" — "till death do us part!" Unlike agencies, a personal manager, if he's the right one, can be a great aid and campanion throughout the rough road ahead!

Jack Benny — Irving Fein

One of the greatest relationships between a client and his personal manager, took place between Jack Benny and Irving

Fein. They were together for many years right up until Jack passed away.

I would like to tell you a story which took place prior to, and during, Jack's first engagement at Harrah's which illustrates how a good personal manager functions in behalf of his client.

When I was hired by Bill Harrah, one of the terms of my agreement was that my name was to appear on all of the print ads for the stars as, "Bob Vincent Presents."

Several weeks before Jack Benny was to appear for us, I received a phone call from Irving Fein asking me not to have my name in the ads for Jack, because Mr. Benny preferred that *his* name be the only name in the ads.

It sounded like a reasonable request, in view of Jack's stature in the business, so I called our advertising department, and asked them to delete my name from the Jack Benny ads.

When Jack Benny arrived for his engagement, Irving Fein took me aside and explained that their show was all rehearsed, and that they would not need my help in putting it together at Harrah's. It was obvious to me that Irving was afraid that I might attempt to re-produce their show. At this point, it was early in my career as Entertainment Director, and I realized that Irving was uncertain as to my qualifications for the job, so I made it my business to stay in the background during rehearsals and let them put their own show together.

All during rehearsal, I could see little details that needed some changing in order for the show to run smoothly. Even though I said nothing at the time, I made notes for myself. There were technical mistakes like curtains opening at the wrong time, members of my crew caught in full-light setting microphones, etc. There was nothing drastically wrong, but with some minor changes, we could eliminate these mistakes.

Bill Harrah and I had a habit of sitting in what we called "Kings Row" in the back of the South Shore Room, so that we had a good view of the show, and so we could discuss the merits or mistakes of each show we presented.

During Jack's first show, it was obvious to both Bill and myself that there were stage moves which needed to be rectified. I assured Bill Harrah that I was aware of them, and that they

155

would be corrected during the intermission between the first and second shows.

As soon as the first show finished, I had a martini with Irving, and together we made some changes in the mechanical routining of the show in order to eliminate the flaws. As a result of this meeting, the second show ran like clockwork.

After the second show, I happened to be walking through the stars' dressing room area, and as I passed Jack Benny's door, I heard Irving Fein call to me. I stopped and went into the dressing room. Jack was relaxed in his robe and I told him how pleased both Bill Harrah and I were with his show, and how happy we were that he had decided to play for us.

With this, I left Jack and Irving and went up on stage to finish up my night's work before leaving for the evening.

The next night, I had an occasion to sit with Mary Livingston who was having dinner in the South Shore Room watching Jack's show, and it turned out that Mary and I got along fine. She's a nice lady, and I told her how beautiful she looked, and how I've loved her as part of the Jack Benny show for years.

About the fourth or fifth night Jack was there, he called me into his dressing room and said, "Mary tells me you're a pretty nice guy."

"Well," I said, "you know, she's a nice lady and I've enjoyed having dinner with her."

"Well, sit down," he said, "I want to get acquainted with you."

We talked for a few minutes and then Irving Fein walked in and we continued trading stories about the funny things that had happened to us in entertainment. At this point I felt a personal acceptance by both Jack and Irving.

About the end of Jack's first week, I noticed that Irving Fein started calling me "Palsie," which is kind of a favorite expression of Irving's. I think he sensed I wasn't trying to force my Entertainment Director's title upon Jack and himself in order to satisfy my ego. So, by the end of the engagement, we were very good friends, and we negotiated a return engagement for about six months hence.

The point of the story is that one day, about three months

before Jack's second engagement, I got a phone call from Irving Fein.

"Palsie, you know things are a little different than the first time we played up in Tahoe," he said. "We've enjoyed it so much, and we love coming back. Incidentally, we don't mind you *presenting* Jack Benny this time!"

Two Types of Agents

There are basically two categories of agents. One works in the variety department of one of the major agencies that we have mentioned previously in this chapter. Because these agencies handle stars who are in demand, there is less need for these agents to do a lot of creative hard selling. Most of their time is taken up with answering phone inquiries from buyers who call in requesting one of their name artists.

Before we go any further, I should point out that these major agencies, with a few exceptions, handle artists who are signed with them exclusively. This means that anyone desiring the services of these stars **must** deal with their particular agency.

I don't mean to imply that the agents with major agencies do not have to sell. Their problem may not be securing engagements for these desirable artists. Their real job of selling is trying to get the stars and their personal managers to **accept** the engagements once they are sold.

The other type of agent is the man or woman who works for a smaller agency, where the artists are practically unknown talents, who want more money than they are worth from operators who didn't really want them in the first place. They were "hard sold" by an agent who needed the commission to keep his doors open. This type of agent and his small, but very necessary agency, is where I've spent most of my years, and I will now describe this "hard" selling, "hard" working agent to you.

It has been said that an agent was once an artist who had his brains kicked out. Actually, most of these agents were once musicians, singers, or performers of some kind.

Speaking from experience, I can honestly verify that this "small time" agent has the most thankless job in the world. The acts think he's a necessary evil and a parasite. The club owners think he's preying on the poor, defenseless artists, and doesn't deserve to be paid his commission. His wife and children can't see why he has to travel so much, and stay out so late every night, and his fellow agents can't see how he holds onto any of his artists or accounts. In fact, they lay in wait for him to make one mistake and, because they are such good friends, they attempt to relieve him of both his artists and his "hard-won" accounts.

It's been said by some wise man that "the small agency business is the only business in the world where the 'rats eat the cats'." The only way to exist in this business is to either be a "rat," or a "cat" with "rat" tendencies.

It is difficult to describe the qualifications needed to be in the small agency business.

Qualifications of an Agent

First of all, you must have the guts and determination of a tiger, and the persistence of a Marine Corp Drill-Sergeant. Your percentage of sales, per call is about 10 percent. This means you are nailed to an average of 12 working hours per day, at least six days (and nights) per week. You cannot get away from your work at any time, because every telephone booth is your office.

Besides the above, you must also have some background in the business, either as a performer, musician, singer, comic, or club owner. It's practically impossible for someone with no "working" knowledge of show business to become successful as an agent. There are a few, but damn few.

Because entertainment is an intangible art form, a good agent must have super intuitive powers, and must sense immediately how to improvise an answer, even before the question has been asked. When you're dealing with eccentric, ego-bound artists, and sharp club owners, and you've got your so-called "friendly" fellow agents breathing down your neck, you'd better be able to improvise instantaneously, or they will devour you.

Where's the reward? Why work all of those hours for such poor hourly wages? Let me tell you why I've stayed in this game for 28 years.

First of all, you've got to like a challenge, not one, but

several each day. You've got to like to get into the ring with Muhammad Ali every time the phone rings, or every time you talk to an act, or a club owner. It's you against the adversary, all by yourself — no time to prepare your answers in advance, no time to write out your speech in advance, and no way of knowing where the next "punch" is coming from. Sometimes you win, and sometimes you lose. The test of your mental agility is unbelievable.

This form of selling is by far the most intricate and involved in the entire field. Here you are selling intangible objects to an operator who never saw the artist perform, in most cases, for money he doesn't want to spend. Now, after you've got him sold on your artists, you've got to call your artist and convince him that you didn't take an order, and that he's actually being well paid.

How's that for a challenge? Multiply this by twelve-hour days, and you've got the picture.

The second reward is, no boredom! There are no two days alike, no two deals alike. The only reason an agent can work the amount of hours he does, without tiring, is because of the constant excitement and lack of monotony. Also, because of the atmosphere surrounding show business, what with music, dancing, floor shows, liquor, and happy people. You tend to forget how long you've been working, and how late the hour is getting.

The third reward is money. The reason I mention money third, and not first, is because when you consider how many hours and how many days you spend doing your job, you are working for the lowest hourly wage possible! I figure that the average hourly wage for an agent is somewhere between $5.00 to $7.50 per hour. Plumbers, electricians, and all of the other craftsmen, all get two to three times this hourly wage, and their products don't talk back to them.

Speaking of money, the biggest drawback to this is the reluctance of the artist to pay his commission. Unfortunately, in most cases, the artist is paid in full, including your commission, and then it becomes your obligation to collect your percentage from the artist.

I'm not implying that all artists do not pay commission promptly, but there are many who feel that you don't deserve it and you don't need it. For one reason or the other, it becomes an aggravation to collect it. In many cases, when the artist doesn't pay your commission, he has used the money for something else, and as the debt becomes rather large he resents paying it, because he's already spent it.

Now comes the breakdown of a relationship which started out healthy — to the degree whereby the agent stops booking the artist. This utimately leads to a union or civil suit. Both the artist and the agent lose and it is completely unnecessary.

When I was a working artist, thanks to my upbringing, I paid my commissions on time. In fact, there were times when I paid my agent **one week in advance**, figuring if I threw "bread" upon the waters, it would come back a thousand fold.

Most artists realize that the agent is earning his money, and needs it to operate in their behalf, so most commissions are paid immediately. There are times when the contract reads that the commission is deducted by the operator, and is to be sent to the agent. Even then, from time to time, you will run into an operator who feels that you don't need or don't deserve the money, so he doesn't send it to you. Again, comes a breakdown in a relationship and a possible law suit.

Basically, I think this happens from time to time because of the relaxed nature of our business. Agents do not work in a strict financial atmosphere, what with the fun aspects of show business, and because agents tend to be relaxed, fun-loving individuals, who look prosperous (deceptive!), drive good cars (with 100,000 miles on the odometer), both the artist and the club owner feel that the commission is insignificant to this wealthy (?), "Charming Charley." Naturally, the agent hates to lose a good artist, or a good account, so he doesn't lean on them as quickly as he should. It's a vicious circle, and this one failing takes much of the fun out of a job which could be a joy.

In a subsequent chapter I will cover a possible solution to this problem, having to do with the establishment of an agents association called "The International Theatrical Agencies Association" (I.T.A.A.)

The fourth and most "spiritual" reward, is the occasional act that you helped make it to the big time. In most cases, you are no longer his or her agent, but you still get a sense of satisfaction from knowing that you had a hand in their success.

I think when you become an agent, you must resign yourself to the fact that most of your efforts in behalf of the artists, and the operators, will go unnoticed, and unappreciated, and that if there is a reward for your conscientious efforts in their behalf, it will be *in heaven*, and not on earth. On the whole, for the amount of hours, sweat, concern, and grief you go through, it's a thankless job. Many times I've said to myself, "Why are you doing it, if it's such a thankless job?" The answer always comes up the same, "What else do you know?"

I didn't mean to paint such a "black" picture of agentry. There are many small and large triumphs, that happen to you from time to time. There is that occasional artist who really appreciates you, and writes you a letter saying so, or he might even send you a gift. There's also that occasional artist who stays with you for years and years, even though he's been propositioned by every other agent in the country. These people are rare, but do exist.

Recently, the commission was increased up to 15 percent, after having been 10 percent since the beginning of show business. There has been some resistance to this increase by the artists, only because they are not business orientated enough to realize that the cost of operation of an agency has increased, like everything else.

Another big reason that the commission needs to be increased to 15 percent, is due to the large increase of "house buyers" that have sprung up all over the country in the cocktail lounges. The owners and managers of lounges and night clubs have turned the buying of entertainment over to these buyers, on an exclusive basis, with the understanding that the exclusive buyer will get his compensation from the agency on what is called "split-commission." In essence, this means that the agent representing the artist only receive 7½ percent of the 15 percent. The house buyer receives 7½ percent, out of which he pays his cost of operation.

Under the old 10 percent commission arrangement, neither the agent nor the exclusive buyer would net any profit under their increased cost of operation, where they would have ended up with 5 percent commission each.

The major agencies, booking name stars, and receiving large commissions, are primarily still charging 10 percent commission to their artists. None of the majors split commission with house buyers, so they get the entire 10 percent.

With the large salaries received by the stars, plus the fact that they never split commission, plus the fact that the majors do not usually need to "hard-sell" their stars, their margin of profits are considerably higher than the smaller agencies. For all of these reasons, they get along quite well on 10 percent.

"What It Takes To Be A Good Agent"

In 1952, I became a junior partner, and General Manager of an agency in Chicago called, Mutual Entertainment Agency Inc. We also had offices in Las Vegas, Nevada, and Beverly Hills, California. From the time I became General Manager of Mutual, until I became Entertainment Director at Harrah's Club in Reno and Lake Tahoe in 1962, I hired and trained at least 10 agents, who worked under my direction.

Between the time I resigned from Harrah's Club in 1965, and the printing of this book, I have hired and trained an additional 25 agents, which should make me some kind of an authority on what it takes to become a successful agent. Incidentally, out of these 35 total agents I hired and trained, only about five of these people became successful in some degree, and are still in the business. The rest of the potential agents usually only lasted about three to four months before they, or I, decided to throw in the towel. These statistics alone should tell you how difficult it is to survive in this jungle called agentry.

To my mind, the most important ingredient necessary to become a successful agent is *self-motivation*. There is no way that the owner of the agency, or the Sales Manager, can program the agent's time, or the manner in which he functions. There are too many variables in this crazy business to establish any kind of set rules, or time schedules.

You've got to remember that you are not dealing with hard-good's item which can remain in the warehouse if you don't sell it. Your product has to eat, travel, pay motel bills, and other expenses such as, automobiles or truck payments, new costumes, upkeep of instruments and equipment, insurance on their vehicles and instruments, sometimes their rent on a home or apartment (which they rarely see), union dues and taxes, repayment of the original loan they took out from a bank, or their parents, in the amount of approximately $25,000, to get into the business in the first place. These expenses continue every week, 52 weeks a year. Now you can begin to see why you, as a conscientious agent, need to work 12 to 14 hours a day, and why I say you must be self-motivated. If you don't keep these artists working at least 44 weeks per year, they have giant teeth and will bite you.

Besides trying to keep your artist happy, you've also got some club owners who rely on you for their supply of entertainment. If you happen to put in an occasional act that doesn't quite fit their rooms, they too, have hugh teeth, and you could possibly end up with a case of rabies from both the artist and/or operator.

Your primary function as an agent is to fit the *right* artist into the *right* club or lounge and because of your "good judgment," you have made two people happy. As a reward for your good services, you receive a commission (sometimes).

As you can see, the second most important ingredient of a good agent is good judgment.

There are many agents who survive in this business but who book artists into clubs where the artist lays the biggest bomb of all time! He meant well when he booked the date, but he lacked this most important ingredient, "good judgment." An agent like this, who **just doesn't know,** is more to be feared by a club owner than an agent who has good judgment, but tells an occasional lie.

A good agent must know whether the "hole" takes a round peg or a square peg, and puts the right one in at least 85 percent of the time. If you, as a person buying entertainment, can find one of these rare individuals, hang on to him. He's valuable to you.

The next most important ingredients, in my opinion are dedication and loyalty to his agency.

Because of the nature of the entertainment business, what with all of its human frailties, it's difficult to find agents who will give you dedication and loyalty. Either they are not making their salaries and expenses, and you as the agency owner, have to carry them, or they leave your agency. This is usually after much investment of the owner's time and money.

These people, who have very little dedication, or loyalty, are much like some artists who continually jump from one agency to another, seeking that magical agent who will wave his magic wand over their heads, and make them instantaneous stars. If you, as an agency owner, can find that rare agent who is loyal and true, and dedicated to your agency, hang on to him because he, too, is rare.

The fourth most important ingredient for a good agent is honesty. Because of the bad reputation that all agents have carried for many years, it may seem strange for me to even list honesty at all. The popular opinion of agents is that they would lie on their mother's grave about everything. Nothing could be farther from the truth.

For the last 45 years, I have been involved with hundreds of agents, either as an artist, as a purchaser of entertainment, as a personal manager, or as an agent-owner of two agencies. In all of these years, and in all of my contacts with agents, I can honestly tell you that at least 90 percent of these people attempt, in all sincerity, to be honest in their business dealings at all times. You must remember that the entertainment business is a mercurial business, so what you say today in all honesty, could become reversed totally by tomorrow, without any control by you. This unfortunate, uncontrollable change of events could make you, as an agent, look like one of the biggest liars of the century! This is one of the many frustrations of an agent's life, and is probably the major reason for the high rate of agents quitting show business. You can get killed, without knowing why, or without knowing what or who killed you.

The fifth most important ingredient is good business sense.

Again, realizing that many agents were once artists there is a carry over of bad business sense from their entertaining days, when all they had on your mind was "wine, women, and song." Most performers are not good businessmen, which is the way it should be, because their primary job as artists is to create intangible, emotional reactions in the minds and hearts of the audience. It's difficult for an artist to do this successfully, and at the same time, do his own tax returns, pay his own bills, invest his own money, etc. There are a few artists who can do both, but damn few. That's why they need personal managers, agents, and business managers.

An agent must have good business sense, because on the surface, it looks like the agency is making tons of money, due to the large gross commissions they receive weekly. The "net" is something else!

A good agent has to realize that there is a tremendous cost of operation in running an agency, and it's his job, besides selling acts, to figure out what the cost of operation is, so he can estimate whether or not he is profitable to his agency.

In my experience as a small agency owner, you are fortunate if your agency can net 2 percent out of the 10 percent or 15 percent commission you receive. The margin of profit is so small, that every agent in his company has to limit his business expenses, such as telephone, travel, entertainment, motels, food, automobile, etc., so that the net profit doesn't completely disappear.

The sixth ingredients a good agent needs to be a success are a *computerized mind* and a *great memory*.

When you, as an agent, deal with so many intangibles every day, it's impossible to write on a memo pad, everything you're going to say and everything you're going to do. Most of your business is done by telephone, and there is no way you can anticipate what's going to come out of that next telephone ring, so you can prepare yourself. You've got to have those answers at the tip of your tongue at all times, and they had better be the right ones. Any "heming and hawing" you go through while the person on the other end of the line is waiting for the answer, is the "kiss of death." Chances are, if you don't have the immediate right answer on the tip of your tongue, you've lost the deal, whatever it was!

Your mind must be like a sponge. It must soak up and retain everything you see and hear all of the time. If there is a question asked, you must spit out the right answer immediately. The more readily you can do this, the more deals you will make and the more money you will accumulate for both yourself and your agency. If you have a bad memory and you can't develop it, take my advice — either get out of the business, or don't get into it in the first place. Answers and information are the tools of your trade.

The seventh ingredient you must have to become successful as an agent, is *time* — *time* to build a good national reputation, *time* to accumulate all of the right answers, *time* to become well known among all of your fellow agents, *time* to build a good reputation among all of the accounts, *time* to develop a good rapport with the artists, *time* to learn how to pace your work day, so you don't end up with stomach ulcers or a heart attack, *time* to build your list of artists and accounts, with the knowledge that neither will last forever, and that they will eventually have to be replaced with other artists, and other accounts, *time* to study the changing trends in the entertainment business, and the good sense to change your directions immediately, *time* to develop the right instincts like when to say "No," as well as "Yes," *time* to know how much punishment your mind and body can take each day, so your "computerized" mind can tell you when to go to bed.

The eighth and last ingredient a good agent needs is the "courage of his convictions." Whatever you believe in, based on a combination of experience, information, good sense, and sometimes natural instincts, you must make a total commitment to selling your product or service. Once you believe in an artist, and you are positive that he has the in-born charisma which an audience will buy, all you've got to do is find the right physical facility where you definitely feel the artist will fit, and sell!

You must either believe in your artist totally, or you've got to give the artist a release, and find someone who you really believe in. The worst thing you can do is to get involved in the grey areas of "semi-believability."

Some years ago in about 1960, I became acquainted with Major Riddle, who at that time was the Managing Director of the Dunes Hotel in Las Vegas, and in addition to all of his other duties, was also the Entertainment Director.

I was talking to Major by phone from my office in Chicago, where I was the General Manager of Mutual Entertainment Agency, Inc. During the course of our conversation Major Riddle mentioned that he was coming to Chicago to visit with his daughter. He said that he would have one evening free, if I wanted to show him some small entertaining groups for his lounge.

I arranged to meet Major at the airport and took him to see his daughter. We all went out to dinner, and during the meal I mentioned that I was handling a theatrical hypnotist by the name of Ted Boyer (sometimes known as Trian Boyer).

Major Riddle was quite upset about the mention of a hypnotist and said, "I do not want to see a hypnotist. They're all phoneys! All of their so-called subjects are shills, and the gamblers in Vegas aren't going to fall for that bullshit!"

No matter how much I tried to convince Major Riddle that Ted Boyer was probably the best entertaining hypnotist in the business, and that all of his so-called "subjects" were not shills, and were just normal customers in the club, I could not change Major Riddle's opinion about hynotism.

Before we parted company that evening, I made arrangements to take Major Riddle to see a couple of small lounge groups. I further explained that one of the best restaurants in Chicago was the Cairo Restaurant and lounge, where Ted Boyer happened to be appearing.

Before Major got upset about it, I explained that we would have dinner, and be out of the restaurant before Ted's show started. He agreed to go to the Cairo under those conditions, again reminding me that he definitely *did not want to see a hypnotist!*

Because I was so sold on Ted Boyer's ability, plus the fact that I felt a colorful hypnotist would be a big attraction in Las Vegas, I decided to gamble on my convictions, and set up our dinner at the Cairo, so that Major Riddle could see the beginning of Ted's show, and if he got interested, we would stay for the complete performance. If major Riddle was really upset, we would finish dinner and leave.

I called Ted Boyer and told him the whole story about Major Riddle's feelings towards hypnotism, and how important it was for Ted to start his show that evening 30 minutes earlier, so that we would just about be having our desert and coffee, when the show started. Ted said, "Okay." The stage was set! Either I was going to make an important booking for both Ted and myself in Las Vegas, or I was about to lose an important client. No entertainment buyer in Las Vegas at that time had ever played a hypnotist. This made my gamble even greater.

Major Riddle and I arrived at the Cairo Restaurant about 8:00 p.m., and I had arranged a table in the back of the restaurant, but located where Major could still see the stage in the lounge. Ted Boyer was to start his show at 8:45 p.m.

Dinner was excellent and Major was enjoying himself. I was naturally nervous, and was doing my best to hold his interest so that he wouldn't notice Ted Boyer's band setting up, and the other preparations going on on stage.

Ted had also invited some of his friends who had become good subjects over the many weeks that he had appeared at the Cairo, so that there was a good crowd assembled at 8:45 p.m. Some of his potential subjects were very pretty young girls. I had hopes that they would keep Major Riddle interested until Ted could get into his performance.

I was really apprehensive about my whole scheme until I noticed out of the corner of my eye, that Major Riddle was getting interested in the show.

By the time the show was over, I felt that possibly Major was convinced that hypnotism was not fake, and that Ted was a great performer.

As I was paying the bill, Ted came to our table and I introduced him to Major Riddle. In front of Major I told Ted that he still had some misgivings about hypnotism, and that he still felt that all of Ted's subjects were shills.

With this, Ted walked over to a pretty, well-built young lady, who was one of the subjects who appeared with him on stage. He leaned over and whispered something in her ear.

The young lady got up, walked very slowly over to our table, sat herself in Major Riddle's lap and locked her fingers together behind Major Riddle's head.

Naturally, everyone in the restaurant was watching this scene, and Major was getting embarrassed and angry. He said to the young lady, "All right, the joke's over, get off my lap!"

The young girl didn't make a move, and her hands were still locked behind his head.

Now Major was really getting mad, so he reached behind his head intending to break her head lock, so that he could force

168

her to get off his lap. All this time, Ted Boyer was standing near us, with his arms folded across his chest, with a smug smile on his face.

When Major Riddle grabbed her hands, he got the funniest look on his face! He knew, in order to unlock her hands, he would have to break all of her fingers!

In total frustration he looked up at Ted Boyer and said, "All right, you son-of-a-bitch, get her off my lap and I'll buy you!"

With this, Ted snapped is fingers and the young lady came out of her trance and returned to her table.

Ted Boyer opened in the lounge at the Dunes Hotel a few weeks later, and packed the lounge and casino for months. In fact, he was so fascinating to the gamblers in the casino, that they would quit gambling just to watch the show. It became necessary for Major Riddle to hang a curtain between the lounge and the casino, so that the "games of chance" could continue uninterrupted.

My gamble, and the courage of my convictions paid off.

There are naturally more ingredients necessary for all good agents to have, but I think I have covered the most important ones. If you want my advice, don't get into the agency business unless you have a strong constitution, and the determination and dedication to pick yourself up and dust yourself off at least 10 times a day. This form of selling is the toughest profession in the entire sales game.

You can count yourself a successful agent, if you are not sitting in the park feeding the pigeons, and mumbling things like "Please pay our commissions.", or "Why won't you take the job?", or "What do you mean, you are breaking up the group?",or "What do you mean, you want a release?", or "Why are you giving your account to some other agency?"

If you are still in the business and reasonably happy, you can consider yourself one hell-of-a-guy.

nine

Hotel and Club Owners and Managers

Hotel and Club Owners and Managers

Because of the excitement that surrounds the entertainers, and the entertainment industry, men and women who have accumulated a fortune in other kinds of business, oftentimes invest in a hotel or night club so they can "touch a star" and become a part of Show-Business. From the outside it looks fairly simple. You put in a stage, add some spot lights, hang a pretty curtain on the back wall behind the band stand, and then call the nearest agent to supply you with the artists who will fill your room with happy drinkers, and dancers, right?...Wrong!

Anybody who is about to build a facility that will be used for entertainment, needs to make a detailed study of the most complicated business there is before he or she spend one dime on the building. I'm not trying to discourage these people from getting involved in show biz. I just hate to see the continued waste of money, time, and energy that has gone on for as long as I can remember.

Not only has there been money, time, and energy spent foolishly, but the resultant impractical entertainment plants have actually retarded the entertainment industry. Once the owner has his money invested, it's mandatory that he buy entertainers for the room. This is where the real problems start.

Just picture an example of the typical lounge or club with the grand opening night invitational party for the purveyors and guests of the management. The band is hired, complete with uniforms or rented tuxes, the club is loaded with flowers sent by well wishers, the owner and his wife are standing at the door greeting the arriving guests, and suddenly the orchestra hits the first note of music. No longer can you hear anyone's conversation. Now people are *shouting* at each other.

The room manager dashes to the bandstand and screams at the band to quit playing so loud. The band leader informs the manager that he's not playing loud, and that the reason the music is too loud is the bad acoustics. The band leader is usually right.

Owners & Architects

When the owner decides to build this entertainment "palace," he selects an architect to design his facility, based on some recommendation of the architect's work, and after having visited some of the office buildings, hospitals, and possibly another hotel or night club. Unfortunately, 90 percent of all appraisals are based on the "visual" appeal of the building, and very little attention is paid to the "audible" or "emotional" effect of the entertainment area.

First of all, chances are the owner has little or no knowledge of what makes sound travel in an either pleasant or unpleasant manner. This is a highly technical matter and should be left in the hands of the experts. The owner assumes that the architect is an expert in all things pertaining to the building and, therefore leaves the "audible" and "emotional" problems in his hands.

Unfortunately, there is no college or university that teaches architects what happens to a cymbal when a drummer hits it with a drumstick, or what happens when an organist plays a chord on his organ, which is amplified through one or two Leslie speakers, or what happens when four or five voices are amplified through microphones powered with 600 watts of power. They don't learn what happens when a band of seven musicians and singers crank up to create the necessary excitement, so that the disco dancers can feel the beat and go home with the feeling that they have had a good time.

Please understand that the acoustics of your entertainment area is very important to you gentlemen and ladies who have, or are about to, invest millions of dollars in what you hope will be a successful, and pleasant business venture. I have covered this same subject more thoroughly in another chapter called "Architects and Interior Designers."

The reason I have started this chapter with a description of the physical problems is because, for the last 40 years, I myself have been involved both as an artist, and as an agent, in trying to correct these built-in flaws after it's too late, and also have tried to convince my artists to "do the best you can under the circumstances."

Before you prospective hotel or club owners select an architect, please find out how much they really know about sound, acoustics, stage crafts and how many seats you need in your room so you can make a profit, based on the actual cost of entertainment. What size should the bandstand be? How high should the ceiling be? Where should the dance floor be located? What kind of spot lighting equipment should be installed, and where? What's the best, most practical sound system to install for the kind of customer you are trying to entice? What type of wall, ceiling and floor treatment should be installed so your customers can carry on a conversation in normal speaking voices during the time the band is playing? These and many more questions need to be answered by you and your prospective architect **before** you sign a commitment with him, and put your entire fate in his hands.

I'm not implying that there are no capable architects available. I'm just warning you that there are very few who thoroughly understand this intangible business, which involves the emotional, unpredictable needs of the audience.

Knowledge of Show-Business

Let's assume for the moment that you are one of the fortunate owners who does have a fairly practical, physical facility. Now comes the job of deciding how to go about buying your entertainment. Before you start buying talent, you need to ask yourself some questions, namely:

1. Do you know what the tastes of the immediate "local" market are within a radius of ten miles of your club or hotel?

2. If you have a hotel, do you know what kind of customer you will attract into your hotel as room guests, and what are their tastes for entertainment?

3. Do you know where to buy the talent you need to satisfy the tastes of the above customers?

4. Do you know what your budget for entertainment should be, based upon your seating capacity and other factors?

5. Do you know how many weeks you should keep each act, in order not to have the act "overstay" their welcome?

6. Do you know how many bartenders and waitresses you will need in order to service the amount of customers you anticipate will attend your club weekdays? Weekends?

7. Do you know whether or not you should have a "lounge" supervisor every night of the week, and how much authority should he or she be given?

8. To what extent should you "build in" security measures so that you get "most" of the money due from the sale of beverages. Also, do you know what security measures are available to you?

9. Should you operate with entertainment from Monday through Saturday, or Tuesday through Sunday? What hours should the entertainment be on duty?

10. Should you house the entertainers on the premises of your hotel, or off the premises, or should you house them at all? What are the advantages and disadvantages of either method?

11. What kind of "attitude" should you and your management people have toward the performers?

12. Should you have a printed sheet of house rules and company policy to present to the performer, so that they will know your personal tastes in this regard? What should be included in these house rules, so they do not appear to be unreasonable to the artists?

13. Should you allow one theatrical agency to handle all of your entertainment problems, or should you deal with all "agencies?" What are the advantages and disadvantages of either method?

14. What interim period of time should lapse before returning a successful act to your club?

15. Should you attempt to make your entertainment cover both your dining room and your lounge, or should you restrict the entertainment to only your beverage area? What are the dangers of trying to service both the dining customer and the beverage customer at the same time.

16. What will your advertising budget for entertainment be, and what kind: Radio? Newspapers? Direct mail?

17. Should you have a "show and dance" policy? What time should the shows be?

18. What kind of dance music shall the band provide? "Pop," "soft contemporary," heavy "top 40," "disco?"

19. Should you have recorded disco dance music without a live band, or should you combine recorded disco music with a live disc-jockey, plus a live dance band?

20. What size band stand, and what size dance floor? Where should the dance floor, or floors be located?

21. Should you provide a "quick-change" dressing room for the artists behind, or near the stage? How large should it be? Should it have toilet facilities in it? How many dressing rooms?

22. Should you provide a "house" sound system, and if so, what kind? Or should you allow the musicians, and singers to provide their own? What are the ramifications of either method?

23. Should you build in your own stage lighting system, and if so, how extensive should it be? What kind of "low voltage" dimmer system should you use, and how many dimmers should you have? How many "lekos" and "fresnels" should you install, with what candlepower? Also, should you install a sound and lighting control booth, and should you provide a "follow spot?"

You, as the owner, should have the answers to the above questions, before the architect and interior designer begin their work, because much of what they draw should be based upon what your answers are to the above questions.

Buying of Entertainment

Now we come to the buying of entertainment. There are many theories regarding the methods of contracting for entertainers, and entertainment. Many of the operators feel that they must see all the acts before they buy them. Some of the operators do a lot of traveling in order to stay on top of the business. There are other operators who rely on one or two agents who are knowledgeable enough to know what the room calls for. There are some operators who allow the entertainment to be bought by the Food and Beverage Managers, who in some cases have little or no knowledge of the entertainment business.

I must tell you that buying talent is a very intricate, involved and important function of your entertainment policy. The man who buys the talent must have a lot of information, and a good "gut" instinct about what to buy, and what not to buy. I don't believe there are any really bad acts in the country that are working consistently. I think there are just acts who fit, or don't fit your particular needs, under your policy.

If you're running a food operation with a heavy dinner participation in the same room where you have entertainment, you must make certain that the performers are able to give you interesting but low-level music, or floor shows for the dinner show, and then gradually get heavier into the contemporary sounds, for the rest of the evening.

Know What Policy You Want

I firmly *do not* recommend that you try to combine a dining room, and entertainment lounge in the same area. It's almost impossible to please a mature audience, who are eating and trying to talk to each other during dinner, and at the same time, please your young adult, contemporary customer who comes later.

Naturally, it's reasonable to understand that if you cater to a 50 or 60-year-old clientele, you are really catering to a customer who might come in one day a week, on Friday or Saturday. This means that the whole front part of your week is very slim, and non-profitable.

In order to be in the entertainment business, you must design the entertainment policy, so that it will be appealing to the young adult between 21 and 30 years of age. There are more of this age group available for entertainment, and it keeps you abreast of the current demands of the business. Generally speaking, when you're buying good quality entertainment, and you're spending $2,500 a week or more for your act, you'll find that these artists are more consistently successful, than if you are trying to maintain a budget of $1,500 per week.

It's the same old story, when you get into a better class entertainer. He is able to buy material, his pictures are of better quality, and in general, he's much more professional.

I've been on the buying end of the entertainment picture too, and I think I can make some recommendations here, in regard to your method of buying acts and entertainers, so that you have some guideline to go by.

Who's Going to Buy the Entertainment

Naturally, when it's possible for you to travel then it's wise for you to see as many acts as you can before you buy them. However, there are many times when an operator is so busy in the operation of his own hotel, or supper club that he's too busy to get around. There are so many things happening in the business, and so many new acts coming up all the time, that it's practically impossible for a man who is running his own business to get around often enough to see what's happening. I personally recommend that an operator find two or three agents that he highly respects, that he feels are aware of his operation, and who have spent some time with him in the club analyzing his needs, and also who handle a good supply of entertainers that will fit his club. I do not recommend that a man allow one agent to handle his account exclusively, unless that agent is totally aware of what he needs, and also **unless that agent has enough acts to supply him with at least 80 percent of all of his entertainment.** If you, as an operator, hire an agent, or a person who does not have enough product, then you are involved with a man who must buy talent from other agencies, whereby he either has to split commissions with the other agencies, or you have to pay him a fee for doing this job for you.

Personally, if you're going to hire a man to buy all your talent, I recommend you pay him an adequate salary and forbid him from taking any commission from the artists, or from outside agencies, for this reason. No agent in the business wants to split commissions on his acts, because it costs between six and eight percent of the 10 or 15-percent commission he receives to operate an agency. If the agent is subjected to giving away five or 7½ percent of this commission to an entertainment buyer of a club or hotel, you can see why he would hesitate to deal with a house buyer. If you don't pay him a fee, you can see where it's only human nature for the entertainment director of a hotel or supper club to try to get a full 10 or 15 percent for himself, which means that he will look far and wide for acts who are free from any agency-ties. He may even buy an act that is inferior in order to get his full 10 or 15 percent, rather than buy an act from an agency, where he'll only end up with five or 7½ percent split commission. If you can't afford to hire an Entertainment

Director and pay him out of your own receipts, then I recommend you refrain from contracting with an individual person who must get his income by splitting commissions with the agents, and deal with two or three agents you can trust.

When you select the agency you're going to buy your entertainment from, you've got to analyze whether:

1. They have the proper information and instincts, and know what kind of entertainment your room calls for.

2. That they have the integrity and good business sense to consider a long term arrangement with you important enough, to give you the attention necessary to do the job.

There are many agents around the country who take a personal interest in their accounts, to the extent of being willing to sacrifice half of their commission to put in a superior act, rather than putting in one of their own acts at a full commission.

Contracts

In thinking about the negotiations for entertainment, it is necessary that a union contract be signed between the operator and the artists when it's a musical attraction, and the musicians belong to a union. If it's a non-union band, all you need is a letter of agreement.

These are of course, negotiated between the operator and an agent or a manager, and sometimes directly with the act. Once the deal is confirmed by all parties, the contract must be filled out and signed by both parties. When you contract for a group of self-contained musicians, I recommend that the important members of each group be listed on the contract, and a clause typed in which says, "Should any of the above performers not appear on this engagement, this contact shall be subject to cancellation by the operator."

This is a very important clause because, there are times when a principal member quits or gets fired, and you've contracted for the group through the leader, who may be a drummer or a bass player and who is not one of the prominent members. As you probably know, once that contract is signed by you and the leader of the group, you are obligated to play that group, regardless of who is in it, with the exception of the leader, unless you put in this clause. The rider must be signed, as well as the face of the contract, in the appropriate places.

Once this contract is typed by the agency and sent to you for signature, it should be signed immediately. I'm aware that there are several operators who become insecure after they have confirmed an engagement over the phone, and do not sign them immediately. This is a bad arrangement because before that contract can be considered firm, it must also be signed by the artist, and then distributed for completion. Now there are times after you as the operator have signed the contract and sent it back to the agency, that the agency either does not send it to the artist immediately, or the artist does not sign it for one reason or another. There are times when agencies are not able to get their artist to confirm engagements, or the artist changes his mind, and then it is necessary for the agent to get back to the operator and ask him to either cancel the date or accept a substitute attraction. Naturally, if that contract is not completed and signed by both the artist and the operator, there is no firm deal, regardless of what anybody has said verbally. Even a wire of confirmation is not considered a binding contract or a firm agreement. It's merely an indication that you have an understanding.

If it becomes necessary for the agent to call the operator and ask him to postpone, or cancel the date, or change the dates around to some other dates, please be tolerant because again, the agent probably is trying to maneuver the act into your area at a time when it is more appropriate and more convenient. The artist is the one who has to do all the traveling, all the driving, and has to put himself through a lot of inconveniences, in order for him to appear in your club.

My basic philosophy regarding this situation has always been that the operator should be understanding and cooperative, providing the request for a change of date or cancellation is done before ads have been placed or money has been spent. The attitude should be that both the agent and the operator should make it as convenient as possible for the artist, so that he doesn't have to drive thousands of miles uselessly. The best thing we can do with good performers, and good acts, is to **keep them in business,** so that everybody can make a dollar.

Over the many years I have been in the business, I find that a three-week engagement is probably the ideal length, particularly in the self-contained lounge business, where the artist and the name of the group is unknown. If you open with an unknown group and they're in for three weeks, generally the pattern is that the first week is "get-acquainted" week, with the first weekend really making the community aware of the calibre of the act. The second week is much bigger, building to a great Friday and Saturday and the third week is proportionately bigger and better than the second week.

If you keep an act for the fourth week, generally that fourth week will begin to fall off, and generally the customers and the help are kind of happy that the act is closing. My philosophy is that you should keep your acts in good condition by keeping them only for the proper length of time, so they don't burn themselves out, and so you can return them perhaps twice a year. If they overstay their welcome, and stay for that fourth, fifth, or maybe sixth week, chances are that your customers will have had too much of them by that time, and you won't be able to return that act.

Generally, the hours of an engagement fall between 8:30 p.m. and 1:30 a.m. Sometimes, it's adjusted to 9:00 p.m. to 2:00 a.m., depending upon the actual closing hour of each club. This means that your performer is in the building for five hours. I strongly urge that the first set, or first hour, should be involved in pleasing your early customers without too much volume. Later, if you have a show policy, I recommend it be put on about 10:00 p.m. I further recommend that you only do one show per night, and the rest of the evening should be spent in dancing. The show should be no longer than an hour maximum, and preferably 45 to 50 minutes in length.

When buying entertainment in the lounge business, it's wise to stay booked about eight to 10 weeks minimum, and as far as five to six months maximum, because if you're buying quality entertainment, every operator in the country wants those same quality entertainers, and as a result, the artists get booked up pretty far in advance.

Any agent or any talent buyer who tells you to wait and buy at the last minute so you can get bargain prices is foolish, because there aren't that many great acts, and you have to get your bid in for those acts well in advance.

181

You're better off to keep that act alive and keep your customers interested in return dates, so you can play them for years and years. Of course, when you buy this same act on a return date, chances are, if you've advertised well in front, you're going to have a pretty big opening night, and you'll probably end up with three strong weeks.

What you're doing is establishing that act in your area as a name, and ultimately they will become drawing cards for you.

Naturally, as they return and as they are successful, and as they are not deaf, dumb, or blind, you're probably going to have to give them an increase in money each time they come back, or until they reach a point whereby they are getting the top of your budget. At that point, you've got to make a decision whether to exceed your budget, or find yourself a new act.

Playing Semi-Name Acts

Let me point out the dangers of playing name attractions or semi-name acts. Unless you have at least an 800-seat facility, I recommend that you do not get in the trap of playing any kind of act with any kind of national name value, even though you may get one at a bargain price. You might want to play a name for one week, or 10 days, every six months, just as an extra shot in the arm, but don't mistake this success as being a new answer to your entertainment policy. If you start playing name acts fairly consistently, or almost steadily, you're going to find yourself in a one-way tunnel to oblivion, because your customer begins to expect a name every week, and when you try to go back to just good talent, your customers won't let you.

The thing I recommend is that you play consistently good talent, just the same as you're consistent in buying your food, giving good service, and pouring quality liquor. Be consistent, don't get into the trap of buying name attractions, unless you have the seating capacity and can play the best. Most operators with comparitively small seating capacity have found this so-called answer to their profit picture to be the kiss of death, because you cannot stay in the name category steadily. There aren't that many names that fall into the price bracket that you can afford.

When you've reached the point where there aren't any

more names in your price category, you're going to have to go from $10,000 up to $30,000 to continue this star policy. At that point, you have trapped yourself, and you cannot revert back to talent at $2,500 per week.

My firm recommendation is that you develop your own names, give them an additional $100 or $200 when they return until they get beyond your budget, and in the meantime, develop other good young acts to replace those acts that get too expensive for you.

Attitude Towards Entertainers

Let's spend a few moments considering the psychological aspects of the operator's attitude toward entertainers and entertainment. If you're going to be in the entertainment business at all, you must realize that you're dealing with a human being, subject to all sorts of emotional traumas and frailities, so you have to have a certain kind of sympathy and understanding for this kind of person. When you really stop to think of it, for a performer to travel to a strange city every two or three weeks, to pack up all his equipment, all his instruments, all that hauling in and out of a truck or van, packing up his own personal clothing, plus possibly a wife and a baby, and traveling 500 to 1,000 miles in a day and a half, and then unpacking, setting up all his equipment, checking into a motel, you've got to be sympathetic toward his problems.

When he gets to the club and begins to set up, I would personally see to it that someone give him all the assistance possible, even to the extent of having a couple of bus boys, or housemen, or bellhops available. All of this special consideration will ultimately give you a stronger, better show on the stage, because you are getting started with a better relationship.

I'm also aware that many operators have been abused by entertainers from time to time, and as a result they have become bitter and they've lost some of their tolerances and understanding of these artists. I suggest that you do not allow the few to affect your feelings toward the many. Most entertainers will give you everything they have, regardless how you treat them. However, any kindness you show them, will give you a much better performance. It's only smart to give them some special consideration, and treat them kindly without being too condescending to them. As long as you're in the business of entertainment, you've got to realize that you're dealing with a person who is subject to emotional feelings, more so than nonperformers. I don't want to give you the impression that you should fawn over the entertainers. I feel you should be firm, but at least helpful and considerate.

You should have a room in the immediate area of the lounge where they can change their clothes, sort of a dressing room where they can hang their uniforms and costumes, unless they are housed in your hotel. If your club is not in a hotel, then you should provide them with dressing rooms and a washroom facility. There should be a small dressing table for the girl singer to repair her makeup, and proper lighting so that she can see what she's doing. If you provide this dressing room facility for the group, it tends to make them leave their uniforms in the club and change costumes between shows, so that you get a new fresh costume each time they do a floor show. This is much better than ending up with a performer who must wear the same uniform for an entire evening.

Wherein you talk about the real strong performers — the best in the business — you're talking about people who like to change costumes, who work so hard they perspire and would like to change their uniforms between shows and wash up a bit. The facilities you provide for them will again help to give you a better show, and also will give you a performer with a better attitude.

Speaking of the entertainer's attitude, there seems to be some confusion between the operators who own hotels, or motels using entertainment, and the artists they employ. The confusion centers around the giving of "gratis rooms" as part of the contract price.

In the artists' mind, the gratis rooms are actually coming out of their salaries, and in the operators' minds the gratis rooms are "gifts" from the management. Somewhere between these two opinions lies the real answer.

From talking to hotel and motel operators, I get the impression that they feel that the cash salary they are paying is *approximately* the value of the act, and as long as they are not running

Billy Kay   The Checkmates

100 percent occupancy, they are "sweetening the deal" with the giving of gratis rooms.

In most cases when an operator gives gratis rooms, he is actually getting an act worth about $200.00 per week more than the cash he is paying them. If he is not running 100 percent occupancy, it is costing him about $9.00 per day, covering his service of each room. Most operators realize this fact, and are satisfied with it. There *are* a few hotel men who resent the "gratis room" set-up.

In my experience, if the artists were not getting gratis rooms and they were being paid their normal full salary without rooms, they would probably be staying in a motel where they would get a weekly rate, and as such, it would be less expensive, but not quite as high quality as the hotel or motel he is working

185

Skiles & Henderson

in. Also, it would not be as convenient, because of the distance between his sleeping facility and where he is working. From the artists' standpoint, it is a definite advantage for him to live on the premises.

From the operators' standpoint, he is somewhat resentful of having the artists staying in his facility for several reasons.

One, he often has a full house and as such, loses his fully

daily rate for each room that the artists are occupying. This could amount to a financial loss of between $25 to $65 per day of revenue for each room.

Two, depending on how the artists, and sometimes their families, treat the rooms, he resents the condition of the rooms when the artists leaves.

Three, in the operator's mind, he generally figures that the artist is getting the value of his room at "full-rate" which, if this were true, makes the artists' salary considerably *over* what his true market value really is. Here again, it depends on his occupancy.

As you can see, there are logical arguments to support both sides of this coin.

Whenever an operator is working with the artists on a cash, plus gratis room basis, the operator's attitude should be geared to getting the most entertainment value that he can out of the artist, and as such, he would be wise not to take the wrong attitude toward giving gratis rooms. It would pay him to treat the artist as if he were a "paying guest." After all, the operator's purpose is, or should be, to get as much value out of his artist while he's on stage as he can, and of course, the artists mental attitude at night is greatly influenced by what has happened to him during the day.

Another big mistake some hotel operators make is to rent or lease furnished apartments, or a house, which he feels will suffice as gratis rooms, and at the same time will be a financial savings to him. There are several valid reasons why this **does not work successfully.**

You can readily see where a five or six-piece group with two or three wives, plus a small child or two, would present a giant problem if they were all thrown together in apartments, or worse yet, in one big house, regardless of how many bedrooms the house had. There is little or no privacy, and it doesn't take long for this uncomfortable condition to negatively affect the group's attitude when they hit the bandstand.

Also, there have been instances where operators have rented furnished facilities off the premises, without television sets, and in some cases, with no telephones. If the musicians are single, it's not too big a problem, but, if the operator is playing show groups, the rented houses or apartments are disturbing to

187

both the wives and their husbands. This condition has got to affect the group's performance on the job.

My firm recommendations to the owners and operators are as follows:

1. If you don't intend, or can't house your entertainers in your hotel, I suggest you pay the act their regular full salary, and let them find and pay for their own accommodations. In this instance, you can't be blamed for their living circumstances.

2. If you do rent furnished apartments or a house, please be certain that there is a sufficient amount of *private* sleeping rooms and at least *two* bathrooms. Also, be sure that there is some kind of maid service provided at least three times a week, if for no other reason than to make certain that the apartments or house is kept in decent living condition. Needless to say, entertainers, by nature, are "free-form" livers and usually are not as careful about their living conditions as most other people.

3. If you do not house all of the entertainers and their families on the premises, I strongly suggest you give them at least *one* gratis room for several good reasons.

In order for your act to look clean and neat on stage, they need a room to wash up between shows, or dance sets. Also, some acts like to make at least one full change of costume during the evening. This is very effective and gives your customers a better impression of the "class" of your act.

Another good reason for having at least one room on the premises is so that the members of the group can make a change out of their "stage clothes" into their street clothes at the end of the evening, and leave their "stage clothes" in the room. In this manner, their costumes will look much fresher on stage. If the weather was rainy or snowy, and they had to wear their stage clothes back to where they were staying, you can see where their appearance would suffer.

I recommend that whenever you do give gratis rooms, that you make the entertainer feel that he is being treated the same as your other paying guests, because in a sense, he is paying for the rooms.

As an owner or operator, it is wise for you to put that entertainer on stage every night in as happy and relaxed mood as you can, so that the artists gives *your* customers 100 percent satisfaction.

As an operator, I recommend that you do not get too friendly with your entertainers. I would stay away from any personal friendships, or contacts with your performers, other than possibly a going-away party of some nature in your club, or your restaurant in order to show your appreciation for a job well-done. It's a good idea to give the entertainer access to free coffee or free coke. It's very seldom you're going to find that entertainers overdrink Coca-Cola, 7-Up, or coffee.

If they're going to buy liquor over the bar, I suggest you charge them straight prices.

Upon the act's arrival, I recommend that you have a meeting with all of the people involved in the group, or in the act, and lay out the ground rules of your own particular operation. It would be best if you had a house policy printed on a memorandum so you could give each member of the group a copy. It could have on it your policy; your exact show times; and whatever rules and regulations that you feel are reasonable.

In thinking about your supervision around the lounge and club, I strongly suggest that you inform your employees, cocktail waitresses, and bartenders that there should be no fraternizing on the job, during the hours of performance, or during the time the girls, or the boys are working. I think this is only good for relationships, and it eliminates the wasted time and conversation between a performer and a waitress, when she should be taking care of her customers. As part of your rules of behavior, I think on this memorandum to the artists, you should also ask them to refrain from bringing their wives, or girlfriends into the club, when you are anticipating capacity business, such as on a Friday or Saturday night. I think the wives of the performers should be allowed to come into the club during the week, but they should not be allowed to take up the best seats in the house.

You will find, as an operator, that if you give the performer all the physical assets that we have described already, with great sound and great lighting, a dressing room, large stage, and good acoustics, you'll find that you're going to have performers anxious to come back to your club for return engagements. Because of this great treatment, you will also find that it's going to be less difficult for you to get them to come back to work for you at the same price, or for a very little increase. They are going to be anxious to play for you because artistically, they're presented properly. They are happy while they're there knowing they sound good and look good. Money then isn't really as all important as it would be, if they were working under bad conditions.

In regards to your other employees working in the entertainment area, it's very important that they be instructed that it is not up to them whether or not the new act is better than the last. It's really up to the customer, and it's wise to inform your help that they are **not** to express anything but an **optimistic opinion of the attraction at all times.**

Waitresses and bartenders at times have a tendency to attach themselves to favorite entertainers or favorite groups, and no one else can possible be better than their favorites. Your employees must help sell the *current group* to the customers. It is important that you inform them that no matter what their personal opinions are of the entertainment, the new act is here. It's contracted, and there's nothing you can do about it. For everyone's benefit, they should be enthusiastic about the new act to all of their customers.

In thinking, and writing about a good sound entertainment policy, you have to take into consideration that when you're playing the top acts in the country, you're also dealing with entertainers who have good photographic pictures and biographies, and who are public relations minded. It's wise to get as much publicity out on the entertainers as possible.

Advertising and Publicity

The relationship between the operator, or the owner of the hotel, and the local newspaper critics is important. As each act comes in, a written invitation should be sent to the entertainment editor, or the entertainment columnist of the local paper, and he should be invited as your guest to the opening, or the second night, if possible. Sometimes it's not wise to have the writers at the opening night event, because there is always an adjustment period for each entertainer. No matter how good they are, until they get used to the room and get used to the physical equipment, it's probably wiser to have your newspaper writer, or other media people come to the second night. These people can be very important to you in free, unpaid advertising.

Also, in your paid ads, you're much better off to take a larger ad for fewer days of the week, than to have small ads several days of the week. You've got to shout loud and clear to the reading public that you've got good entertainment, and whenever possible where you have a two or three column ad of six or eight inches, I would include a picture of the entertainer in the ad. It is wise to have this ad appear about three or four days before the artists open, and also have another ad appear on opening day.

Most of the business you will do with unknown, but good talent, has got to be from word of mouth. Once you've put these two ads in, it's really up to the act to draw people, based on how strong they are on stage. No amount of paid advertising will make a bad act, into a good drawing card. The best you can do is make your towns people aware that you are changing your entertainment to a different act, and give them the name of the act, in the event that someone might know them, or in the event they may have played the club before. From that point on the rest is up to the entertainer.

I think of all the advertising media, newspapers are your best bet, unless of course, you're playing an act who has had some record activity. Then you ought to couple your newspaper ads with some radio advertising, so that the disc jockeys will play the records on the air, and give you some additional free advertising. In many of the bigger cities, there is an entertainment nightlife magazine, and I think it's wise to keep your name alive by taking a constant ad in this magazine.

The biggest deterrent to a successful entertainment policy is the operator who considers entertainment as a necessary evil, and really doesn't want to be in the entertainment business. With that kind of an attitude, generally the whole operation is wrong. The physical set up is bad, the stage location is an afterthought, the sound and lighting is minimal, and in most cases, the operator is rarely in the club. In other words, because the operator really didn't want to be in the entertainment business, the attitude of everyone connected with it was pessimistic.

191

Expanding Lounge Entertainment Policy

For many years, going back to the beginning of restaurants, and cocktail lounges, entertainers were considered third rate citizens, and in the early days around the 1900's, they were just strolling minstrels who worked for whatever money people would put into a "kitty." There was no guaranteed salary by the operator, or if there was a guaranteed salary, it was very slim, and the operator sold the entertainers on the fact that they would be getting tips from the customers.

In the early days of the entertainment business, there were no bandstands, there were no sound systems, and there was no spotlighting. They were usually strolling guitarists, or a piano player and a violin, and possibly a drummer, and conditions were really bad.

In bringing it up to the present, 1979, there is a big increase in the Motor Inn or Hotel business, and more and more operators of today, are realizing that entertainment could be almost as profitable as the room business.

Many of the motor inn chains have gone to hiring entertainment directors, who are specialists in the field, and who handle all of the entertainment for the motor inns. Even some of the franchise motor inns have hired entertainment directors to handle their entertainment problems. This is a great step forward, and will hopefully lead to a more sophisticated entertainment policy.

In the last five years I became involved with two of the largest chain operated hotels in the world, the Holiday Inns, Inc., and the Ramada Inns Inc. I saw them change their attitudes toward entertainment going from casual piano bars, to full-blown lounges and night clubs.

As it became obvious that there was money to be made with these expanded facilities, the new hotels, still on the drawing boards, were now being designed with a more sophisticated entertainment policy in mind.

Even with my advice, the interior design departments were slow to realize, that the visual effects were not as important as the audible effects. Even with the new hotels, more often than not, the entertainment areas had to be modified after opening, in order to correct the flaws that should have been obvious in the beginning.

It is my firm recommendation to all hotel owners, either chain or individually owned, that a contingency, say of $50,000 be set aside in the construction fund, only to be used **after** the opening of the building, to correct the unforseen errors which will drastically effect the profit picture.

First impressions are most lasting as you know, and if these flaws are not corrected immediately, it could badly effect the success of the project. Usually every nickel in the building fund is spent to complete the building, and even though major errors are detected after opening, the Innkeeper or General Manager must live with these mistakes, and still meet their forecasts. I consider it a major flaw in planning, and I trust that those in power who determine the construction costs, will heed the advice in this paragraph.

Separation of Food and Beverage Departments

While I'm giving advice to hotel owners and operators, I would like you to consider this change from tradition. This is especially applicable to hotel chains.

When the early hotels were built in the days of the small piano bars, it was natural to turn the hiring of the piano player, and the running of the bar, over to the Food and Beverage Director. It was a fairly simple job to find a new piano player from time to time, so anyone with half a "musical ear" could handle this minimal entertainment need.

Now that the lounges in most hotels using live entertainment, seat from 150 to 300 people, the job of not only buying entertainment, but also supervising ten waitresses, four bartenders, and a lounge supervisor, becomes much more complicated.

Remembering that the primary function of a Food and Beverage Director is the preparation and serving of food, he is, by training, up at 6:00 a.m. ordering food, and supervising his kitchen help. Furthermore, he is involved in seeing that his lunch and dinner customers are satisfied. This now keeps him busy from 6:00 a.m. to 10:00 p.m. There's no way, even if he's qualified, that he is then going to spend his time after the dinner hour is over, in supervising his evening entertainment program.

Most Food and Beverage Directors were born in Europe, or are first generation children of mothers, and fathers who were schooled in the restaurants of Europe. Their experience in the entertainment, and music business is limited, because to be a good food man, your hours, by necessity, must be daytime hours.

My recommendation to the hotel industry, and the chain hotels in particular, is to separate the Food and Beverage Departments into two distinctive departments, under the supervision of different directors, each specifically trained in their own speciality.

It's obvious that the Food Director would already have guidelines to determine his duties and responsibilities, but with the Beverage and Entertainment Director, new guidelines would have to be established.

This new department should be handled by a young man or woman who is geared to night hours, and who has a liking for the kind of people who prowl the face of the earth after 10:00 p.m. The evening person is younger naturally. He loves the bright lights and live music. He likes to dance, loves the ladies, and he doesn't mind getting up for work after only five hours of sleep.

Beverage and Entertainment Director

Whoever becomes the Beverage and Entertainment Director, must like and understand this "nighttime cat." Not only must he understand this type of customer, but he must also understand, and be able to motiviate his nighttime employees. In other words, after 9:00 p.m. in the lounge, this new director is the captain of the ship until 2:00 a.m.

In addition to physically supervising the night activities, it should be his further responsibility to:

A. Turn in a report daily as to the major events of the previous evening to his Innkeeper or General Manager.

B. Handle all of the problems of the entertainers. Enforce house policy.

C. See that all of the money spent for liquor reaches the cash registers safely and stays there.

D. Study the new trends in the entertainment industry, and see to it that whoever is buying the entertainment, is made aware of these changes.

E. Meet and talk to every customer he can so that they feel recognized and wanted.

F. Make certain that unruly customers are diplomatically subdued or removed.

G. Stay on top of all local, competitive clubs with entertainment, so that he is in constant touch with the whereabouts of the night-time customers.

H. Keep evaluation sheets on each act that appears, with his recommendations as to the advisibility of return engagements; increased money, and other pertinent information.

As you can see by the above, there is a need for a change in the old outmoded policy of having one Food and Beverage Director handling everything. The amount of money that a full night time supervisor could save, just from money that leaves the club in the bartenders' and waitresses' pockets alone, could pay his salary.

I'm not maintaining that all waitresses and bartenders are not honest, but in my experience, it helps to have someone around to keep an eye on your cash register.

Many, men who have made a lot of money in some other kind of business such as, plumbing, electronics, lumber, automobiles, etc., have harbored an urge to get into "glamorous" show-biz. They found much to their dismay, that the new "toy" they became involved with practically took every nickel they had saved in the business they really knew, and understood. Some of them found out too late that they knew nothing about the entertainment business, and were forced into bankruptcy.

Please don't get into show business until you have sought out expert advice on all phases of it. It's a great business, and a lot of money has been made in it . . . but not by amateurs.

EGO KILLS MORE PEOPLE THAN CANCER

ten

Architects and Interior Designers

Architects and Interior Designers

You may wonder why this chapter has been included in "Show Business Is *Two* Words." Only a performer who has been subjected to bad acoustics, bad sound, bad lighting, bad stage locations, bad traffic patterns of the waiters and waitresses, and bad atmosphere, can attest to the importance of this chapter in the total entertainment picture.

I can't fault the architects and interior designers totally for these conditions, because sometimes the owners and operators of these entertainment facilities are not clear in their own minds exactly what they want in the way of entertainment. In some cases, the owners themselves dictate what they want in the way of decor and interior design, which the architect and interior designer is forced to install, contrary to their better judgment.

Acoustics

In any event, other than the main show rooms in Las Vegas, Reno, and Lake Tahoe, it is rare that a facility, which obviously is going to use music and entertainment, is functionally and practically designed.

Instead of dwelling further on the negative aspects of what mistakes have been made in the past, let's go on to a positive look at what should happen to all buildings being designed and decorated for entertainment. Transmittal of words and music to the ears of the paying customers should be the purpose of those ladies and gentlemen who have received their diplomas in architecture and interior design, in order to assist the musician and the performer in carrying that tangible, and intangible message to those "ears," without irritation and distortion. Before you ladies and gentlemen of the drafting board can successfully perform your work in this field, I believe you need to know what happens to words and music, if these rooms are **not** designed and decorated properly. Basically, I'm not writing about the "look" of these entertainment rooms, as much as the "sound" of these rooms.

Architects and interior designers have for many, many years beautified the face of the earth with outstanding looking edifices, but something is wrong, and has been wrong since the very beginning of their profession. It's almost like the word "acoustics" was never discussed at any time during their education.

It's rare that I have ever performed, or attended a performance in an entertainment facility, where the words and music of the performer, were transmitted to the ears of the audience without having "bounced" off the wood, glass, plastic, or concrete walls, floors, and ceilings. By the time those "pure" chords were released from the throat, horn, guitar, or keyboard, etc., to the time it landed in the ear of the customer, it had met other chords (or discords) which were also bouncing around these hard surfaces, thereby having lost it's pureness of tone.

Outside of the main theatres in Las Vegas, Reno, and Lake Tahoe and now Atlantic City, there are very few places of entertainment where you will find ideal acoustics, and sound reproduction. I'm also aware that the architects and interior designers are subjected to the whims and demands of the owners of these projects, and often the mistakes in sound reproduction can be attributed to the unreasonable demands of the man who is paying the bill. I believe this situation is a rarity, however, and in most cases, the owner selected the architect because he assumed that he was a qualified, and highly educated professional in his business.

Let's examine what happens when a typical small contemporary band of seven musicians and singers play for a dance with a young adult clientele, who like the current "disco-top 40" tunes that millions of customers are buying today.

In the band you have multiple keyboards, (organ, electric piano, moog synthesizer, string machine, etc.), amplified guitar, amplified bass, drums, (and percussion) and two trumpets and a trombone. Out of the seven musicians, probably at least four of them are also singers. Not only are they carrying all of the amplified instruments listed in this paragraph, but they are also using a public address system which cost them at least $5,000. Every type of sound reproduction they have, is of the best quality that money can buy.

In order for the band to be successful with their 25 to 40-year-old clientele, they must be "exciting" (notice I didn't say "loud"), so that the dance floor is filled at all times. There is no way that any band, whether it is a rock band, or a jazz orchestra such as Harry James, Woody Herman, Count Basie, Maynard Ferguson, or Buddy Rich, can be successful at a concert, or a dance, without reaching some "peaks" of sound during their performance. It's during these "peaks" that the audience "climaxes" and feels that they've gotten their money's worth.

Now where do you architects, and interior designers fit into this picture? It is simply your duty to see that the words, melody, and chords that emanate from those throats and instruments hit the ears of the audience in as pure a state as possible, without being distorted on the way.

If you now realize this, I believe with your endless amount of information, plus your knowledge of many different "surface" materials available to you, you can come up with an entertainment facility which will greatly reduce this irritation.

"Uncontrollable " and "Controllable" Sound

For your further information, there are two kinds of sound emanating from musical groups, or orchestras. There's what I call "uncontrollable sound" and "controllable sound."

"Uncontrollable sound" comes off a snare drum being hit, or a bass drum, or a cymbal and the sounds coming out of an organ speaker, a guitar amp, a bass amp, or any horns being blown. These sounds are all "percussive" and once they are released, they wander "at will" all over the room. Your job as architects and interior designers is to see that they do not wander **at all**, or as little as possible.

The "controllable sound" comes from the vocal public address system, which has volume controls on the amplifier so that these sounds can be controlled.

Now we come to the usual problem. Assuming that the audience wants to hear the vocal message, the public address system must be turned up sufficiently loud enough, so that the vocals can be heard over the "uncontrollable sounds", which is usually impossible in poorly designed rooms.

You ask "Why doesn't the band turn down their volume controls on their amplifiers so that the vocalists can be heard?" The answer to that is, if the room is acoustically bad, by the time the musicians turn their amps down enough for the vocals to be heard, the "guts" and "climax" is gone from the performance, and the audience has never reached the "point of excitement" which is necessary for a successful concert or dance.

Wouldn't it be much more simple, for you architects, and interior designers, to build "sound traps" in the ceilings; or cover the walls and ceilings with cork or cloth; or any other material which has a minimum bounce potential, so that those "uncontrollable sounds" will hit a surface and "die" without wandering all over the room, **forever?**

I know that you can do it, if you feel that it is important enough. Believe me, when I tell you that your profession has *unintentionally* killed more performers, and performances than you can imagine. Without knowing it, you have doomed many places of entertainment to failure before the doors were open. What's more, the poor owner of these rooms of fun and pleasure, never did figure out why his place was dying. *I* knew the reason because, as a performer in these rooms, I watched his death, knowing full well he was doomed before he started.

In addition to acoustics, let me point out some other things you can do for the benefit of the owners, the performers, and the audience who come to see them.

Establish Entertainment Policy

The first thing that the owner and his architect must decide is, what is this room going to be used for? Is it going to be a dining room-lounge combination? Is it going to be a night club for the presentation of name attractions? Is it going to be a "show" cocktail lounge, or a combination "show and dance" lounge? Is it going to be primarily a banquet hall, which at times, will be used for dancing and shows? In other words, and in fairness to the architect, the owner has to definitely make up his mind what he intends to do with this room, so that the architect, and the interior designer will know better how to design it.

Each of the above "types" of rooms call for a different type of design, in order to get maximum efficiency. If the owner intends to have a large show room, presenting "star" name attractions, it is necessary that it seat at least 800 people, in order for the operator to be able to afford to pay the present salaries

201

demanded by stars who will definitely draw.

At today's prices, excluding the gaming areas, it costs approximately $25,000 to $40,000 per week to put a star on stage, who is a guaranteed drawing power. If you have your architect design a 600-seat theatre, you are doomed to buying "semi-name" stars in the $15,000 per week price category, which means that you are taking big gambles that these stars will be profitable. You are better off to spend $30,000 per week for a "solid star" than to spend $15,000 for a "semi name."

In my experience, the customers today would rather spend $8.00 per person for a name they really want to see, than to spend $5.00 per person for someone that they're really not thrilled about. Therefore, my advice is that you make this decision in advance, so that your architect will know how many seats are necessary to design in your theatre.

On the other hand, if you're going to present self-contained entertainment, and good lounge acts, it would be foolish to design a room that seats more than 350 people. Unless you are going to build the usual cocktail lounge, you're better off to fill a 350-seat house every night than to have a half full house that seats 500 people during the week days, and then only fills up on Saturday night.

Physical Layout of Room

The ceiling height is important because if you're going to present entertainment, you have to raise the entertainment up off the floor a minimum of 30 inches. This means that if you only have an eight or eight-and-one-half- foot ceiling, by the time you get that stage built, and get the performers standing on that stage, they're going to look very "squashed" down by the low ceiling.

If you're going to present any kind of entertainment, you should get them 30 inches off the floor, and you should have at least three to four feet over their heads, which means that the ceiling height in the room should be anywhere from 11 to 12 feet from the floor. At this height, the performers do not have that "squashed down" look, so that they will seem much more comfortable, and it makes a better total look from the audience standpoint.

Stage Type and Size

The stage itself, to be ideal, should be at least 16 feet wide across the front, and 14 feet deep from the front of the stage to the back wall, with a "sub-stage" under the main stage. Naturally, the better groups you get, the more people there are per group.

Generally when you're talking about buying a $2,500 a week lounge group, you're talking about anywhere from six to eight people in the group. Well, if you put on stage a set of drums; which takes up 7' x 7', plus an organ, and one or two organ speakers; plus a guitar amp; a bass amp; and several horns; and possibly a piano, you're talking about quite a bit of space necessary just for the equipment. Of course, you have to have enough room for about four people in front, with about three to four feet of depth for them to move and dance.

When you design a stage, it should be built with heavy construction under the main floor, whether it be steel girders or whether it be 4 x 4's laid closely enough so you can build a shelf underneath the main part of the stage, or a drawer-type "sub-stage" on rubber casters, so that when you have a group that does a lot of choreography, you can pull this shelf out from underneath the stage. It will be a step down of about six inches, and it will pull out about 10 feet over your dance floor, and be about 12 feet wide. With this kind of arrangement, you can put the dance floor in front of the bandstand, because during your floor shows, when you pull that lower shelf out over the dance floor, the sub-stage will cover it. This keeps the customers from dancing during the floor shows. When the floor show is over, you can push the sub-stage back under the main stage, which leaves your dance floor free. This is the most ideal way to present entertainment, where you have a show and dance policy.

The back wall behind the bandstand should be covered with a light colored cloth backdrop that will take lights, so when you put on blue lights, the backdrop will look blue, and when you put on red lights, the back drop will look red. Any kind of light material, with maybe a silver or gold fleck in it is ideal.

If you're going to be really sophisticated, you should also cover the front and sides of your stage with a curtain on a traveler, motor driven. That means that during the daytime, you don't have your customers seeing a bunch of drums, horns, and instruments on stage. It completely dresses up your stage, and makes it look a lot better.

If, for some reason, you cannot have your dance floor right in front of the bandstand, and you want a dance floor in the room, the best place to put it is off in the corners, adjacent to the stage; far enough away so that your customers will have a choice of whether they want to watch the shows, or whether they want to dance. There's nothing worse than having a dance floor right in front of the bandstand, or right alongside of the bandstand, whereby when the group starts to do their floor-shows, the customers get up and dance, and obsecure the view of the people who are sitting at the tables.

In the design of the room, you have to keep in mind that the traffic pattern of the waitresses and the customers, in and out of the room, should **not** be anywhere near the bandstand. If you have your service bars in a position where the waitresses have to walk across the dance floor in order to get to the service bar, or if they have to walk right in front of the bandstand, this is a distraction, both to the customer, and to the performer. Be careful where you put your service bars, and also make sure your traffic pattern of the customers going to the restrooms, or going in or out of the lounge is far away from the bandstand, so that you don't have these distractions.

Personally, I feel that every room should have a sit-down bar somewhere. Naturally, it should be placed somewhere away from the bandstand area, so that it gives the room a certain amount of warmth and informality, and also gives the single boys and.girls a place to sit at the bar, rather than having to sit at a table. The right location for this bar is important from every aspect.

Sound Equipment

In regards to installing sound equipment for "live" entertainment, I highly recommend that you never use overhead ceiling speakers, except for background music. Most of all; I firmly recommend that you never, never allow a background music company to sell you on using background music speakers for the *dual purpose* of handling both background music, and your live entertainment.

These background music systems were designed for low level music and they're fine for intermission, but they will **not work for live entertainment.** When you start pushing the volume of sound vocally, and instrumentally, through the microphones into these inexpensive 8 or 10 inch conal speakers in the ceiling, they will distort, and become very irritating to your customers. Just keep in mind that you are selling two things when it comes to entertainment, sound and vision. If you can hear the act beautifully and comfortably without high level volume, and if you can see the act with a flexibility of colors and special lighting, then you're presenting your act properly.

Sound and Spot Lighting

Even though many Motor Inns, Hotels, and free-standing lounges are installing their own "house" sound systems, I recommend that every group should carry its own sound. Often the system installed by the operator is great, and is as good as you can possibly buy, but there are many times that the house system falls short, not so much from the lack of money spent, but because of the lack of experience by the owner or the man who sold him the equipment.

Since the advent of the rock artists, sound systems have become very sophisticated. Because of the high degree of amplification from the organs, guitars, basses, and even amplified horns, the public address business had to keep up or get lost in the shuffle. The musicians, particularly in the rock field, became experts in sound, because they realized that their success in concerts depended upon good, clear sound reproduction, with enough power to cover 15,000 to 25,000 screaming kids. Also, they were playing in outdoor arenas where, at times, there were 100,000 people in attendance.

Granted, the rock musicians began to "rupture" the ear drums of the older generation, but there is no doubt about the fact that they provided the current generation with a new high-quality, electronic, reproduction process. God knows, we needed it!

Going back to the 1940's and the 1950's, sound reproduction for public address systems were terrible. They were barely good enough for paging, utilizing a 35-watt amp with two 10-inch speakers. For many years, in the beginning of the lounge business, the early groups had to suffer with inadequate sound systems. In most cases, you were almost better off to sing through a megaphone.

Fortunately, today it's a whole different story. There is an unlimited amount of great amplifiers, mixers, microphones, speakers, and everything else imaginable to choose from, and reasonably priced, when you figure that if you do it right the first time, once is enough. There is no reason for anyone today to be subjected to bad sound. The only major problem we have with sound is the bad acoustics built into the lounges by unaware owners, architects, and interior designers.

In order for all of you artists (and owners, architects, and interior designers), to better understand what kind of sound and lighting equipment will give you the right audible and visual effects you need, I have asked two friends of mine, who both happen to be experts in their respective fields, to draw a diagram of what the typical lounge of 250 seats should be equipped with, in regards to a reasonable sound and lighting system.

Jacques Vogt, who is the current stage manager at Harrah's Club at Lake Tahoe, and Herb Swartz, who is the chief sound engineer, both have been kind enough to draw the following schematic of the typical lounge sound, and lighting installation, so that all of you owners who are interested, can understand more easily what equipment you should install and where to install it in order to solve both of these important necessities.

Naturally, depending on the shape and size of your lounge, this diagram may have to be modified somewhat, but it will give you a suggested stage set-up.

As you can see by the following diagram we suggest using 4-6" fresnel quartz lamps on each side of the main stage (500 watts each) for general lighting during the dance music period.

During the floor shows (with the thrust stage in the out position), we are suggesting the use of 8-6" fresnel, quartz lamps (500 watts each) on the front pipe for four color fill, plus 5-3½" Face Specials (Test Lamp used was Kliegl Model 1343 Series, with narrow angle lens).

206

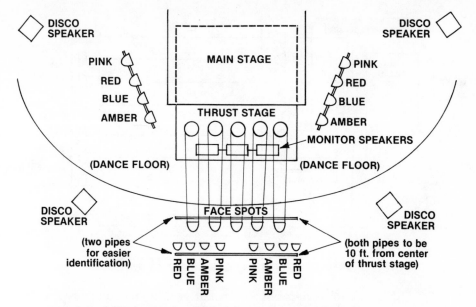

In addition to the Kleigl lamps mentioned above, we are much impressed with the Berkey Colortran Mini-Ellipse Model #213-155. This is an excellent unit for the purpose of lighting the area we are referring to. It accepts a range of high output Tungsten-Halogen Lamps from 250 watts to 500 watts, at 120 volts, and 500 watts at 240 volts. There are other desirable features found on this fixture not found on others.

To operate the above lights, we recommend the use of the Kliegl 9 Control Console. It has nine (9) Control Channels in a 2-scene preset arrangement, with a "Group-Off-Independent" selection switch for each channel, and a Submaster Controller for each scene.

Additional Kliegl 9's may be added as "slave" units in order to expand the controls.

Also recommended is the use of the Kliegpac 9 Dimmer Package, which carries 2400 watts, full load, per dimmer. Each dimmer is fully filtered for both lamp filament, and R.F. interference, plus being protected by individually fully-magnetic circuit breaker.

The groups, in most cases, are not able to carry complete spot lighting. They are too bulky, what with all of the other equipment and instruments they have to carry. I do recommend to the groups that it is a wise idea to buy and carry a small incandescent "follow spot." You can always get one of the wives or girlfriends to operate it.

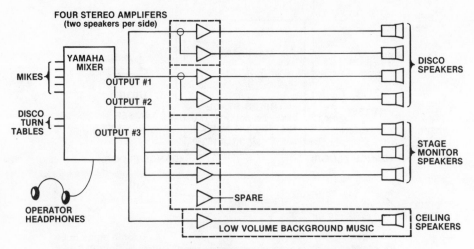

FOUR STEREO AMPLIFERS
(two speakers per side)

YAMAHA MIXER

MIKES

OUTPUT #1

OUTPUT #2

DISCO TURN TABLES

OUTPUT #3

OPERATOR HEADPHONES

SPARE

LOW VOLUME BACKGROUND MUSIC

DISCO SPEAKERS

STAGE MONITOR SPEAKERS

CEILING SPEAKERS

SOUND CONSOLE "LASH UP"

Should you owners wish to install your own sound system there are excellent speakers manufactured by J.B.L., Electro-Voice, and the professional model Shure Speakers.

Recommended "Disco" Speakers are the EV S-15-3; and for monitor and audience speakers, E.V. FM12-2. Also recommended is the use of 2-200 watts per channel stereo amplifier for disco speakers; and 2-150 watt per channel stereo amplifiers for monitor speakers.

Recommended mixing console is either the Yamaha P.M. 700 which has 12 inputs; or the Yamaha P.M. 1000 which has 16 inputs.

Getting back to the groups carrying their own sound systems, I recommend that they buy a good, low-impedance system, with at least 600 watts of power in stereo, with a good mixer, and with at least eight mike outputs. They should also carry at least two good quality speakers, assuming you only need to cover rooms with a maximum seating capacity of 300 people. There is no need to get speakers to cover a concert hall, if you, for the moment, are going to be playing in lounges.

In addition to the two speakers, which will be used to cover your audience, you will need two or three floor monitor speakers, so you can hear what is coming out of the audience speakers. By using a stereo power amp and mixer, you can increase the volume of sound coming out of the monitor speakers, without increasing the volume of sound going to the customer.

Good monitor sound, at the level the artists feel they need, is most vital to their feeling of security. Good monitor sounds coming back to the ears of the artists begins a chain reaction. The better they sound to themselves, the better they sing and so on. It's somewhat like the amateur singer singing in the shower. He can never understand why he doesn't sound that good all of the time. It's really the "echos" and "overtones" he hears in the shower that he loves.

I recommend to all of you owners, architects, and interior designers, that you search very carefully for the right sound and lighting "experts," before you make a commitment for their services. Make certain that whoever does the job has had more than "book learning" in both of these fields. Ask to see some of their installations before signing a contract. I recommend further that you take a professional singer, and a professional working lounge group with you, in order to get their opinions. After all, these people will either sink or swim by what you install. Once you get the right equipment installed in the right places, it will last a lifetime.

Artist Domination of Audience

It makes it difficult for the entertainer to control an audience when he can't see them, and they can't see him. Bear in mind that the success of a performer is based on whether or not he can control his audience, and whether or not they can see him visually enough, so that they can get the "message" the performer is sending out. The performer must, at all times, dominate the entire room so that his "actions" can have the necessary "reactions" from the audience. If there is a constant amount of noise and conversation in the room, there must be something wrong with the design, the sound, the lighting, or the acoustics. When a professional performer loses control of his audience, he's lost the game.

Another important factor, if it can be done, is to design the room so that the musicians, and performers, can enter the stage directly without walking through the main part of the dining room or the lounge. Sometimes this is not feasible, but if it can be done, it adds something to the performance, when the audience is not subjected to the entrance of the band, and all of the subsequent moving of instruments, and the necessary movement of people, prior to their performance.

Let us now consider the biggest problem areas and let me identify the "do's" and "don'ts" for you.

First of all, the most prevalent problem is the **room acoustics!** No matter how small or large the lounge, the same basic principles apply. In order for the owner or operator to make a profit, he must do business six nights per week. In order to do business six nights a week, he must buy entertainment that is appealing to a youngish (21-35) clientele, because these are the only people who are out looking for entertainment six nights a week. The only type of music these young adults are looking for is contemporary, or disco-rock, and as we all know, current contemporary music must contain the sounds of the hit records of today, which are recorded with groups playing organs, guitars, basses, drums, percussionists, horns, multi vocalists, etc.

The main point I'm trying to get across to you is, in order for the operator to make a weekly profit, he must present the current contemporary "sounds" to his customers, however, and this is where you interior designers come in, the "sounds" *must not reverberate off of the walls and ceilings!* They should not be totally covered with glass, plastics, wood, metal, or any other *hard surfaced material.*

I can't honestly fault you up to this point, because to my knowledge, there has never been any instructional education, or books which defines this problem in detail. We can forgive you for your sins of the past, but now that you are aware of this situation, there is no longer any excuse. I beg of you to please give this universal problem your serious consideration. Let's try to keep the entertainment business profitable.

In a large way, if we can solve these problems before they occur, you will be contributing, more than you realize, in the development of the stars of tomorrow. We badly need new star attractions to succeed such artists as Bobby Darin, Louis Armstrong, Elvis Presley, Wayne Newton, Paul Anka, Neil Sedaka, Barry Manilow, The Eagles, The Beach Boys, Chicago, etc. Please bear in mind that all of the above stars started playing lounges and they all suffered through the acoustical sound problems we have described herein.

We must naturally assume that architects and interior

designers are not entertainers, and as such, do not understand that the performer is attempting to captivate his audience, so that they are under his complete control. Call it hypnosis, if you will.

As we all know, it is impossible for a hypnotist to hypnotize anyone, if there are any distractions. The same is true of a performer. For this reason his voice, whether singing or talking, must "dominate" the entire room. He must create an intangible "aura", so that his one-on-one contact with each person in the audience is under his control. For this reason, the acoustical treatment must be such that any conversation, or any noise of any kind does not bounce from one wall to another. Any reverberation of sound that bounces from one surface to another, and then on to another, will ruin the hypnotic effect the artist is trying to achieve.

Any architect who is aware of his limited knowledge and experience in this "school of audibles", would be smart to seek some advice, not from another layman, but from a professional performer, or an experienced agent, or a professional "show" lounge group, who can give him the benefit of some practical advice, in the acoustical control of sound.

In summary, let's not let the various chords that are emanating from the musical instruments wander from wall to wall, or floor to ceiling, so that a C^7 chord is hitting a D minor chord, and they are eventually joined by an E chord, and all together they "bounce" all over the room, continually hitting the ears of the customers in an irritating dissonance. Each chord as it hits a surface must "die," so that the next chord has a chance to enter the ear of the audience, just as "pure" as it left the musician's instruments or voices.

I'm certain, now that you are aware of the importance of proper accoustics in an entertainment facility, that you architects, and interior designers will put as much thought into the "audibles," as you have into the "visuals."

eleven

Fairs and Expositions

Fairs and Expositions

Around the 1900's, farm people in small communities all over America, gathered together once a year, usually after their harvest time, to sort of show off their animals, and trade information regarding new farming methods, comparing livestock, and of course, enjoying each other in a social gathering of old friends. These fairs naturally became more and more sophisticated as the years went by. The larger fairs, in the larger cities, sometimes came under state control, and were run by a Commissioner appointed by the Governor's office. There were others, however, who were owned and operated, by a group of local businessmen, working on a non-profit basis. All profits were reinvested back into the grounds and buildings, in an effort to improve the fair each year.

Under the state controlled fairs, naturally, each time there was a new election the Governor's office sometimes appointed a new Commissioner to run the state fair.

I will not attempt to explain the running of various types of fairs, except in regards as to how it effects the entertainment program of each fair.

Early Beginnings — First 50 Years

When fairs first began, the only purpose of these "gatherings" was to trade "farming" information. Because of our normal American ingenuity, the fair managers, in an effort to increase the amount of people attending their fairs, began to import visual "circus type" acts, such as "high wire acts," animal acts, trapeze acts, trampolines, etc. These attractions began to increase the "social" reasons for people to attend the fairs, and many people came, who were not particularly interested in the farming aspects of the fair, but enjoyed the entertainment.

As state fairs, and county fairs grew in size, and importance to the community, and as the need for more money for expansion became necessary, the fair managers began to look to the record industry, and the movie and television media, for star attractions to present on their stages. They enclosed their

214

entertainment areas first with fences, and later with enclosed grandstands, and coliseums, so that they could charge admission, not only at the front gates to get into the fair grounds, but also an extra ticket charge to get into the grandstand to see the stars.

From 1935 to 1940, fairs started to become big business. During the heyday of the big bands, such orchestras as Tommy Dorsey, Benny Goodman, Glen Miller, Harry James, Guy Lombardo, etc., were big attractions at the major fairs. The big band attraction was finally followed with the popular singer era, which was prevalent for 15 years after 1940. In the 40's such singers as Frank Sinatra, Helen Forest, Dick Haymes, Rudy Vallee, Helen O'Connell, Bob Eberle, Nat King Cole, Ray Eberle, and many others became the big attractions in the main arenas.

In addition to the star attractions, there were what was called "free acts" presented throughout the grounds on little stages spotted all over the fair area. These were free to the general public in order to justify part of the value the fairgoer received, for the price of the general front gate admission. The acts on the free stages were naturally less expensive and were small circus type acts — clowns, acrobats, small lounge groups, puppet acts, etc.

For the first 50 years of "fairs", the average age of the fairgoers were approximately 45 years of age, primarily because the main emphasis was on farming and "agriculture". As the fairs became more diversified with, not only star entertainment, but also carnival rides, carnival games, plus exhibits which were of interest to all ages, the average age became more in the middle 30's. In spite of these more "youthful" attractions, the majority of the fair population is still centered around farming and agriculture.

Getting back to entertainment at fairs, until about 1975, most of the star attractions were slanted to the adult market of 40 to 65 years of age. One of the main reasons that this existed, was due to the fact that the fair boards, and the fair managers, were usually men and women in their late 50's and early 60's, which meant that the tastes of these buyers of talent, lent themselves to buying such stars as Lawrence Welk, Jack Benny,

Roy Rogers and Dale Evans, Red Skelton, etc. Naturally, these stars drew very well, but the grandstand was mostly filled with an older clientele.

Contemporary Artists

About 1975, some of the younger, more adventuresome fair buyers experimented with buying such names as Roy Clark, The Beach Boys, Chicago, Wayne Newton, The Carpenters, Kenny Rogers, Tony Orlando & Dawn, Neil Sedaka, etc., and much to their surprise, they doubled and tripled their gross business, not only in their grandstands, but also at their main admission gates. Besides this large source of profit, they also found that all of their concessions, also increased proportionately in their grosses.

We are now at a point today, where fair buyers are beginning to realize that the average fair goer is no longer a husband and wife of about 50 years of age, who came to the fair solely because of the cows, horses and poultry. The average fair goer today is there to have a good time. The more variety you give them, the more you gross *all over the fair.*

Talent Buyers — General Managers Or Professional Producers

Again, returning to the entertainment program, there has been a difference of opinion for years as to what policy to pursue, in regards to "who is best qualified to select and purchase the entertainment for the fair?" The general manager with very little or no experience in show-biz, or a professional theatrical agent, or producer? Who would do the best job? There are two schools of thought on this delicate question.

Who Buys The Talent?

The school of thought that prefers to allow the general manager of the fair to select and buy the talent, feels that he has the pulse of his fairgoer and as such, he knows best what kind of acts to buy. Also, with him buying the acts, there is no necessity for the fair to pay out any commissions, or fees to an outsider.

I believe, in some cases where the fair is rather small, and

Bob Vincent   Kenny Rogers

where the budget is limited, the general manager should, with his board's assistance, select and buy the talent. These smaller fairs are not very competitive, in the sense that their customers are not overly demanding regarding the sophistication of the entertainment program.

On the other hand, if a fair is big, and they are located in a competitive market, either in or near a major city, I firmly believe that no one, without a great deal of knowledge and experience in the entire entertainment business, can do a successful job of selecting, and negotiating for the stars, and all of the supporting talent necessary to please the varied tastes of these more discriminating audiences.

In order for the general manager or one of the members of

217

his board of directors, to be qualified to buy the entertainment, he would have to be able to:

A. Anticipate the ever-changing tastes of the public.

B. Have detailed knowledge of what is happening currently with the artist's record activity, both single and album releases.

C. Have "inside" projections of what is planned in the way of "future" record releases on each artist.

D. Research the television guest appearances of each artist, and the "viewing" dates of each television appearance, in relation to the dates of the fair.

E. What, if any, movie appearances are forthcoming in the artist's future.

F. What the "track" record of each artist is, in regards to other fair appearances.

G. What the "fair market" value is of each artist, and what was his track record in regards to his drawing power at other fairs, in comparable market areas.

H. What the personality "hang-ups" might be for each artist, and his cooperativeness.

Even if that rare general manager could be found who has all of the above answers, the amount of time it would take for him to do the job, could be better spent in improving all of the other aspects of the fair. Also, if a professional producer is hired, it is normal for him to be in attendance throughout the entire run of the fair, in order to supervise all of the artistic duties, for a smooth running performance; as well as handling all of the possible problems which may arise, between the star, and the management of the fair. In addition to selecting and negotiating for each star, his presence on the premises during the fair alone, is well worth his fee.

The general manager is too busy with a hundred and one things having to do with running a successful fair, so that he couldn't possibly spend enough time staying on top of what's happening **currently** in the entertainment business. If he relies on what was right for him last year, it could be wrong for him this year. If he's going to rely on reports from other fair managers as to what they think, or what was a big drawing card for them *last year*, he could be wrong again. As I said before, *nothing is constant, or consistent* in show business.

Cindy Vincent   Mel Tillus   Bob Vincent

"Chic" Hogan   Roy Rogers   Dale Evans   Bob Vincent

What was hot last year could be "cold" this year. That is why I believe major fairs need a professional entertainment buyer and producer.

I do not maintain that any outside agent, or buyer of talent should have a "free hand" in buying the talent, but I do maintain that the major fairs need an expert, and they would be foolish not to listen to him. His fee, whatever it is, can easily be justified by the amount of money that might be lost by *selecting one wrong* star. He will not *always* pick a winner, but he will certainly be much more right than a talent buyer, who has very little current information, and professional background.

Artist's Material For Fairs

In my experience, I find that an artist playing fairs, where there is a matinee, and an evening performance, should design his or her show, so that the material for the matinee audience is geared to an older age group, due to the fact that the older people attend the fair during the daylight hours, and naturally, they also attend the variety show in the matinee period. For this reason, the star's performance for the matinee should include songs, stories, jokes, etc., that would appeal to an older audience.

Also in the same vein, the excess sound volume of the band should be reduced in the afternoon, bearing in mind again that the 50 and 60-year-olds' hearing is not tuned to the rock sounds of the young adults. What material you might do in the evening performance, which would be acceptable, possibly might kill your act during the matinee with the "older folks".

Western Washington Fair

In 1972, I was hired by the board of directors of the Western Washington Fair, located in Puyallup, Washington, to become their entertainment agent-producer, to work under their Entertainment Director. When I first took over this function, I worked under James Blair, Sr., who had been the Entertainment Director for some 30-odd years. Until my appointment, the Western Washington Fair had been primarily playing the circus-type acts, and some semi-names. The fair was originally nine days long, and up until my entry into their enter-

Dolly Parton   Greg Stewart

tainment world, they pretty much played the same acts for the entire nine days.

It didn't take long for me to convince them to change acts every two or three days, so that they would have a chance at the *same* customer two, or three times. I was also able to convince them that they would be wise to play some younger attractions, rather than sticking strictly with acts that would only appeal to a 50 to 70-year-old customer.

Jim Blair, Sr., retired and his job as Entertainment Director was taken over by "Chic" Hogan, another 30-odd year veteran of the Western Washington Fair. "Chic" allowed me to buy some younger stars, such as, John Davidson, Bobby Vinton, etc., which together with some Lawrence Welk stars, Roy Rogers and Dale Evans, Jim Nabors, etc., gave us a more well rounded program, in order to satisfy *all* ages of fair goers.

221

Revamping Sound & Lighting

Also, when I first took over, the sound system, and spot lighting was not adequate for the increased sophisticated tastes of the bigger stars, so I began to re-vamp all of the sound and lighting, including the operation of same. Besides the technical improvements, we also updated our dressing room facilities. By the year 1978, the Western Washington Fair was second to none in the mechanical facilities for the proper presentation of any superstar in the business.

In regards to the updating of lights and sound, I called upon a gentleman by the name of Gary Gonter, who is the owner of a company called Bandstand Music. Gary, in addition to being a sound and lighting expert, also owns several musical instrument stores in the Seattle-Tacoma, Washington area.

I explained my sound and lighting problems to Gary, and together, we designed a whole new installation of these facilities for the Western Washington Fair.

A contemporary sound reinforcement system should provide the audience with a full spectrum sound. Audiences expect and deserve to hear a quality performance equal to "recording studio quality" along with the excitement of a "live performance."

Basically, a sound system consist of a house or main system, and a monitor or on stage system. The purpose of the main system is to provide a balanced, distortion free reinforcement of the performance. The system should provide full frequency response (80 to 15,000 hertz) at a sound pressure level of 75 to 95 db. It is ideal if the seats in the audience receive sound pressure varying not more than $\pm 3db$.

Why monitors? Obviously, the performer must hear what is going on musically. On a large stage, with several performers and back-up musicians, it is practically impossible to hear specific musical sounds and literally a singer cannot hear himself sing without an adequate monitor system.

Generally, one sound man or crew of men will mix sound for the performers on stage while a separate sound man or crew of men will mix sound in the audience seating area. Although the two (2) systems share some components i.e., microphones, the two systems allow for independent sound production.

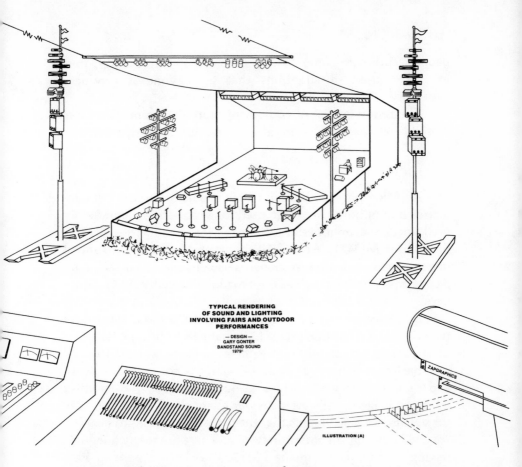

TYPICAL RENDERING
OF SOUND AND LIGHTING
INVOLVING FAIRS AND OUTDOOR
PERFORMANCES
— DESIGN —
GARY GONTER
BANDSTAND SOUND
1979¹

ZAPGRAPHICS

ILLUSTRATION (A)

One of the most common complaints concerning a concert is the sound pressure level. Occasionally a person in the audience will indicate he has trouble hearing a performance but more commonly, the complaint is "it's to loud." How loud is loud? A live performance must provide impact or drama without offending the listener. Since the sound pressure level is in the hands of the sound operator, it is essential that this person has a grasp of not only electronics but has had musical experience as a performer himself. In a sense, the sound man is really a second conductor.

In the rapidly expanding field of audio electronics there is a myriad of electronics components. All manufacturers strive to present their products in the best light through the use of printed specifications. Although audio specifications cannot be ignored, the final proof is "does the system sound good musically," is it dependable, and is it commonly used by professional sound people? Although some products are of excellent quality, they are often used in situations that go beyond a product's capability.

The following list of equipment represents items that have worked well for productions at fairs and outdoor performances.

Sound

A. Microphones: Both dynamic magnetic and electret condensor microphones are often used for vocals. Some commonly used vocal microphones are: Shure SM58, Sennheizer MD413, Sennheizer MD421, AKG D1000, Beyer M69. For instrument micing, a mic with a flat response is usually favored. Many condensor microphones such as ones manufactured by AKG, Sennheizer, and E-V, are suitable.

B. Mixers: For most sound production, a mixer must have twenty-four (24) to thirty-two (32) channels to be acceptable by most performers. In addition to main outputs, at least four (4) sub-masters are needed. Four (4) outputs for monitor sends and/or effects (reverb, echo), are also necessary. A monitor mixer on stage usually needs fewer channels (8-16), since only the vocals and instruments that the performer wishes to hear are "mixed" through the monitor system. There are many adequate mixing boards. The Yamaha PM1000 has been a popular item among sound men and performers. The Tapco C-12, and Soundcraft boards are also recommended.

C. Amplifiers: Eight (8) to ten (10), two (2) channel amplifiers are needed to supply a main system. The amplifiers may range from two hundred (200) watts per channel in order to drive bass speaker cabinets, seventy-five (75) to one hundred (100) watts per channel for mid-range speakers and thirty (30) to forty-five (45) watts for high frequency speakers. The Crown model DC300A, Crown D150A, Crown D75, Yamaha 2200, and the Yamaha 2100, are highly recommended.

D. Speakers: The number of speakers used in a outdoor system will vary according to the seating capability of the establishment. For an audience of five to six thousand, a total of six (6) bass horns, six (6) to eight (8) mid-range horns and drivers, and six (6) to eight (8) high frequency drivers would be adequate. To cover larger audiences proportionately more

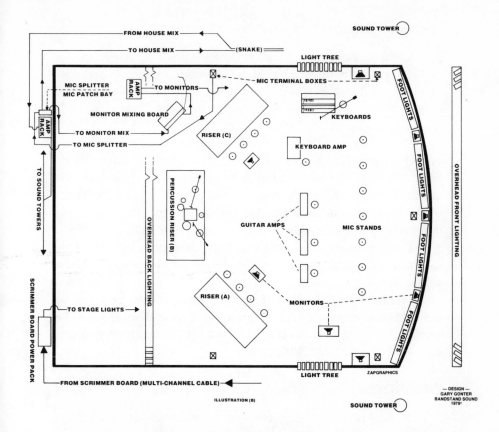

amplifiers and speakers would be needed. The main speaker system should consist of a JBL type bass cabinet, model 4560 loaded with 2220 transducers (cone speakers). JBL 2440 and JBL 2482 drivers coupled with JBL ninety (90) degree, sixty (60) degree and defraction lenses will supply adequate mid-range frequency. JBL high frequency drivers, model 2420 and model 2405, are recommended.

   E. Crossovers: The use of electronic crossovers for bi-amping purposes is recommended. The crossover points of 1000 hertz and 8000 hertz is recommended. JBL, Crown, and Yamaha all manufacture a dependable crossover unit.

   F. Equalizer: Graphic equalizers that allow a one-third octave frequency adjustment are necessary. Recently, parametric equalizers are being used. Although parametric equalizers allow finer adjustment, they are somewhat more difficult to operate. Urie, MXR, Tapco, and Ashly, are recommended.

   G. Special Effect: A compressor/limiter is helpful, in that, protection against high volume peaks is insured. Urie, model LA-4, is recommended. Digital and analog delay units are now available and can be used to provide echo and reverb. Also, these units can be used to delay audio signals so that all sounds reach the audience at the same time.

H. Monitor System: A monitor system consist of a mixer, amplifier, equalizers and speakers. The on-stage microphone lines are split and designated mics are then run through the monitor system. Monitor speakers are generally placed in front of the stage, at least one speaker on each side of the stage, and individually where needed.

The monitor sound operator should be on stage where he can hear what is going on and also have visual contact with the performer.

The quality of the monitor component should be equal to the main system but scaled down in size and quanity. The specific brands and models mentioned for the main system can also apply to the monitor system.

Lighting

A. Lighting: Lighting consists of follow spots and stage lighting. For an audience of five thousand (5000) to six thousand (6000) at least two (2) Super Trooper carbon arch follow spots are needed. The follow spots should be placed in cages but above the audience seating area. Strong is a recommended manufacturer.

For most performances at least forty-eight (48) stage lights are desirable. The lights can be fixed permanently on the stage front overhead, stage rear and sides of the stage. An alternative is to have a cluster of twelve (12) lights fixed to a "light tree." A total of four (4) pneumatic light trees will give more than adequate lighting. Par 1000 watt lights are recommended in that they are not easily damaged by rain. Various color gels are needed in that every performer has their own choice of color.

A light mixing board with twenty-four (24) channels is required to allow control of the stage lighting. Foot-lights are useful, but not entirely necessary, for most performances. Foot-lights can be useful for non-musical groups such as acrobatics and circus type performances.

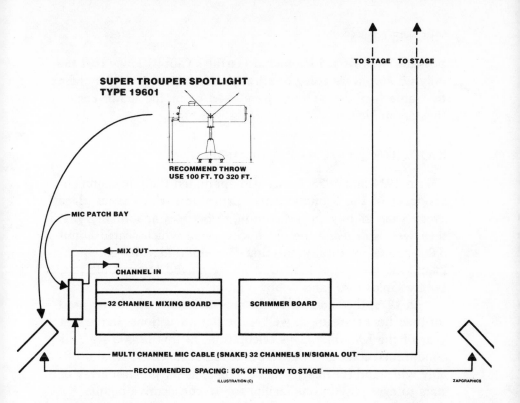

SUPER TROUPER SPOTLIGHT
TYPE 19601

RECOMMEND THROW
USE 100 FT. TO 320 FT.

TO STAGE   TO STAGE

MIC PATCH BAY

MIX OUT

CHANNEL IN

32 CHANNEL MIXING BOARD

SCRIMMER BOARD

MULTI CHANNEL MIC CABLE (SNAKE) 32 CHANNELS IN/SIGNAL OUT

RECOMMENDED SPACING: 50% OF THROW TO STAGE

ILLUSTRATION (C)

ZAPGRAPHICS

Intercom

A. To coordinate the various sound and lighting stations, a
high quality intercom system is needed. A headset with one (1)
muff and attached microphone, such as are manufactured by
Clear-Com, would be adequate.

Following the installation of this sophisticated equipment,
all of the superstars that we played were ecstatic when they
realized that we were almost as well equipped as the casino
theatres in Nevada. Naturally, my purpose in improving this
most important area, was to make it easier for me to buy bigger,
and better stars in the future.

The improved sound and lighting must have helped us get
these top artists because in 1978, I was able to entice such people
to play for us as, Roy Clark, Myron Floren and all the Lawrence
Welk T.V. personalities, Johnny Cash, Mel Tillis, and Neil
Sedaka.

Again, much of the knowledge that made all of the above

227

possible, was what I learned at Harrah's Club. I knew that the only way we were going to attract superstars, was to give them the same facilities as they were used to in the major casino theaters in Nevada.

Klondike Days — Edmonton

In 1974 and 1975, I was also appointed the Entertainment Producer of the Klondike Days Exposition which takes place every year in July, in Edmonton, Alberta, Canada. In 1974, they were still using the old hockey area which seated about 5,000 people. Naturally, this first year, our budget for entertainment was somewhat limited, but, we played Lynn Anderson, Bobby Goldsboro, and Bobby Vinton.

In 1975, they completed the new coliseum, which was used for their hockey team, as well as the star attractions. In the first year of the Klondike Days celebration, in this 12,000 seat, air conditioned coliseum, we were able to put together, what probably will stand for many years to come, as the greatest array of stars to ever play in one facility for 10 consecutive nights.

They were, in order of their appearance, Paul Anka, Dionne Warwick and Ray Stevens, Jeff Beck and Commander Cody, Bobby Vinton and Tanya Tucker, Johnny Cash, Gladys Knight and the Pips, Guess Who, Charley Rich, the Beach Boys, and the Osmonds. I think it's going to be a long time before any celebration will be able to provide their audiences with a more impressive line-up of stars in 10 consecutive nights.

It took at least six months and six million phone calls, trips, meetings, etc., for me to put this complete show together. I had a whole lot of help from Mike North at I.C.M., Sid Epstein at William Morris Agency, Marty Klein at A.P.A., and Johnny Hitt of the Jim Halsey agency, in order to make it all become possible.

In addition to the help I received from the above friends of mine, I also dealt directly with personal managers, and in many cases, I had to use my friendship with the stars, in order to get them to agree to play Edmonton, Alberta, Canada. At that time, most of the stars hardly knew where Edmonton was.

One of my reasons for telling you all of this, is so that the board of directors of the various fairs, and expositions, will

Zella Lehr

more clearly understand how difficult it is to properly put the right shows together, and how much experience, connections, and time it takes to come up with a financially successful program. It looks easy from the outside, but many have tried ... and many have failed.

Another problem which we ran into in the Edmonton Coliseum was the house sound system, which was adequate for announcements during the hockey games, but was totally unacceptable for the stars during Klondike Days. We had to import various special sound system companies, and in some cases, we had to change these companies every night. Can you imagine what a monsterous job it was in presenting a different star, (or stars) every night, with rehearsals in the afternoon sometimes with a 36 piece symphony orchestra (for Paul Anka)? Following rehearsal we did two shows at night, and then broke down all of the equipment after the second show (working all night), and then started the whole process all over again the next afternoon. Mulitply this by 10 straight days and nights, and you can easily see why you need professional help, if you are trying to operate in the major leagues of show business.

Central Washington Fair

In 1976, I was also appointed as Entertainment Producer for the Central Washington State Fair, located in Yakima, Washington. The General Manager, Greg Stewart, became aware of what had happened at the Western Washington Fair in Puyallup, and felt that it was time for the Central Washington State Fair to upgrade their entertainment program.

In 1976, we made some technical improvements in the facilities, again by Gary Gonter, and we had a successful fair by playing such stars as John Davidson, Roy Rogers and Dale Evans.

The following year, 1977, we made further improvements of our sound and lighting and played Jim Nabors, Mel Tillis, and Bill Cosby.

With the success of the previous two years, in 1978 Greg Stewart and his board of directors went all out and rebuilt the stage, adding a large canopy and greatly improved our sound and spot lighting. We were fortunate in buying Neil Sedaka, Pablo Cruise and Dolly Parton. Two days after we played Dolly she was voted the "Country Western Entertainer" of the year.

With all of our improvements, plus these fine performers, we set an all-time high in attendance, both at the main gate and in the grandstand.

If you can analyze my description of what happened with both Washington fairs, and the Edmonton Klondike Celebration, you will notice that we not only played great artists, but

Bob Vincent   Ken (Festus) Curtis

we also brought the standards of lighting, and sound, up to the
finest money could buy. You general managers cannot afford to
have any "weak links" between the message the stars are trying
to transmit to the ears, eyes, and hearts of your customers.
Several of these stars have gone on major television shows, and

231

raved about the sound and lighting, plus the star treatment they received.

As I've stated before, there was a method to our madness. By giving the stars this kind of treatment, we knew that our reputation would spread all over Hollywood, Nashville, and Beverly Hills, so that it would become easier each year for us to entice bigger and bigger stars to Puyallup, and Yakima. After all, these two cities are not exactly the best known towns in America. At least they weren't until we began playing such stars as I have mentioned previously in this chapter.

You can readily see where the fair entertainment business is no longer considered "amateur night" in the country. The fair business no longer takes a back seat to Nevada in the stature of stars that they are playing. With many of the fairs buying bigger stars, plus the advent of gambling casinos in Atlantic City, you can also see where the entire industry had better start taking a serious look into the manufacturing of a whole new crop of commercial stars, in order to satisfy the huge appetitite for attractions, which we will need to fill in the future.

"Free Acts"

For unknown acts who would like to get into the fair circuits, I recommend that you contact the general managers of each fair directly. They often have a special events chairman who they may refer you to for auditions, etc. Once you become known, and successful working for the fair managers, they will recommend you to other fair managers, so that it's entirely possible for you to make the major portion of your yearly income, solely from fairs. The fair season generally extends from the middle of July through the middle of October, so you can see where there is money to be made on the fair circuit.

With the small county fairs, plus the major city, and state fairs, there are literally thousands of possible jobs available to young performers, provided of course, you have an act that is primarily geared to a "fair" customer. I have covered this requirement elsewhere in this chapter.

If you young, unkown artists are interested in working the fair circuit, *Amusement Business* magazine lists national, and regional fair conventions, and at most of the meetings there are "showcases" scheduled in order to present new talent to the buyers. If you can contact the chairman of the talent committee well in advance they may want you to audition for them.

Also, there are theatrical agents around the country who specialize in booking fairs, and if you can audition for one of these agents, chances are, if he likes your act, he can arrange your appearance at one of these "showcases", without your having to audition any further.

Another method for acts to get involved in working the fair circuit is to get a star who plays a lot of fair dates interested in using you as an "opening act" for them. Most stars use supporting acts to "warm-up" the audience for about 30 minutes, before they come on stage. If you have the right kind of act for the "warm-up", and if the star's personal manager takes an active interest in you as a potential new star, there's a good chance you can become a steady member of the star's supporting cast.

If you new, young artists have read this chapter carefully, you must realize that there is a decided difference between playing fair dates, and playing night clubs. I would say that at least 80 percent of all fair goers have probably never set foot into a night club in their entire lives. That's hard to believe, but it's true. They are the kind of people who work hard all of their lives, very seldom take a drink, unless it's a special occasion, go to church every Sunday, vote in every election, pay all of their taxes, and fight in every war. They are the backbone of this country, and because of the way they are, they have to be entertained differently than the typical "city folks!"

They will not stand for any "suggestive" material. They will not stand for excessively loud music (except the young adults, during rock concerts), and they love performers who are sincerely honest, and dedicated in their efforts to give them the kind of simple songs, and clean comedy that they are looking for.

EGO KILLS MORE PEOPLE THAN CANCER

twelve
Musicians Unions

Musicians Unions

The American Federation of Musicians, by far the largest musicians union, representing most of the professional "card carrying" players in the United States and Canada, have reached the crossroads of its existence, which began around the year 1900. From that year, till now they have virtually dominated all of the music business in both the United States and Canada.

Big Band Days

The American Federation of Musicians (A.F. of M.), had a big spurt in their increased membership around 1930 to 1945. During those years, the "big bands" flourished, and every kid who could bang on a percussion instrument, pick a string, finger the ivories, or blow a horn, ran down to the local A.F. of M. office to join up, so that he or she (remember Ina Ray Hutton's all girl band?), could audition for one of the big name bands such as Tommy Dorsey, Duke Ellington, Jimmy Dorsey, Benny Goodman, Chick Webb, Jimmy Lunceford, Glen Miller, Harry James, Gene Krupa, Buddy Rich, Lionel Hampton, Les Brown, Count Basie, Woody Herman, and many others. At the peak of the big bands, there had to have been at least 500 "name" orchestras, and God knows how many semi-name and unknown territory bands were traveling all over the country, playing in Elks Clubs, skating rinks, school gymnasiums, theatres, dance halls, and even street dances. When you figure that there were from a minimum of 10 musicians to as many as 25 musicians, per orchestra, you can readily see why there was such a large membership increase in the A.F. of M. during those years.

Since their inception, the American Federation of Musicians, have been a dominant force in the promotion and protection of "live" music throughout the North American continent. Their original purpose was to bring all professional musicians together for mutual information, protection, and financial benefit, and in so doing, bring a higher caliber of music to the peoples of the world.

To a great extent, A.F. of M. have been successful, but, as in many organizations, as they grew in size and power, they lost

236

Count Basie

some of the original purpose, and their rules and regulations did not keep up with the changes in the total musical entertainment picture.

Incidentally, so that you will know that I write with some credibility, I joined the Detroit chapter of the A.F. of M. as a saxophone player in 1936, and played on a full-time basis from 1937 until 1952. I continued playing on a part-time basis, as well as working as a full-time theatrical agent, from 1952 until 1962. During all of these years I not only belonged to the Detroit A.F. of M. local, but I also joined the musicians unions in New York City, Chicago, and Los Angeles. I still hold paid up cards in these latter three locals.

In the beginning of the musicians union, their jurisdiction was delegated to regulating the musicians who were playing in their "home" locals. As each local chapter grew, they applied for a charter from the national office.

Early Administrative Problems

Before the advent of the "big band" days of traveling orchestras, most musicians only played in their home cities, and the administration of these local orchestras was comparatively simple. With the introduction of famous traveling orchestras, the administration of these bands became more complex, so a new set of rules was designed by the A.F. of M. governing these large orchestras.

In an effort to keep the traveling musicians from taking too many jobs away from the local musicians, the Federation levied a 10 percent travel tax on every traveling band, even though some of the members of said traveling bands belonged to the same local where they were appearing.

Another bone of contention, in an effort to discourage traveling bands from playing in outside locals, A.F. of M. forced the members of each orchestra to pay one-quarter dues in each foreign local.

Despite all of this taxation, if there was a problem with a traveling orchestra in a city where they were not *all* members of that local, the A.F. of M. local officers in that city would not attempt to solve any problems, and informed the band leader that he or she would have to take their problem to the national office for legislation. You can readily see why this taxation without representation was resented by the traveling orchestra leaders.

Advent of "Lounge" Groups

Since the demise of practically all of the big bands around the year 1950, musicians began to form themselves into smaller bands of three, four and five members, and began to play small clubs or lounges in their home towns. In an effort to make the music more entertaining and worth more money, they began to use group vocals, comedy, record-pantomime, etc., which was really the beginning of the lounge groups as we know them today.

Naturally their fame spread to other cities outside their home towns, and they began to travel to wherever they could make the most money. Here again, the local chapter of the A.F. of M., in an effort to protect their own local members from being replaced by these "outside" groups, charged "work dues," plus one-quarter temporary membership dues on each outside member who played in "their" local.

It's perfectly natural for the local officers to try to protect

Harry James   Bob Vincent

their own members, but they almost forgot that they are *all* members of the A.F. of M., and under our free enterprise system, are entitled to work in any part of this country, wherever their services were desired and needed.

Taxation Problems

About the time the popularity of the big name orchestras began to diminish, there began to be unrest in the ranks of the big band orchestra leaders, who had been forced to operate under what they felt was undue taxation. Many of the leaders refused to continue paying the 10 percent traveling dues, plus temporary membership dues to each "foreign" local, thereby creating a large rift between many of these orchestra leaders and the American Federation of Musicians.

Around the late Fifties, a group of band leaders engaged the services of a labor attorney, and proceeded to appeal to the civil courts for relief from the 10 percent dues on their basic scale wages. Some of the name orchestra leaders who were involved

239

in these cases were Stan Kenton, Sy Zentner, and Hank Thompson.

After much litigation, the United States courts decreed that the 10 percent travel dues on the orchestra leader's gross scale wages for the entire band was unwarranted, so the A.F. of M. eliminated the 10 percent work dues. Following the loss of the 10 percent revenues, the musicians union instituted new rulings which allowed each of the member locals, to charge up to 4 percent work dues on all traveling bands or groups, plus they also had the option to levy a quarter-of-the-year temporary membership dues, on each individual musician who played in a foreign local.

This taxation, continued until February of 1978, at which time the International Executive Board of the A.F. of M. changed their rulings to read that, the traveling members playing in a foreign local can be charged *either* the *work dues,* or the *temporary membership dues, but not both.*

National Association of Orchestra Leaders

Because of all of this tension and civil court hearings, a new association came into being called the National Association of Orchestra Leaders (N.A.O.L.). It was made up of the dissenting orchestra leaders, plus some local New York and New Jersey small band leaders, agents, and individual musicians.

Allied Musicians Union —

In addition to the American Federation of Musicians, one other musicians union sprung up, namely the Allied Musicians Union of New York, which is headquartered in Yonkers, New York.

It is not the intent of this author to enter an opinion as to the merits of any of the musicians unions, or associations, but there is definitely a need for all musicians unions to take a "new" look at themselves, in order to determine whether or not they haven't lost some of their perspective regarding their aims and goals. Are they truly representing *all* of the individual member musicians in the best possible manner, or is there a large segment of traveling members who have been, and are being treated as *step-children?* In any event, it is obvious, even to the officials of the A.F. of M., that something drastic has to be done soon to relieve the tension between themselves, and musicians, agents, personal managers, purchasers of musical entertainment, and the National Labor Relations Board.

Taft-Hartley Act - Landrum-Griffin Act

Many musicians and agents are not aware that under the Taft-Hartley Act, it is not mandatory that they belong to any union in order for them to work. However, a union may require in a collective bargaining agreement, that employees join the union 30 days after they became employed. There are also 20 "Right To Work" states in the country, in which no worker can be refused employment, if he or she does not belong to a union. The current Right To Work States are as follows:

November 5, 1978 — Right To Work States

1. Nevada	11. Arkansas
2. Utah	12. Louisiana
3. Arizona	13. Mississippi
4. Wyoming	14. Alabama
5. North Dakota	15. Georgia
6. South Dakota	16. Florida
7. Nebraska	17. Tennessee
8. Kansas	18. North Carolina
9. Iowa	19. South Carolina
10. Texas	20. Virginia

In addition, there is an act called the Landrum-Griffin Act (section 29, U.S.C., 411, section 101 (3A), which states that no local labor organization can increase the rate of dues and initiation fees, without a majority vote, by secret ballot, of members in good standing, voting at a general or special meeting, after reasonable notice of the intention to vote upon such question; or in the case of a federation of national labor organizations, by majority vote of the delegates voting at a regular convention; or by vote of the members of the executive board, provided they

241

have expressed authority contained in the constitution and bylaws to do so.

Musicians Unions —
National Labor Relations Board

The National Labor Relations Board (N.L.R.B.) has recently come into a more active role of settling claims in civil court because of the increased problems between the American Federation of Musicians and members of their union, agents franchised by the A.F. of M., hotel and club owners who are using union musicians, theatre and concert halls using musicians, and the lounges and casino theatres in the gambling areas.

As musicians, agents, and owners became aware that the N.L.R.B. was available to unravel the inconsistencies of some of the state laws, versus the federal laws, and the confusing question as to "who is the employer?", the N.L.R.B. became more actively involved. This prime question as yet has not been firmly established.

Prior to the new N.L.R.B. rulings covering the question of "who is the employer," the A.F. of M. were attempting to make the purchaser of the bands the employer, which would put the operators under the obligation of paying all of the payroll taxes on each musician in each band.

In spite of the A.F. of M. suggestion that the operator was the employer in their Form B contract, there was a clause printed on the contract, and I quote, "this contract does not conclusively determine the person liable to report and pay employment taxes and similar employer levies, under rulings of the U.S. Revenue Service, and of some state agencies," (end of quote).

The only exception to this would be in a case where the purchaser of the musicians, "hand picked" each musician himself, and where he had complete control of the band in regards to their style of music, hours of employement, costumes, etc., and he also had the right to hire, and fire, the individual musicians, at his own discretion. The operator, in this case, would truly be the employer, and as such, would be obligated to pay each of the musicians' state and federal taxes, just the same as he does for his bartenders, waitresses, cooks, etc.

Also, as of January 1, 1979, it is my understanding that Article #25 of the A.F. of M. constitution and bylaws is under consideration for revision. This article covers the activities of all franchised agencies, who are involved in selling A.F. of M. member musicians.

In Article #25, it states that all agencies, working under an A.F. of M. franchise, must submit all claims to the International Executive Board (I.E.B.) of the A.F. of M. for settlement, without the right of appeal by a civil board of arbitration. Under this article, it also is mandatory that all agencies must sell their bands for at least minimum union scale, regardless of how high the scale may be.

Excessively High Minimum Scales

The basic principle of all business, and the fundamental manner of setting the price of any products, whether it be a solid item or a service, is *supply* and *demand,* If the product is in demand, the price goes up, and the less it's in demand, the price goes down. This has always been, and will always be, the basic law of the market place.

In the last few years, the A.F. of M. has gradually increased their minimum scales, so that in certain locals, primarily in the major cities such as Las Vegas, Reno, Lake Tahoe, Chicago, Detroit, San Francisco, New York, and Nashville, the minimum scales are so high that a large majority of musicians are working *under* the minimum scale by filing "phoney" contracts, or even worse, by not filing contracts at all.

What is happening in these cities, where excessively high scales prevail, is that the new, young musical groups who know that they are not worth the minimum scale, do not join the union at all. They take a job for the kind of money they are really worth. Naturally as they develop and improve, they begin to get more money, and are in greater demand. Unfortunately, by this time they have learned how to get along without belonging to any musicians union.

What certain locals of the A.F. of M., in essence, are trying to do, is to force the price of all groups to conform to the price of a seasoned, polished band that have been together for some time, and who have established their price, *based on their de-*

243

mand! These excessively high minimum scales have also forced the agents who are trying to sell these musicians, to enter into illegal (according to the A.F. of M. rules) contracts, or non-union contracts.

This manner of by-passing the high scales has become a necessity, in order for the agencies to stay in business. There isn't an agent alive who enjoys selling a musical group **under** the prevailing scale, unless he has to do it in order to keep his doors open. Also, there isn't a good agent in the business who will sell an act for $2,500 per week, if he knows in his heart that it's only worth $1,800 per week.

The effects of these excessively high minimum scales hurts everyone, and it is particularly damaging to the A.F. of M. Granted, the local musicians union collects their 4 percent work dues based on the contract price on the face of the contract, regardless of what the group actually receives, but there are more musicians who are resigning their membership, or who aren't joining the A.F. of M. in the first place, so that whatever extra taxes the musicians union collect based on the increased minimums, they are losing in revenues caused by the decreasing memberships. The increased taxes may seem to be the road to increased revenues, but it's obviously self defeating.

Advent of "Rock n' Roll"

About the time the big bands began to lose their popularity, a new form of small bands came into being. These small bands, or "combos" as they were sometimes called, fell into two basic types: the entertaining comedy, novelty groups who were primarily "show" groups, and the "rock and roll" groups who were primarily "dance" groups.

The rock groups originally were principally from the East Coast and most of the first ones came out of Philadelphia. Dick Clark and his American Bandstand T.V. show, gave the rest of the country their first look at a new form of music, with a new visual form of choreography by the band members, called the "Philadelphia Two-Step." The first rock groups borrowed their "two steps" from the black groups, who also became popular with a soul-sound called "rhythm and blues."

Just about the time the new generation became aware of

244

The Big Beats

this new rock sound, along came The Beatles. They captured the hearts and souls, and the imagination of the entire younger generation, all over the world, and at the same time, welded the young adults into a solid, unified, mass of humanity.

The new generation had their champions, and with this unification caused by The Beatles, many sociological changes came with it. There were new attitudes regarding dress codes, hair styles, new religions, new attitudes regarding sex, and a togetherness feeling between all of the young people of the world.

It was inevitable that all of these changes in the new generation was not to be appreciated by the older generation, which caused a great deal of misunderstanding between the two.

At the time of this social revolution, there was a radical change in the music business. The old, big jazz bands were going out of style, and the rock and roll musical groups were getting more popular. Granted, the first rock groups were primarily made up of musicians who had very little musical training. Most of the early rock groups only knew three or four

245

D.D. Smith & Co.

chord changes, but the new rock beat gave the entertainment business a whole new dancing generation. No longer did they touch when they danced. They just got on the dance floor and did "their own thing."

A.F. of M. Early Attitudes Towards "Rock"

Regarding the American Federation of Musicians, which was the only musicians' union in existence at the beginning of the rock craze, they too resented the new, loud playing "rockers," who were taking jobs away from the older players. In the beginning, the officials of the A.F. of M. ignored these three-chord players, figuring that it was a temporary condition, that would soon disappear.

My reason for giving you a history of the new contemporary music and musicians is to point out that the majority of the full-time working musicians today are made up of these same contemporary rock musicians, only in the music of today, the players in these so called rock groups are some of the **finest musicians** in the country.

The A.F. of M. officials have now recognized the value of these new musicians as an important asset to their union, and have made aggressive overtures to convince them to become members of the American Federation of Musicians.

One of the basic problems is that the majority of full-time musicians who belong to these "home" locals are **traveling** musicians. They probably spend 80 percent of their time working in other cities, and in other locals than their own.

Because of this large amount of time traveling away from their home local, the full time working musician is not at home to vote for the election of the new officers. Naturally the musicians who attend the elections, and represent the majority of *voters* are the "older" members who are at home, and who only play an occasional park concert, Saturday night dance at the Elks Club, or a wedding in the local church.

I'm certain that proxy ballots are available for every election, but as is usually the case, the traveling musician who is busy building his career, never thinks to request a proxy ballot, or if he does, it's done too late for it to catch up with him. It is my recommendation that all musicians, both traveling, and non-traveling, take a more active interest in their "home local" business, particularly at election time.

As a result of this circumstance, the same officials seem to be re-elected, particularly in the smaller cities, and often they are not sympathetic to this new rock sound, or the new rock musicians. This makes for an unhealthy condition in the local union, because the smallest number of *part-time musicians*, or gold-card holders, who are also no longer in the current music scene, are making most of the decisions which govern the activities of the missing majority of active full time players.

It is my recommendation that the I.E.B., with the vote of the general membership, seek to find some means whereby each local union will make a more determined effort to get the younger union members involved in the business of the local, even though they are out of town considerably. Also, I feel that there should be a more determined effort made by the election committee of each local, to make certain that the proxy ballots are mailed to the traveling members of each home local early enough so that the newly elected officials truly represent the majority of *all* of the paid up musicians in each local.

Goodwill Gestures — A.F. of M.

Because a large majority of the full-time working musicians are out of town working in other cities, they tend to be forgotten by their home union officials. Because they also feel unwelcome in the foreign locals, it almost gives them the feeling of being a "man without a country."

There is much that both their home local union officials, and the "foreign" officials could do, to improve their relationship with these "wandering minstrels." Some of these goodwill gestures could be:

1. Establishing a fire and theft insurance fund to cover the musicians' instruments, and sound equipment, if they are lost, or stolen.

2. Send a representative to the club opening night of each engagement, in order to help them with any possible problems with the owner, or lounge manager. At that time he could answer any questions from the leader, especially if this is the group's first time in a strange town.

3. Assisting the groups with suggested replacements of musicians, if someone is seeking replacements. The field representative of the local union should collect a list of musicians from his local, who would like to join a group.

4. The local union secretary should keep track of all of his "traveling" members, and he should know *at all times* where his "traveling" members are located, or at least keep a permanent address and telephone number that is current, so that the travel-

ing member does not have the feeling that he has been forgotten, and that all they want from him is his money!

5. At tax time, the union could have several of their "older" members, who are wise in the ways of filing tax returns and getting all of their deductions, assist the younger members in answering questions regarding tax matters.

6. Administrate the E.P.W., and Health and Welfare funds, so that **every** musician who contributes to it, get's his proportionate share of the fund.

7. The field representatives should be in constant touch with the major purchasers of music in their city, and keep a good relationship with these owners, so that when a small problem does arise, it doesn't become a major one.

8. Making certain that the minimum scales *are not excessive*, so that the club owners don't turn to non-union musicians for their bands.

Civil Laws — Regulations

During my early years as an agent, the A.F. of M. was ruled with an iron hand, and whether or not you agreed with the conditions, you as an agent lived in fear that any infraction of the A.F. of M. rules and regulations would cause you to lose your license or franchise, and literally put you out of business.

With the advent of the Taft-Hartley Act, plus the right-to-work states, and the National Labor Relations Board, the agents have begun to realize that the old manner of working under the jurisdiction of A.F.of M. no longer exists.

International Theatrical Agencies Association

In January of 1975, I was one of the founders, and the first President of an association called, the International Theatrical Agencies Association. The intention of the original 20 founding fathers was to attempt to convince the A.F. of M. that these unfavorable conditions, which were direly affecting the agents, musicians, and the A.F. of M., had to be changed.

In this chapter on musicians' unions, I won't dwell further on the I.T.A.A. because it will be covered more thoroughly in a separate chapter. I only mentioned it in this chapter so that the readers will be aware of all of the "causes," which led up to the formation of the I.T.A.A.

Recommendations for the A.F. of M.

To bring this chapter to a close, I want to go on record as a former musician and a current member of A.F. of M., to see that all musicians are represented by a strong union, one that realizes that all of it's members should get equal representation, not only in their home local, but also in *any local* where they happen to be playing. After all, musicians are meant to be traveling couriers of happiness, spreading musical cheer all over the country.

I'd like to see the new generation musicians treated with respect, and I'd like to see the excess union scales reduced to a reasonable level, so that the **real value** of each musician, or each group will determine the money they receive, in relationship to how many customers they can put in the seats every night. This will give them the incentive to work a little harder, think a little more about their business, and sweat a little more in order to increase the owners' revenues, and their own income.

I'd like to see the musicians unions' attitude toward theatrical agents improved, in relation to the amount of benefit the agents are to **both** the musicians and the A.F. of M. Without agents, at least 80 percent of all musical groups would be working for flat scale, or less.

During the national convention of the A.F. of M. held in Spokane, Washington on Monday, June 19, 1978, Victor Fuentealba, the new president, said "The majority of young musicians who join the Federation today do so at the suggestion of booking agents who sincerely feel that these young musicians will enhance their careers by being members of our Federation. The booking agents are also responsible for practically all of the traveling engagements performed by our members, and for many of the local engagements. Without the booking agencies," he admitted, "there would be no music business today."

This statement alone indicates that the American Federation of Musicians, and the agencies are making some progress in their mutual relationship, for the betterment of the music industry.

We'd like to see younger musicians elected to the board of directors of each local, so that the attitude and conditions of each local can be more current.

We'd like to see a completely different type of working arrangement between all theatrical agencies, and all of the musicians unions, so that there is an equitable compromise for everybody's benefit. I definitely would like to see Article 25 of the A.F. of M. bylaws *revamped,* and a new separate working agreement drawn up following a meeting of the A.F. of M. and a committee of agents from the "International Theatrical Agencies Association."

If the A.F. of M. officials in each local continue to refuse to legislate any disputes involving "traveling" musicians, working in their jurisdiction, I would like to see the elimination of any travel dues paid to the local union, and a small percentage of gross salary received by the traveling musician, paid *directly* to the national office of the A.F. of M. After all, if the disputes can only be settled by the I.E.B. in New York, why should the local union benefit from the receipt of any dues money, where *no* representation is given?

Summary

As I stated in the first paragraph of this chapter, the American Federation of Musicians are at the crossroads of their existence. My hope is that the A.F. of M. will make the right choice in the future path they pursue, so that I, and all of my fellow members, can continue with our main purpose in life, which is to bring a lot of "fine music" to a lot of "fine people" all over the world. Let's eliminate all of this controversy that clouds our minds and our playing, so that we can all get the notes out "nice and clear."

EGO KILLS MORE PEOPLE THAN CANCER

International Theatrical Agencies Association

International Theatrical Agencies Association

On January 25, 1975 in St. Louis, Missouri, a meeting of 20 lounge booking agencies was held for the prime purpose of forming an association that would represent all musical agencies

Founding Fathers I.T.A.A.

Facing camera left to right; Sam Colton, Greg Hayes, Don Faber, George Harness, Edna Whiting, Norman Joyce, Augie Morin, Billy Rizzo, Dave Jackson, Ted Purcell, and Art Raye. Back to camera left to right; Gary Van Zeeland, C.W. Kendall, Charley Johnston, Dave Mills, Irene Fuerst and Bob Vincent.

under one protective umbrella. This meeting brought together the largest agencies in this field, and was the beginning of the International Theatrical Agencies Association (I.T.A.A.). From its small beginning, the I.T.A.A. in 1978 has grown to approximately 90 member agencies.

If you have read the chapter on "Musicians Unions," you already have an understanding as to some of the reasons for the necessity of having an association of musical agents. Besides the agents' problems with the A.F. of M., the members of I.T.A.A. sincerely felt that it was necessary for them to clean up "their own house."

Founding Fathers

At this first meeting in St. Louis, it was decided that the 20 "founding fathers" would elect temporary officers until a general membership meeting could be held, which would take place in Chicago on March 14, 15, and 16, 1975, for the purpose of holding their first full-term election of officers. The temporary officers were as follows:

Bob Vincent — President
Gary Van Zeeland — First Vice-President
Don Anderson — Second Vice-President
Augie Morin — Secretary
Dave Jackson — Treasurer

Steering Committees were:
Finance — Dave Mills, Sam Colton,
and Charlie Johnston
Constitution and By-Laws — Lane Erskine,
Don Faber, and Norman Joyce
Aims and Goals — Jack Belmont, Don Anderson,
Arnie Prager, Gary Van Zeeland,
and Art Raye

For many years, prior to the formation of the I.T.A.A., agents in the musical lounge field had been dealing with each other on a "split commission" basis in a loose association. Agents in Los Angeles, for example, in an effort to book their attractions in Chicago or New York, would, in most cases, contact another agent in the city where he wanted his act booked, instead of trying to do it himself, and in this manner a "business" friendship was initiated between two agents. Considerable business was transacted often between agents, without them having met in person.

Major Irritations

Naturally in the course of conversation over the telephone, they began to discuss their mutual problems in the industry.

The major irritations with all of the agents seemed to be:

A. The increased cost of operation, and the fact that they no longer could stay in business on 10 percent commission.

B. The threat of having their francises revoked by the A.F. of M., over any little infraction.

C. Their own lack of any "Code of Ethics," in order to govern the manner of doing business between themselves.

D. The *unwarranted* bad name all agents had gotten over the years.

E. Their inability to collect their commissions promptly from the musicians.

F. Their inability to pursue the collection of due commissions in civil court, because of the restrictions of the agreement signed by the agencies with the A.F. of M.

G. The general feeling that their status as independent brokers, representing both the musician and the operator, was not truly reflected in the francise agreement that each agency had signed with the A.F. of M., in order to obtain a franchise.

H. The unwarranted high union scales in some locals.

Because of the increasing exchange of telephone calls and letters between agents, in the pursuit of a working relationship, the above problems began to surface more and more. These discussions really perpetrated the formation of the I.T.A.A.

In addition to the problems between agencies and the A.F. of M., the agents were receiving complaints from each of their group leaders regarding; the excessive dues and taxes they were being charged in every "foreign" local where they appeared, the antagonistic attitude of the musicians union officials in these "foreign" locals, and the general feeling that they were not being represented properly by their own "home" locals.

With all of these problems landing on the agent's desk, several of the major lounge agencies felt that the time was ripe to organize themselves into an association that could possibly solve some, or all, of these ills.

On March 15, 1975, the first full-time slate of officers were elected, and the aims and goals were established. It was also decided to incorporate as a non-profit organization in the state of Delaware. This was accomplished in May of 1975, with the help of the attorney for the I.T.A.A., Mr. Dick Shelton of Chicago.

Meetings with A.F. of M.

In September of 1976 under the new President of I.T.A.A., Ted Purcell, a meeting was held in the New York City A.F. of M. offices between a committee of the I.T.A.A. made up of Ted Purcell, Arnie Prager, Ross White (Canadian agent) and Jack Belmont, and members of the International Executive Board of the A.F. of M. This was the first in a series of meetings between the I.T.A.A. and the A.F. of M.

The formation of I.T.A.A. was done with the full knowledge of the President's office of the A.F. of M., and I, as the first President of I.T.A.A. explained that the purpose of I.T.A.A. was to assist the A.F. of M. in the regulation of musicians activities all over the country. This attitude made the meeting between the negotiating committee of the I.T.A.A., and the Executive Board of A.F. of M. most pleasant and somewhat productive.

At these various meetings, all of the problems were laid on the table — not only the problems concerning the agents, but also grievances of the musicians who were members of the A.F. of M. Some headway was made in each meeting, and as a result of these meetings, on April 15, 1976, the President of the A.F. of M. sent out a document to all agencies, allowing them to increase their commission up to 15 percent.

At the time that I and my fellow agents were trying to organize an association of agencies in the lounge field, many agents loudly proclaimed, that we were crazy to think that we could bring all of these "free-form" salesmen into one organization and have them all agree to conform to a Code of Ethics.

Many of these same scoffers have now become avid members of I.T.A.A., and the proof of it's value to the industry, is the increasing number of agencies who are joining. In many respects, it is surprising how agents, who are quite independent thinkers, when thrown together with other agents "face to face," are found to be "upstanding citizens" who have morals, a conscience, and a great desire to bring credit to their profession. I realize that this is hard to believe, what with the bad name, and bad press we have suffered for years. Agents have been maligned by comics, and have unjustly been the butt of their jokes since the beginning of show-biz! All artists, if the truth were known, would admit that they would not be enjoying their present success, without the help and guidance of some agent, somewhere.

Article 25 — A.F. of M.

Since 1935, at a national meeting of A.F. of M. Article #25 was made a part of the by-laws regulating the activities of all franchised agencies. It was obviously designed to dictate the manner in which agencies, under the franchise issued to them by the A.F. of M., operated their business in behalf of the musicians they represented.

In actuality, agents do not **solely** represent the musician. In actual practice, all agents are "brokers," not solely representing the musician or the operator, but attempting to satisfy both parties, in exchange for which the agent receives a commission. The more successfully he presents **both** parties, the more successful his agency becomes.

Since the inception of I.T.A.A., there have been many hours spent in discussing the A.F. of M. problem, trying to convince the A.F. of M. that the agents do not, and cannot, represent the musicians solely, without hurting all parties concerned. If a musician, or group is mis-booked into the wrong club, and the customers disapprove of the act, everybody suffers, and everybody loses.

The I.T.A.A. attitude is that agents are no different than real estate brokers. The object is to fit the customer to the kind of home where he feels comfortable, and when money and property have exchanged hands, a commission is paid. It's just as simple as that.

In 1935, when Article #25 was written and adopted by the A.F. of M., conditions were totally different. The big bands were flourishing at that time, there weren't many traveling

I.T.A.A. Board of Directors 1979
Gary Van Zeeland — President

Standing left to right; Norman Joyce, Bill Rothe, Arne Prager, Bob Vincent, Craig Nicolson, Charlie Johnston, Charley Penta, Keith Lance, John Vinatieri and Frank Wiener. Seated left to right; Jack Belmont, John Sansone, Linda Menche, Pam Pribble, Dave Snowden, Garry Van Zeeland, Augie Morin, C.W. Kendall, Barry Ano and Dave Jackson.

lounge groups working around the country, and the music business was much simpler to regulate.

It stands to reason that there has been a radical change in the total entertainment business since 1935, and in spite of these changes, the agencies are still working under the same By-Laws.

Code of Ethics Adopted

In 1978, the I.T.A.A. general membership adopted a Code of Ethics, which primarily was designed to regulate their own internal manner of doing business with each other. It establishes the "ground rules" so to speak, so that the day-to-day business between agencies would be governed by guidelines which were directly related to the musical booking business. Just the fact that an assembly of "agents" would take the time to establish their own rules and regulations, shows that the original purpose of the I.T.A.A., which was to uplift the image of agentry, *is working*.

Canadian Agencies

Since it's inception, the I.T.A.A. has embraced it's fellow agencies from Canada. For many years, there has been an exchange of musical acts between the United States and Canada. There is an independent branch of the American Federation of Musicians, operating out of their headquarters in Toronto. It's rules are somewhat similar to its American "cousin," with some minor variations, because of Canadian laws.

When I.T.A.A. was first formed, it was operated for a short period under the name, "Theatrical Agencies Association," but with the addition of some fine agencies from Canada, the word "International" was added.

Back in the days between 1950 to 1960, there was a larger segment of American acts playing in Canada, than vice-versa. They were playing in Vancouver, Calgary, Edmonton, Winnepeg, Saskatoon, Toronto, and Montreal. The reason for this unbalanced exchange was that the American entertainers at that time were a little more advanced in their professional showmanship abilities.

Since 1960, the Canadian musicians, and singers, have developed rapidly in their entertaining and musical prowess, to a point where the balance of exchange is a great deal more equal.

Canadian-American Tax Problems

Another thing that slowed down the migration of Canadian artists to America was an unbalanced regulatory income tax, which was in existence between the two countries. When American artists played in Canada, there was a 15 percent work tax payable to the Canadian internal revenue department, some of which could be recovered by the American artists, at the time when he, or she made out their end-of-the-year income tax returns.

The imbalance came as a result of a U.S. tax imposed on Canadian entertainers coming to America, of **30 percent** on gross monies received, which, as you can readily see, kept many operators in America from buying Canadian acts. As this book goes to print, changes in these tax laws are happening almost daily, so it is difficult to predict where it will all end up. I feel that both countries will soon work out the tax rates for everyone's benefit.

The I.T.A.A. is doing some lobbying in both Ottawa and Washington, D.C., in an effort to reduce the taxes in both countries, so that there can be an even exchange of entertainers and entertainment between America and Canada.

Several top agents from Canada such as Ron Scribner, Ross White, Bud Matton, and Craig Nicolson from Toronto, Frank Wiener and Doug MacFarlane from Winnepeg, Barry Holden from Windsor, Ann Randle from Calgary, Don McKenzie from Edmonton, and Robert Tyrala from Islington, Ontario, have all become members of I.T.A.A., and have worked diligently in an effort to promote a good working relationship between Canadian and American agencies. They are also doing everything possible to get the Canadian tax department to meet with the U.S. regarding a mutual reduction of the unreasonable taxes which are hindering the exchange of entertainment, between the two countries.

New Agreement with A.F. of M.

Getting back to the main purpose of I.T.A.A., which is to have a new working agreement between agencies and the A.F. of M., the board of directors of I.T.A.A. see no way that working under Article #25 of the A.F. of M. by-laws, in it's present form, is going to be feasible. In drawing up a new agreement there are certain conditions which have to be resolved before any arrangement will work.

Forgetting the I.T.A.A. for the moment, the board of directors of the A.F. of M. must be worn out from reading the hundreds of claim cases that they get almost weekly, from musicians, club owners, agents, attorneys, other unions, etc. They must spend thousands of hours, and thousands of dollars trying to settle these cases.

It would be so much simpler for the A.F. of M. to let the agents settle their own problems with musicians, and other agents through the civil courts, and then the I.E.B. could concentrate on the main objective of their existence, which is, "Keep Music Alive — Support Live Music!"

I sincerely believe that *if* the officials of the American Federation of Musicians would look at their total picture without past pre-conceived notions, they would welcome with enthusiasm, the opportunity to be rid of those pesky agency problems.

Agents as Independent Brokers

Let's assume, for the moment, that there were no longer any franchised agents under the A.F. of M. regulations, and that all agencies were "brokers" of entertainment, operating *under civil laws*. Also, the American Federation of Musicians were *only* representing the musicians. Here's the way it could work:

A. From the A.F. of M. standpoint, they would:

1. Charge initiation fees and dues to musicians for joining and becoming members.

2. Advise musicians as to the terms of the contracts that they are being asked to sign.

3. Set minimum scales for *each individual* club or lounge, instead of giving them "blanket rates."

4. Receive copies of the civil contracts that the agents will be using to cover engagements in their jurisdiction.

5. Assist the musician in all things pertinent to his career.

6. Negotiate all scales and conditions covering live music on television, movies, and record sessions done in their local jurisdiction.

7. Assist the musician in every way possible.

B. From the Agents' standpoint, they would:

1. Act as *brokers* for entertainment for live talent buyers.

2. Get signed civil contracts covering the engagements. Said contracts would be designed within the laws of the state, and agreeable to both the operator, and the musician.

3. Sign artists to exclusive artist — agency contracts, that would conform to civil laws governing all personal contracts. Again, the contract would have to be reasonable, and the terms would have to be agreeable to both the agency, and the musician.

4. Assist the musicians in their artistic and business direction, in order to further their careers.

5. Collect their just commissions, directly from the musi-

cian, or have it deducted by the operator. Again, the commission would be spelled out in detail on the engagement contract, before it was signed by both the operator and the musician.

6. Operate their agency in a business-like manner, as dictated by the laws of both the state, plus the national law of the land.

7. Assist both the operator and the musician to the best of their ability.

8. Meet with the American Federation of Musicians both regionally, and nationally, in order to discuss the ways to be of help to the musician, and indirectly make life more pleasant for everyone.

If this new attitude would become a reality, much time, money, and man-power would be saved, and the slogan, "Keep Music Alive — Support Live Music" would take on a new meaning.

EGO KILLS MORE PEOPLE THAN CANCER

fourteen

Heads or Tales?

Heads or Tails

Hope you will enjoy this "Heads or Tales" chapter. I felt that these stories would be pleasurable to you readers, and also it might give those of you who are not actively involved in our crazy business, a better insight into the "nature" of the people who prowl throughout this jungle called "show-business."

Ed Sullivan — Frank Sinatra Jr.

I was at Harrah's in 1964 when Frank Sinatra, Jr. was kidnapped. Before I go much further, let me assure you that the kidnapping was not a publicity story to enhance Frank Jr.'s career. It actually happened, even though it was badly handled by amateur kidnappers.

Most of you will remember that Frank Jr. was held by his captors for a few days in a house not too far from Frank's home in Beverly Hills. When the kidnappers realized that not only was the F.B.I. looking for Frank, but also some of Frank Sr.'s "friends," they decided that it might be wise to let the kid go. According to Frank Jr.'s version of what happened after he returned, *they* were more scared than he was.

Following Frank's release, he returned to Harrah's to complete the balance of his contract, which still had three more weeks to run. Naturally, the casino was filled with his fans and well-wishers, so we were doing capacity business with Frank's show, which was playing in our lounge.

About two days after Frank returned, I received a phone call from New York. It was Ed Sullivan.

"Bob, I'd like to have Frank Jr. on my television show this coming Sunday. How about sending him to New York immediately?

I said, "Ed, we've still got about three more weeks to go on his contract, and with the business we're doing in the casino, I'm certain Bill Harrah is not going to be interested in releasing Frank before the end of his contract. How about having him on your show after his contract runs out?"

"I can't use him then. It's too late!," said Sullivan, "What do I have to do to get him *this* Sunday!"

"Ed, I'm awfully sorry, but you understand why we can't

Frank Sinatra Jr.

let him go this weekend. It would be a bad business move!"

Again, Ed Sullivan said, this time with more determination, "I must have him this Sunday, what do I have to do?"

Suddenly, a light went on in my brain, and I said, "If I were able to convince Bill Harrah to release him for this Sunday's T.V. show, would you agree to play a two-week engagement for us this summer with your own show, when you are on hiatus?"

"You've got a deal! Send him out right away!"

Frank Jr. was gone from Harrah's only from Thursday

through Sunday, and of course, Sullivan mentioned that Frank was appearing at Harrah's and that he was on his show as a temporary "loan-out."

Bill Harrah was pleased with the swap. It was a big feather in our cap to play the "king" of all television the following summer, Ed Sullivan.

Gary Moore T.V. Show and "I've Got A Secret"

During my tenure at Harrah's, I made a deal with Gary Moore to tape one of his television shows from our South Shore Room theatre at Lake Tahoe. We also decided to do one segment of "I've Got A Secret," which was Gary's production. We were going to tape both shows during the same week that we had Judy Garland playing for us in the evening.

You can imagine what kind of problems that created. It meant that we had to tear down Judy's stage setting, including lights, curtains, etc., each evening after her one show, in order to get ready for the taping of the television shows the next morning at 7 a.m. This meant constructing camera platforms, running cable all over the casino, and the South Shore Room, plus hanging new curtains, new television lighting, etc. We even had to resurface our complete stage floor, in order to accommodate the dancers that Gary Moore used on his show. Naturally, after a whole afternoon of taping the T.V. shows with a live audience, we had to take out all of the platforms, cameras, cables, and rehang curtains, reset spotlights, etc., in order to get ready to present Judy Garland for her nine-o'clock evening performance.

I don't have to tell you how many hours of sleep I got that week! We had about 80 technicians, stage hands, lighting men, directors, producers, and grips who also got very little sleep.

After we finished taping "I've Got A Secret," we decided to have a going-away party in our banquet hall before the cast left for New York City. Naturally, everybody got very "happy" during the evening. We asked Gary Moore to make a going-away speech to the departing cast.

Before I go much further with the story, I should explain to you readers that before Gary Moore had arrived at Lake Tahoe,

Gary Moore, Carole Burnett and Bob Vincent

I asked his attorney if there was any particular food that Gary was fond of. His attorney said that Gary liked almost any kind of food, but he was absolutely crazy about peanut butter!

When I heard this, I bought about a dozen jars of peanut butter, in all sizes from the very tiniest to the "king size."

I planted all of these jars in the suite of rooms we were providing for Gary ... in the drawers, between the mattress and box spring of the bed, in the medicine chest, bathtub, etc. No matter where he went in his suite, there was a jar of peanut butter.

Of course, Gary was tickled, and pleased that we had found out about his "weakness," and told everybody he talked to about it.

When Gary was making his going-away speech to the cast, he mentioned the peanut butter! In closing his speech he said, "With these people at Harrah's Club, you don't dare mention that you like 'elephants' because you probably will find one in your room the next morning!"

Immediately, I remembered that the Sparks Nugget was using an elephant named Bertha as part of their floor show. I got on the telephone and called Lee Frankovich, who was the Entertainment Director at the Nugget at that time, and I explained that I would like to have Bertha trucked to Lake Tahoe, which was only about 55 miles away, so that we could have Bertha and her trainer come on stage at the conclusion of the taping of the Gary Moore T.V. show, with a big sign held in her trunk which would read, "Bertha likes Gary Moore ... and Peanut Butter too!"

Lee loved the idea and agreed to loan Bertha for the afternoon and, of course, I arranged for Harrah's to cover the expense of transporting Bertha.

Naturally, I hoped to get nationwide publicity over this crazy event, so I called a photographer and all of the local press people to cover the story. Gary Moore, of course, knew nothing about what we had cooked up for his final tape session.

I had to call Bill Harrah and tell him what was going on, assuming that he would be pleased with all of the national publicity we were going to receive. I told him Gary Moore and Durwood Kirby, his announcer, would talk about the incident on their radio and television shows for months afterward.

Bill listened very carefully to my plans and said, "I don't like it!" I was shocked when I heard this and asked him why.

He said, "I agree that there will be a lot of publicity, but much of it would be about Bertha, who belongs to our chief competitor, The Nugget in Sparks."

Unfortunately, I was not able to convince Bill to change his mind, so I had to kill the whole idea. I got a little satisfaction by presenting Gary Moore with a large, stuffed elephant at the going-away party for the cast of the Gary Moore show, but it lost something in substitution.

Jayne Mansfield — "I've Got A Secret"

In the previous story about our taping of the Gary Moore T.V. show, and "I've Got A Secret," another funny or tragic thing happened, depending on how you look at it.

Jayne Mansfield, the sex goddess of the early 1960's, was supposed to be the mystery guest on the show. Jayne was flying up to Reno from Las Vegas, and we were picking her up in our limousine at the airport in Reno, and driving her to Lake Tahoe.

On the day she was to arrive in Reno, I received a phone call from our driver from the airport. He said that "Miss Mansfield and a gentleman friend just got off the plane, and they seem to be a little unsteady. I was shocked, and a little upset because she was due to be on camera in two hours.

I told the driver to get them up to the lake as soon as possible, and before they get in the limousine, take the brandy, which we customarily kept in the back seat compartment, out of the car.

About 30 minutes later, I received another phone call from the driver. He said, that Miss Mansfield insisted he stop in Carson City, so that she and her friend could buy some liquor. I was really upset, so I told him to get them back in the car, and drive to Tahoe as quickly as possible.

I thought that I should, at this point, inform the director and producer of the television show what was taking place. We decided to take precautions by asking Carole Burnett to stand by as a possible substitute for Jayne Mansfield. Carole was there, of course as a member of the cast of the Gary Moore Show.

When the limo arrived, I knocked on the door of the suite and Jayne's friend opened the door.

I've seen some drunks in my time, but I don't think I've every seen two people more drunk than Mansfield and company. Jayne was sitting in a chair, with her feet up on the table, with two martinis, one in each hand! Her friend turned out to be a hairdresser, and in his drunken stupor was attempting to set her hair for the television show.

As I entered, Jayne turned to me and said, "Here, honey, why don't you have a drink?"

I took one of the drinks out of her hand and dumped it into the toilet. "Miss Mansfield, when I work, I don't drink! You've only got 30 minutes before you're due on camera, so if I were you, I'd quit the booze and get over to the South Shore Room!" With this statement, I left and went back to the stage.

I had another meeting with the director and producer and we decided to meet the limousine at the rear door of the stage, and if Jayne and her friend couldn't make the steps leading up to the stage without help, we were going to ask Carole to substitute.

The limousine arrived at the back door and Jayne and friend alighted from the limousine ... no, they *fell* from the limousine! The driver had to half carry both of them up the stairs.

We made our decision immediately, and Carole Burnett was our "mystery guest."

I had two security guards assist Jayne and her drinking buddy to one of the dressing rooms, and gave them instructions to lock the door. Under no circumstances were they to let Miss Mansfield out.

We taped the show with Carole, and about five hours later I had the security guards open the door to Jayne's dressing room. They were both passed out on the floor.

I had the limousine standing by at the rear exit, and with the help of the security guards and the driver, we deposited Jayne and her hairdresser in the back seat, and the driver took them back to the Reno airport for their trip back to Vegas.

I don't believe that Jayne Mansfield ever realized that she *really* became the "mystery guest" of "I've Got A Secret."

Judy Garland — Leighton Noble

I'm sure you all realize how skitish Judy was, particularly in her later years. The day that Judy arrived at Harrah's for rehearsal, her conductor took me aside and explained that he could only stay for three nights, because he had an important picture to score and conduct in London, England. I asked him if Judy knew about his leaving and he said no, so I asked him to let me tell her after opening night.

Realizing that her conductor was leaving, I had a meeting with my house orchestra leader, Leighton Noble. I explained the circumstances to Leighton and asked him to get the albums of Judy's that contained the songs she was doing in her show for us, and memorize all of the arrangements off of the records.

Leighton immediately bought all of the albums and rehearsed the arrangements in his dressing room. Leighton was the most conscientious man I believe I've ever met. He practiced with his baton for hours to make certain that he would be able to successfully take the orchestra over upon the departure of Judy's conductor.

Following our exciting opening night, and after all of the "well-wishers" had departed from Judy's dressing room, she and I were having a quiet glass of wine by ourselves. I thought that the time was right to break the news about her conductor.

Judy hit the ceiling! She said in no uncertain terms, "When he leaves . . . I leave!!"

"Judy, please listen to me for a minute. I have a solution. Tonight Leighton Noble, my conductor, will stand along side your conductor throughout the entire show and follow along with each arrangement. Tomorrow night Leighton will conduct your show, while your conductor stands along side him, just in case you're not happy with the accompaniment. Okay?"

She made me promise that if she wasn't happy with Leighton I would talk her conductor into staying. I promised that I would try.

That evening, as planned, Leighton stood alongside Judy's conductor throughout the entire show. He also had a headset on so that he could hear Judy's interpretation of the songs.

The next night, I was as nervous as Judy. All of my hopes were in Leighton Noble's hands and baton.

After about the first 15 minutes with Leighton doing the conducting and Judy's man standing by, I had the feeling that everything was going well. Judy seem relaxed and was singing beautifully.

After the show was over and all of the guests had left her dressing room, she asked me to stay. I thought that this was my moment of decision.

"Bob," Judy said, "I was against my conductor leaving, as you know, but I've got to tell you something. As good as my man is, I hope he never comes back. I have never felt better in my life. Leighton conducted the arrangements perfectly, and it occurred to me that he was taking me through the original tempos, which my man had inadvertently changed over a period of years, since he took over as my conductor. Leighton brought back the original excitement to the music, which we had lost!

"Please tell Leighton Noble that he can 'send his laundry out.' He can stay with my blessings."

Lena Horne

My predecessor at Harrah's had made a verbal deal with Lena Horne's agency for her to play the South Shore Room at some mutually agreeable date. Before Lena would okay the date, she wanted to fly up to Tahoe to see the theatre.

Lena came up to Harrah's not many days after I took over, and I was thrilled to meet this great lady, and proudly show her around the theatre. After she saw the stage, I took her down to the dressing room area. In those days, in order to get down from the stage level to the dressing rooms, you had to decend by a long set of stairs. We did not have an elevator, as they do now.

After Lena looked over our very lavish dressing rooms for the stars, she returned to the flight of stairs and said, "As much as I'd like to play for you, I couldn't do it because with my tight skirts, there is no way I could climb the stairs to get on stage."

Naturally, I was upset, but I could understand her point. She really couldn't make it up the stairs in those tight, slinky gowns, which were her identification.

After she returned to Los Angeles, and I figured we had lost Lena Horne, I told Bill Harrah in our next entertainment meeting about Lena's visit and the unhappy results.

Again, Bill Harrah, in his pragmatic manner of approaching any problem, said to me, "Get a hold of Bill Wagner, our architect, and see if he can figure a way to install a one-story elevator going from the dressing rooms to the stage. I'm certain there is a way of doing it."

All of us who knew Bill Harrah knew that it would be done even if he had to tear down the entire stage and rebuild it.

I called Bill Wagner in Los Angeles and Bill came up to Tahoe to look the situation over. Bill had the same kind of determination that Bill Harrah had, and he decided that he could redesign the back part of the stage so that we could install an elevator. Naturally, it could be costly, but it was possible.

After several weeks of construction, much of which took place in the early morning hours when our show wasn't going on, the elevator was completed.

I immediately called Lena Horne's personal manager and told him that we now had an elevator and asked him to reconsider. We discussed several potential dates for the future but, while we were constructing our elevator, Lena's agency had made a deal with Frank Sinatra Sr. to play the Cal-Neva Lodge at the north end of Lake Tahoe. Sinatra owned Cal-Neva at that time.

Her date at Cal-Neva prevented Lena from playing anywhere else at Lake Tahoe, so she never has taken advantage of the special elevator which we built to accommodate her tight skirts.

Julius J. (Bookie) Levin — "Super Agent"

For many years now, there have been many stories passed around the entertainment business, particularly in Las Vegas, and Beverly Hills, about a character by the name of Julius J. (Bookie) Levin. He was the most loved and talked about "diamond-in-the-rough" I've ever met and worked for, in my whole life. "Bookie" passed away in 1962, but his stories, and his legend lives on.

Let's backtrack for a moment, so that I can give you the real picture of this character.

"Bookie" was born, but not "raised" in Joliet, Illinois. I say not raised because he had very little formal education, or upbringing. What education he did get was acquired in the streets and alleys of America. He was the prototype Damon Runyon character. Along with his crudeness, he had a heart as big as a house.

When he was growing up, he learned every trick in the trade. His dress was atrocious. His speech and grammar was ridiculous, and his eating habits would have made him unacceptable as a guest at the dinner table in "Tobacco Road."

If you now have a mental picture of Bookie, we can go on with some of the lengendary stories that still circulate in the entertainment industry.

Mind you, Bookie with all of his crudeness and foul language, could be very charming when he wanted to be. Because he was such an interesting character, he was frequently seen at the Friars Club in Beverly Hills, California, playing gin with Jack Benny, Harry Ritz (Ritz Brothers), Tony Martin, Harry Cohn (then President of Columbia Pictures), Georgie Jessel, Sammy Lewis (the Entertainment Director of the Riveria

Hotel in Las Vegas), and every other star and tycoon in our business.

He started in show business by buying a second-hand camera on a tripod, hired the sexiest "broad" he could find to act as a shill, and traveled the circus and carnival circuit taking pictures of the suckers who would pay a dollar, for a picture that cost Bookie a nickel.

Bookie liked to be on the move in his younger days, so the "carny" route was his cup of tea. This picture business lasted for three or four years, just long enough for him to save enough money to invest in a ballroom in Joliet, his home town. He'd always had a fascination for music and musicians. He liked hanging around with these free spirits and swapping stories, and lies, in late-night road houses all over the country.

Now that he had some roots with his ballroom, he started buying an occasional name band for one night now and then. He played such names as, Guy Lombardo (can you imagine what a shock it must have been for Guy, with his sophistication, to listen to "Bookie's" split infinitives?), Tommy Dorsey, Harry James, and several others. It so happened that Bookie got into the ballroom business at the tail end of the big band days, so it didn't take him long to figure out that he should get out while the "gettin' was good."

Before Bookie sold the ballroom, he had been doing some booking on the side, (this is where he got his name), and he was particularly interested in booking lounge groups because in his crafty mind, he figured that with all of these big bands folding, the musicians he hung around with were going to have to work at something, and the small lounge group was the only answer.

After the ballroom was sold, Bookie moved to Chicago and opened an office (who's kiddin' who! ... one room in the Croydon Hotel on Rush Street) and started an agency called Mutual Entertainment Agency, Inc.

Because he liked to be out among the musicians every night, and because he was such a great story teller, it didn't take him long to collect a bunch of entertaining musicians, anywhere from single piano players to five and six piece combos.

He had a knack of knowing what pleased the customer, (no doubt from his "carny" days), and he urged these musicians to not only play their instruments, but be funny and entertaining at the same time!

I can truthfully tell you that Bookie Levin was the grand-daddy of the cocktail lounge group business. From about 1940 up until Bookie died at the Fremont Hotel in Las Vegas in 1962, he was deeply involved in three things, in this order of their importance; the musical lounge business, playing gin with his buddies, and his family which consisted of a wife and five children.

Bookie didn't get married until he was 47 years old, and by the time he was 51 years of age, he had five kids. Somehow, Bookie and a family just didn't fit. Not that he wasn't a good father, (in his manner), but he had absolutely no patience. He also was never home!

I became involved with Bookie in 1951 in Chicago, when I signed an exclusive contract with his agency, Mutual Entertainment Agency, Inc. Bookie, along with Milo Stelt and Eddie Hall, were the first agents I became involved with, following my departure from the Al Trace Orchestra.

After working with my lounge group for about three years, I mentioned to Bookie that I was getting tired of the road and wanted to settle down. Bookie immediately made me an offer to come into his office as an agent, which I accepted.

Working in the office with Bookie (when he was in town), really gave me an insight into his peculiarities. When I joined Mutual, Bookie had already accumulated about one hundred lounge acts, most of whom were working in and around the greater Chicago area. Such groups as the "Novelites" (comic accordianist was Frankie Carr, currently working at the Flamingo in Vegas), The Art Van Damme Quintette, Joe Maize and the Chordsmen, Jerry Murad's Harmonicats, The Metro-Tones, The Zany-acks, and many others.

When Bookie was in Chicago, every day was a new experience. It was nothing for Bookie to come into my office . . . grab the phone out of my hand and hang it up because he had something to tell me, which he felt couldn't wait. I used to say, "For Christ's sake, Bookie, I was talking to a customer! What's he gonna think?"

Bookie's favorite answer was, "Fug 'em. He'll call back! Remember kid, when you've got the acts that they need to make a buck, they'll call back!" You know something? He was right!

Some other mornings I would see Bookie come into the office, snap his finger, turn around and say to me, "I forgot somethin'." With this, he would leave the office. About two hours later I would get a phone call from him from St. Louis. He had thought of something he wanted to tell Harold Koplar at the Chase Hotel so he went to the airport and flew to St. Louis.

Invariably he would forget to take a top coat and his electric razor, or clean shirts or underwear. He was continually buying electric razors and top coats all over the country, and bringing them back to the office in Chicago. At one time in his desk drawer I counted no less than 12 electric razors, and he always had four or five top coats, and overcoats hanging on his coat rack.

There were times when he wanted me to have lunch with him in a deli across the street. We officed at Lake and Wabash Avenues, and if you know this corner in Chicago, it's always busy with traffic. Bookie had a habit of grabbing you by the arm and stopping you to talk, no matter where you and he happened to be. You can't imagine what an experience it was to have him grab you by the arm in the middle of the lunch hour traffic, and stop there to discuss some business deal. I'm surprised I'm still alive!

On Monday nights, we usually worked late in order to plan our activities for the week. Because we were working late this particular Monday, we decided to take our two secretaries down to the delicatessen for a corned beef sandwich. Bookie Milo Stelt, Eddie Hall, and I, plus the secretaries were sitting at the counter, and we all ordered corned beef sandwiches.

It's important to this story that you get the picture of what positions we were sitting in. I was on the stool nearest the door, next came my secretary, Doris Fisk, then came Bookie, with Milo on his right, and the rest of the gang on succeeding stools.

When the waitress brought the sandwiches she placed them in front of each of us. I was talking to Doris and Bookie was talking to Milo. Doris couldn't see what was happening to her sandwich because she was looking at me. But *I could see!*

Now, I must tell you that Bookie dearly loved corned beef, but he very rarely ate the bread. Most times he would lift the top slice of bread off of the meat, pluck all of the meat out of the sandwich, put it all into his mouth, and either put the top slice

Novelites

Jerry Murad's Harmonicats

279

of bread back on the bottom slice, or sometimes he would throw the top slice over his shoulder onto the floor.

On this night I was talking to Doris, and I saw Bookie reach to his left and remove the lid off the meat, and put it all into his mouth without looking to see who's sandwich it was.

I didn't say a word because I could forsee what was going to happen. I quit talking to Doris and started to eat my sandwich, so that Doris could "attempt" to eat hers.

You can imagine the surprise and shock on her face when she went to put the sandwich in her mouth, and discovered that there was no meat in it.

You should have heard the big argument between Doris and the waitress! The waitress claiming that she definitely put corned beef in the sandwich, and Doris yelling that the sandwich was empty!

All the time this argument was going on, I was dying inside, pretending that I didn't see what happened. The funniest thing about the whole situation was that Bookie completely ignored the scene being caused by the two girls, while he continued eating his "other" sandwich.

Inviting Bookie to your home for dinner was another experience. As I said before, he never did anything with any "malice or forethought." He was just undisciplined. You had to learn not to cook spare-ribs with barbecue sauce, unless you wore a washable rubber apron while you were eating. Bookie had a habit of talking with his rib in his hand, and when he got through making a point by waving his rib loaded with sauce at you, you're shirt looked like it was worn by a spotted leopard.

Also, as I said before, Bookie wasn't too choked up about bread. Sometimes he would eat the center of the bread and throw the crusts over his shoulder. When he got through eating, your dining room floor, around his chair, was encircled by half a loaf of bread crusts.

Bookie was also a sucker for anything he could buy wholesale. One time, just before Christmas, he walked into my office carrying a whole load of boxes which contained a Lionel toy train set for his kids. He was flush with his successful bargain and explained to me, "What do you think I paid for these?"

"Bookie, I assume you bought these wholesale!"

"Yes, and I saved $15.00 by buying it from a friend of mine out in Cicero."

"How far is it to Cicero," I asked, "and how did you get there so quick?"

"It's about 25 miles from here."

"How did you get there?"

"By taxi-cab, naturally."

"It must have cost you at least $25.00 in cab fares round-trip to get to Cicero and back, didn't it?" I asked.

With this, Bookie picked up his train set, without answering and disappeared into his office with his "bargain." I'll bet he didn't even get a warranty with it.

When the Fremont Hotel in Las Vegas opened, Bookie and our company was appointed to handle all of the entertainment in the lounge. Jack Davies, one of the owners, and Eddie Torres, the general manager, loved him. They also were aware that Bookie knew the lounge business better than anyone.

Because of our deal with the Fremont, Bookie had to spend considerable time in Las Vegas. Once in a while, in order for Bookie's kids to spend some time with their father, his wife would let Bookie take the children with him to Vegas.

You can imagine Bookie, with five little kids, making sales calls on the entertainment directors of the strip hotels. One day he was calling on Major Riddle and Harold Minsky at the Dunes Hotel. Finally Major Riddle said to Bookie, "For Christ's sake, do you have to bring your kids with you? How can I turn you down staring at five hungry mouths?"

I could go on and on with more stories about Bookie's antics. If you find it hard to believe what I've already told you, please check with Wayne Newton, Frankie Carr, Lee Frankovich, Penny Mayo, Sammy Lewis, Kenny Armstrong, Pat France, Major Riddle, Dick Lane, Eddie Torres (now managing director of the Riveria Hotel in Las Vegas), or any other lounge musician who is over 40 years of age. I'm certain that they all have their own stories to tell. I have yet to mention Bookie's name to someone who's been around the Nevada scene for any length of time, without them laughing.

EGO KILLS MORE PEOPLE THAN CANCER

fifteen

Author's Hopes For The Future

Author's Hopes For The Future

It is hoped that this book will be a new source of information to everyone connected with the entertainment industry, and make their paths toward the "inevitable end" a lot smoother.

To summarize my hopes and dreams, for this great industry I make a fervent wish that:

...All performers, or anyone in the business of mass motivation, will find out what the word "honesty" really means.

...All performers will learn how to successfully "seduce" their audiences, for mutual pleasure and satisfaction.

...The owners and operators of the casino theatres in the gaming industry, will realize that they need to take a hand in the training and development of new name attractions, to replace the fast disappearing old names.

...All architects and interior designers, will make a determined, and sincere effort to find out what the word "acoustics" means, and how to apply it to the entertainment industry.

...The general public begin to realize that agents are men and women who sincerely try to work for the benefit of *all three people* — the operator, the artist, and themselves.

...The buyers of talent shall become gifted with a great deal of "depth-perception."

...The cocktail lounge business becomes known for what it has done, and will do, for the development of past, present, and future stars.

...The artists will become wise enough to realize that all of the money taken in on a night, is not all "net" profit to the operator.

...All artists will realize that the agent's and personal manager's commission is not their money, and to keep it under any circumstances is a form of theft.

284

...Once an artist signs an exclusive contract with an agency, or a personal manager, he will live up to the terms and "spirit" of the contract.

...Artists wives who travel with them on the road, will make a determined effort to help, and not hurt their husbands' careers.

...The artist will realize that the long jumps between engagements that they must make by automobile, was made by his agent several years before him.

...Some of the Entertainment Directors in the gaming area will start buying entertainment, instead of "entertainers."

...The efficiency experts will begin to realize that you cannot "computerize" show business.

...The young musician members of the American Federation of Musicians will take a more active role in the administration of their union.

...All egos will disappear, leaving just self-confidence, based on real talent.

...The marriage between the musical tastes of the old establishment and the contemporary generation, will continue to draw them closer and closer together.

...All new song writers will realize that "old" successful song writers, were also "new" just before their first hit.

...The buyers of entertainment in the lounge field will one day take pen in hand, and figure out what the cost of operation is for a group of five people.

...The Entertainment Directors in Nevada will one day realize that a pair of "bare breasts" on stage, will soon begin to lose their entertaining value. When you've seen one, you've seen them both!

...The colleges will continue to graduate students who have been exposed to jazz, so that possibly big-band jazz rock, might be the next fad, after disco has faded.

...A new "talent discovery" television show will be produced, only this time with producers and directors, who *really* know how to present new talent.

...All performers will realize that fame is often temporary, and that they should save for a rainy day, which could be tomorrow!

...The casinos in Las Vegas will soon resound with the sound of happy people, caused by the change over of the Keno and Bingo areas back to semi-open entertaining lounges, as they were in the days when there was "Fun in Sun City."

...One day soon, the owners and operators of the casino hotels in Nevada, will return to the original premise that they are in the *gambling business*, and quit squeezing the little guy by his room and food prices.

...All singers will learn that there are no bad songs, just bad singers.

...When an artist signs an exclusive contract with an agency, or manager, that he will realize there are *two* signatures on the contract.

...The best critique of your act is not from your friends, but from the *lack* of "silence" from the audience.

...The American Federation of Musicians will realize that they are one big, happy, musical family, and not individual locals.

...I will live long enough to *hear* and *understand* every lyric of every song that is sung or recorded.

> "The pen writes, as the mind remembers
> Millions of victories,
> And just as many defeats."

B.V.

Index

A

ABBA (Rock Group), 64, 133
ACCOMPANIST, 38
ACOUSTICS
    Architects-Interior Designers, 198;
    Hotels & Lounges, 173, 199
ADVERTISING-PUBLICITY, 190
AGENT(S),
    definition, 152; independent brokers (A.F.
    of M.), 262; qualifications, 158; two
    categories, 157
AGENCIES, Country & Western, 144
AGENCY FOR THE PERFORMING ARTS,
    153
ALLEN, GRACIE (Mrs. Geo.Burns), 80, 81
ALLEN, TERRY, 88
ALLIED MUSICIANS UNION (A.M.U.),
    240
AMATO, TOMMY (Wayne Newton), 73-77
AMERICAN FEDERATION OF
    MUSICIANS (A.F. of M.), 236
    administrative problems, 237; attitude
    towards Rock Groups, 246; Article 25
    (By-Laws-Agencies), 243, 258; high
    minimum scales, 243; International
    Executive Board (I.E.B.), 243;
    recommendations, 250; suggested services
    to members, 250; summary, 251
AMERICAN TALENT INTERNATIONAL
    (A.T.I.), 153
AMUSEMENT BUSINESS MAGAZINE,
    130, 232
ANDERSON, DON (I.T.A.A.), 255
ANDERSON, LYNN, 144, 228
ANKA, PAUL, 88
ARCHITECTS, Acoustics, 173, 198-211
ARMSTRONG, KENNY, 281
ARMSTRONG, LOUIS, 103, 210
ARTISTIC CHARISMA, 20-22
ARTIST
    domination of audience, 66-67
    material for Fairs & Expos., 230
ATHENA ARTISTS, 153
AUDIENCE
    climax, 24
AUDITION (proper method), 39-41

B

BAILEY, GLEN, 88
BANDSTAND MUSIC (Gonter), 222
BEACHBOYS, THE, 88, 133, 210, 216, 228
BEACHCOMBERS, THE (Group), 88
BEATLES, THE, 88, 133, 245
BECK, JEFF, 228
BEE GEES, THE (Rock Group), 64, 133
BELLE BARTH, 147
BELEFONTE, HARRY, 11, 142

BELL, FREDDY, 87, 88
BELMONT, JACK (I.T.A.A.), 87, 255, 257,
    259
BELLO, AL, 147, 148
BENNY, JACK
    "Bookie" Levin, gin partner, 275; George
    Burns-Carol Channing at Harrahs Club,
    77-81; Irving Fein, at Harrahs, 154;
    seasoned performer, 11; Vaude star, 143
BENSON, GEORGE, 88, 100
BERKLEE SCHOOL OF MUSIC, 101
BERTHA (Elephant-Sparks Nugget), 269
BEVERAGE DIRECTOR, 193-195
BICHET, SIDNEY, 103
BIG BAND DAYS, 215
BILLBOARD MAGAZINE, 130
BUSINESS MANAGERS, 26, 27
BLAIR, JAMES SR., 220
BLAKE, DICK, 144
BO DIDDLEY, 92
BOONE, DEBBIE, 144
BOREDOM WITH MATERIAL, 26, 34, 56
BOYER, TED (Trian), 167
BREATHING, FROM THE DIAPHRAGM,
    38, 39
BROWN, LES (Big Band), 236
BRYTE, KATHY and JUDY, 88
BURNETT, CAROLE, 25, 66, 269
BOBBY BURNS (G.A.C.), 77
BRIDGE, DANNY, 88
BURNS, GEORGE, 77-81, 143
BURTON, BILLY, 87
BUSHOUSEN, DOUG. (Harrahs), 146
BUTERA, SAM & THE WITNESSES, 87,
    141, 147
BYLOFF, RUSS (Harrahs), 146

C

CAESERS PALACE (Vegas), 148
CAL-NEVA LODGE (Tahoe), 148, 275
CAMPEAU, DON, 88
CAMPBELL, GLENN, 88
CAPTAIN & TENILLE, 88
CARPENTERS, THE, 216
CARR, FRANKIE (Novelites), 88, 277
CARSON, JOHNNY, 66, 68, 143
CARTER, LINDA (Wonder Woman), 143
CASE, KEITH, 144
CASHBOX MAGAZINE, 130
CASH, JOHNNY, 88, 133, 144, 227, 228
CASSIDY, SHAWN, 66
CENTRAL WASHINGTON STATE
    FAIR, 230
CENTURY II PRODS., 144

CHANNING, CAROL, 78-81
CHARACTERS, THE, 87, 141
CHARDON, 144
CHARISSE, CYD (Tony Martin), 81-83
CHARLES, RAY, 88
CHASERS FORE, THE, 88
CHECKMATES, THE, 88, 148
CHICAGO (Rock Group)
early acoustical club problems, 205; Fairs
& Expos., 216; great musicians, 64; lounge
beginnings, 88, 112, 133
CHUBBY CHECKER, 92
CLARK, DICK, 244
CLARK, ROY
country "crossover," 141, 144; Fairs &
Expos., 216; Golden Nugget (Vegas), 147;
Lounge beginnings, 88
CLIMAX (Audience), 52-56
CLOWER, JERRY, 144
COHN, HARRY, 275
COLE, NAT (King), 88, 100, 215
COLE, NATALIE, 88
COLONNA, JERRY, 148
COLTON, SAM (I.T.A.A.), 254
COMMANDER CODY, 228
COMMAND PERFORMANCE (Group), 88
COMMITMENT TO AUDIENCE, 67
COMMODORES, THE (Rock Group), 88
CONTRACTS, ENGAGEMENT, 179
COOPER, ROY, 87
COREA, CHIC, 100
COSBY, BILL, 19, 20, 88, 143, 230
COSTA, FREDDY (I.T.A.A.), 87
COUNTRY MUSIC MAGAZINE, 130
COUNTRY & WESTERN AGENCIES, 144
COUNTRY & WESTERN "CROSSOVERS,"
144
CROSBY'S, BOB (Bob Cats), 103
CROSSMAN, KERI, 88
CUGAT, XAVIER, 148

D

DAE HAN SISTERS, 88
DARIN, BOBBY, 70, 88, 210
DAVIDSON, JOHN, 66, 143, 221, 230
DAVIDSON'S, JOHN, SINGERS
SUMMER WORKSHOP, 43-46
DAVIDSON, WILD BILL, 102
DAVIES, JACK, 281
DAVIS, JOHNNY "SCAT," 148
DAVIS, ROY, 86
DAVIS, SAMMY JR., 11, 142, 143
DEATON, BILLY, 144
DE ANGELIS, BILL (M.G.M.), 147
DEAVILLE HOTEL (Miami), 68-73
DE CASTRO SISTERS, 148
DESERT INN (Vegas), 147
DE WOOD, MITCH, 147
"DISCO," CANNED & LIVE, 103
DONAHUE, PHIL, 68

DORSEY, TOMMY (Big Band), 86, 215,
236, 276
DORSEY, JIMMY (Big Band), 236
DOUD, DAVE (Wm. Morris), 144
DOUGLAS, MIKE, 68
DOWNBEAT MAGAZINE, 130
DUKES OF DIXIELAND, 103
DUNES HOTEL (Vegas), 22, 166
DURANTE, JIMMY, 143
DYLAN, BOB, 100

E

EAGLES (Rock Group)
costume informality, 112; early acoustical
club problems, 198; lounge beginnings,
88, 133, 136
EARTH, WIND, & FIRE (Rock Group), 112,
133
EASTMAN SCHOOL OF MUSIC, 101
EBERLE, BOB, 215
EBERLE, RAY, 215
ECKSTEIN, BILLY, 147
EGLASH, JACK, 147
ELDORADO HOTEL (Reno), 147
ELLINGTON, DUKE (Big Band), 236
ELLIS, HERB, 100
ENTERTAINMENT, BUYING OF, 178
ENTERTAINMENT, POLICY, 201
EPSTEIN, SID (Wm. Morris), 228
ERSKINE, LANE (I.T.A.A.), 255

F

FABER, DON (I.T.A.A.), 255
FAIRS
contemporary artists, 216; first 50 years,
214; free acts, 215, 223; lighting & sound
schematics, 222, 227; talent buyers, 216
FARGO, DONNA, 144
FEIN, IRVING (Jack Benny), 77-81, 154
FERGUSON, MAYNARD (Big Band), 200
FIRST IMPRESSION (Audience), 52
FISK, DORIS, 278
FITZGERALDS HOTEL (Reno), 147
FLAMINGO HOTEL (Vegas), 70-72, 147
FLOREN, MYRON (Welk), 227
FOOD & BEVERAGE DEPTS. (Hotels)
separation of same, 193
FOOD DIRECTOR, Duties of, 193
FOREST, HELEN, 215
FORMAT, SHOW, 30, 52-56
FOUNTAIN, PETE, 103
FOXX, REDD, 87, 88, 141
FRANCE, PAT, 147, 281
FRANKOVICH, LEE, 146, 270, 281
FREMONT HOTEL (Vegas), 147
FRIARS CLUB (Beverly Hills), 275
FRONTIER HOTEL (Vegas), 147, 148
FUENTEALBA, VICTOR (A.F. of M.), 250

G

GALE, CRYSTAL, 144
GARLAND, JUDY, 11-15, 268, 272, 273
GARNER, ERROL, 100
GAYLORD & HOLIDAY, 88, 147
GAYNOR, MITZIE, 143
GENERAL ARTISTS CORP. (G.A.C.), 77
GIBB, ANDY, 133
GIBSON, STEVE (Red Caps), 88
GILLESPIE, DIZZY, 88
GLAZER, JOE, 87
GOLD DUST EAST & WEST (Reno), 147
GOLDEN HOTEL (Reno), 148
GOLDEN NUGGET (Vegas), 147
GOLDSBORO, BOBBY, 228
GOODMAN, BENNY, 86, 236
GOOFERS, THE, 88
GONTER, GARY (Sound & Lighting), 222, 230
GRANT, EARL, 88, 141, 147
GRATIS ROOMS (Artists), 187
GRECCO, BUDDY, 148
GREENE, SHECKY, 87, 88, 141, 143, 147
GREGORY, MATT, 22-23
GRIFFIN, MERV, 68
GRIFFITH, ANDY, 35-36
GUESS WHO (Rock Group), 228

H

HALEY, BILL AND THE COMETS, 88, 92
HALL, EDDIE, 87, 278
HALSEY, JIM, ARTISTS, 144, 153
HAMPTON, LIONEL (Big Band), 236
HAMMERSTEIN, OSCAR, 62
HAMMERSTEIN THEATRE, 62
HANCOCK, HERBIE, 100
HARMONICATS, JERRY MURAD'S, 277
HAROLDS CLUB (Reno), 147
HARRAH, BILL
    Ed Sullivan-Frank Sinatra Jr., 266; Garry Moore, 268; Judy Garland, 14, 15; Jack Benny-George Burns, 77-81; Jack Benny-Irving Fein, 154; Phil Harris, 32; Tony Martin-Cyd Charisse, 81-83
HARRAHS CLUB
    Andy Griffith, 35-37; Bill Cosby, 19-21; Jack Benny-George Burns, 77-81; Judy Garland, 11, 12; Liberace-Barbra Streisand, 46-49; Lawrence Welk, 56-59; Phil Harris, 31-34
HARVEYS RESORT HOTEL, 73, 146, 147
HARRIS, PHIL, 31-34
HAYMES, DICK, 215
HEART (Rock Group), 88
HENRY, HANK (Silver Slipper-Vegas), 147
HERMAN, WOODY (Big Band), 147, 200, 236
HILTON INNS, 90

HILTON INTERNATIONAL HOTEL (Vegas), 147
HIRT, AL, 103, 148
HITT, JOHNNY (Halsey), 228
HOGAN, "CHIC" (W.W. Fair), 221
HOLDEN, BARRY (I.T.A.A.), 261
HOLIDAY HOTEL (Reno), 147
HOLIDAY INNS INC., 90, 192
HOLIDAY INN (Reno), 147
HONESTY, LOSS OF, 26
HOPE, BOB, 143
HORNE, LINA, 274
HOWARD, KEY, 23
HUTTON, INA RAY (Big Band), 236
HYPNOTISM (Ted Boyer), 167

I

IDENTIFICATION, ESTABLISH OWN, 64-65
IMAGE, RETAIN, 25
IMPROVISATION, 30
INSTRUMENTS, THEFT OF, 127
INTERCOM, SOUND & LIGHTING STATIONS, 227
INTERNATIONAL CREATIVE MGT. (I.C.M.), 77, 153
INTERNATIONAL EXECUTIVE BOARD (I.E.B.), 243
INTERNATIONAL THEATRICAL AGENCIES ASSOC. (I.T.A.A.), 249, 254
    code of ethics adopted, 259; founding fathers, 254; meetings with A.F. of M., 257; board of directors, 1979 (picture), 259
IRVING, PETER DR. (Judy Garland), 14
"I'VE GOT A SECRET" (T.V. Show), 268

J

JACKSON, DAVE (I.T.A.A.), 254
JAMES, HARRY (Big Band), 147, 200, 236, 276
JAMES, SONNY, 144
JAY, JIMMY, 144
JENNINGS, WAYLON, 88, 144
JESSEL, GEORGIE, 275
JOHNSTON, CHARLEY (I.T.A.A.), 254
JORDAN, JO ANN, QUINTETTE, 148
JONES, JACK, 46
JOYCE, JOLLY, 87
JOYCE, NORMAN (I.T.A.A.), 254

K

KANE, WALTER (Hughes Hotels), 147
KAY, BILLY, 88

KAYE, MARY, TRIO, 87, 141, 147
KEIRNS, DON, 144
KENTON, STAN (Big Band), 240
KIM SISTERS, THE, 88
KING, CAROLE, 63, 100
KING, SONNY, 147
KINGS FOUR, THE, 88
KINGSTON TRIO, THE, 100
KIRBY, DURWOOD (Garry Moore), 270
KIRBY STONE FOUR (Group), 88
KLEIN, MARTY (A.P.A.), 228
KLONDIKE DAYS (Edmonton, Canada), 228
KNIGHT, GLADYS, & THE PIPS, 228
KNOTTS, DON, 36
KOPLAR, HAROLD, 278
KRAMER, NOEL, 87
KRUPA, GENE (Big Band), 236

L

LABERTO, ROY, 103
LAMB, CHARLEY, 144
LANE, ABBE, 148
LANE, DICK (Hilton), 147, 281
LANCERS, THE, 87
LANDRUM-GRIFFIN ACT, 241
LANSBURG, MORRIS, 70-72
LAS VEGAS
    lounges closed, 142, 145, 146; open lounges, 146, 147, 148
LAVENDER-BLAKE AGENCY, 144
LAYNE, CINDY, 148
LED ZEPPLIN (Rock Group), 88
LEE, BUDDY, AGENCY, 144
LEHR, ZELLA, 144
LEVIN, JULIUS J. (Bookie), 87, 275-281
"LEWIS & CLARK EXPEDITION" (Group), 88
LEWIS, JERRY, 86, 143
LEWIS, SAMMY, 275, 281
LIBERACE, 46-49, 88
LINKE, DICK (Andy Griffith), 36
LIVINGSTON, MARY (Mrs. Jack Benny), 80-81, 156
LOMBARDO, GUY, 215, 276
LOUNGES, TYPES OF
    Las Vegas, 87; coffee houses, 100; jazz, 100; dixieland, 102
LUNCEFORD, JIMMY (Big Band), 236
LUTZ, SAM (Welk), 59
LYNN, LORETTA, 89, 133
LYNN, ROBERTA, 87, 88
LYSDAHL, TORI, 88

M

M.C. ("Rapper") IMPORTANCE OF, 55
MAC FARLANE, DOUG (I.T.A.A.), 261
MAIN STREET SINGERS (Group), 88

MAIZE, JOE AND THE CHORDSMEN (Group), 87, 277
MANGIONE, CHUCK, 100
MANILOW, BARRY, 63, 210
MANSFIELD, JAYNE, 270
MAPES, CHARLES, 147
MAPES HOTEL (Reno), 147, 148
MARGARET, ANN, 88, 143
MARRIOTT HOTELS, 90
MARTIN, DEAN, 25, 48, 142, 143
MARTIN, KAY & HER BODYGUARDS (Group), 87, 148
MARTIN, STEVE, 25
MARTIN, TONY-CHARISSE, CYD, 81-83
MARTIN, TONY, 275
MATERIAL, CURRENT & TOPICAL, 34, 66
    obscene, 43
MATTON, BUD (I.T.A.A.), 261
MATYS BROTHERS (Group), 87
MAYO, PENNY, 87, 281
MC CONKEY, "MAC," 87
MC KENZIE, DON (I.T.A.A.), 261
MC MAHON, ED, 46
MEDIOCRITY, DANGERS OF 41, 64, 65
MERCER, BOBBY, ROADSHOW (Group), 88
METRO-GOLDWYN-MAYER (M.G.M.), 147
METRO-TONES, THE (Group), 87, 277
MILLER, GLEN (Big Band), 86, 215, 236
MILLER, JULIE, 88
MILLS, DAVE (I.T.A.A.), 254
MILSAP, RONNIE, 144
MINONE, WINGY, 103
MINSKY, HAROLD, 281
MOB, THE (Group), 88
MOFFETT, GEORGE, 144
MONTEREY ARTISTS, 153
MONEY TREE, THE (Reno), 147
MOORE, GARY, 268
MORIN, AUGIE (I.T.A.A.), 87, 254
MUGLESTONS, THE (Group), 88
MURRAY, ANNE, 144
MUS-ART CORPORATION OF AMERICA, 153
MUSICIAN, CANADIAN-U.S. TAXES, 260
MUSICIANS UNIONS (N.L.R.B.), 242
MUTUAL ENTERTAINMENT AGENCY, 73, 162, 166, 277
MYTHICAL STORY, DEMISE OF VEGAS LOUNGES, 145

N

NABORS, JIM, 36, 221, 230
NATIONAL ASSOC. OF ORCHESTRA LEADERS (N.A.O.L.), 240
NATIONAL LABOR RELATIONS BOARD (N.L.R.B.), 242, 243, 244

NEAL, SONNY (Wm. Morris), 144
NELSON, STAN (Trio), 88
NELSON, WILLIE, 88
NEWSPAPERS, SOURCE OF MATERIAL, 34-36
NEWTON, WAYNE
"Bookie" Levin, 275; Deauville Hotel-Miami, 68-73; Fremont Hotel (Vegas), 147; lounge beginnings, 88, 141, 143; Newton Bros.-lounge to main room, 73-77; super performer, 11
NICOLSON, CRAIG (I.T.A.A.), 259
NOBLE, LEIGHTON-JUDY GARLAND, 272
NOBLE, LEIGHTON, 14
NORTH, MIKE (I.C.M.), 144, 228
NORTH TEXAS STATE UNIV., 101
NOVELITES, THE, 87, 277

O

O'CONNELL, HELEN, 215
O'JAYS, THE, 88
OLIVIA NEWTON JOHN, 133, 144
OPUS VI (Group), 88
OSMONDS, THE, 228
ONSLOW HOTEL (Reno), 147
ORLANDO, TONY & DAWN, 216
ORIGINAL SONGS, LYRICS OF TODAY, 64
ORIGINAL SONGS, RECORD COMPANIES, 63
ORPHEUM CIRCUIT (Vaude Circuit), 62
OWNERS, KNOWLEDGE OF SHOW-BUSINESS
house policy, 177; attitude towards Artists, 183; attitude towards gratis rooms, 184

P

PABLO CRUISE, 88, 112, 133, 230
PACING OF SHOWS, 52-56
PALACE THEATRE, 62
PARAGON ARTISTS, 153
PARK TAHOE HOTEL, 147
PARTON, DOLLY, 88, 144, 230
PEDDIE, EDDIE and the ZANY-ACKS (Group), 87
PERFORMING MUSICIANS
agent relationship, 114-120; audience reaction, 133, 134; artist-owner relationship, 125-128; artist-customer relationship, 128-130; bass man, 94; costumes, 111; contracts, exclusive, 115-120; comedy material, 108; commissions, 120; cocktail lounge beginnings, 86; creative song writer, 132; dance music, showy, 134-136; drummer, 94; disco-canned & live, 103; front man ("rapper") importance, 106-109; guitarist, 92; girl singers, pros & cons, 95; groups, types (leadership or partners), 96-100;

house public address systems, 127; horn players, 95; hotels, motor inns, 90; instruments, theft, 127; keyboard-man (musical leader), 93; owner-artist relationship, 125-128; pacing of shows, dance sets, 106-108; plastic performance, 107; personnel, keep intact, 136, 137; personal managers, 120-121; pets, on road, 124; pictures, publicity importance, 112-114; rehearsals, 109-111; recording the group, 131-133; salary split, different methods, 96; sound of group, 91; show lounge groups, beginnings, 86; sidemen, hiring importance, 92; sidemen, hiring with wives & families, 92; trade magazines, importance of, 130, 131; trends, changing, 103-106; video-tape for critique, 134; wives and families, 121-125
PERSONAL MANAGERS, (Definition), 153
PETERSON, OSCAR, 88, 100
PETTY, FRED, 87
PHYSICAL LAYOUT, LOUNGES & CLUBS, 202
PICTURES, PROFESSIONAL, 41-43
PLASTIC PERFORMANCE, 18, 26
PRAGER, ARNE (I.T.A.A.), 87, 255, 257, 259
PRESLEY, ELVIS, 92, 133, 210
PRIDE, CHARLEY, 144
PREMIER ARTISTS, 153
PRIMA, LOUIS, 87, 103, 141, 147
PROPER KEYS, MUSICAL, 37, 38
PUBLICIST, IMPORTANCE OF, 25, 67, 68
PURCELL, TED (I.T.A.A.), 254, 257
PURPOSE OF BEING ON STAGE, 52

R

RANDLE, ANN (I.T.A.A.), 261
RAMADA INNS INC., 90, 192
RAYE, ART (I.T.A.A.), 87, 254
RECORD COMPANYS, WRITERS SEARCH, 63, 64
RECORD WORLD MAGAZINE, 130
REGENCY ARTISTS, 153
REYNOLDS, DEBBIE, 143
RICCI, MARLENE, 88
RICE, TANDY, 144
RICH, BUDDY, 200, 236
RICH, CHARLIE, 144, 228
RICKLES, DON, 87, 88, 141, 143, 147
RICK & NEAL (Group), 88
RIDDLE, MAJOR, 147, 166-169, 281
RIGHT TO WORK STATES, 241
RITZ BROS. 148, 275
RIVERIA HOTEL (Vegas) 147, 275
RIVERSIDE HOTEL (Reno), 147
ROBBINS, MARTY, 144
"ROCK & ROLL," ADVENT OF, 244
RODEWAY INNS INC., 90

ROGERS, KENNY
    early lounge beginnings, 88, 133, 141;
    country "crossover," 144; Golden Nugget
    (Vegas), 147; Fairs & Expos, 221
ROLLING STONES, THE, 88, 130
RONSTADT, LINDA, 144
ROONEY, MICKEY, 15
ROSS, JACK, 147
ROTHE, BILL (I.T.A.A.), 87
ROWEN & MARTIN, 88, 147
ROY ROGERS & DALE EVANS, 216, 219
RUPPERT, ALAN, 87
RUSSELL, PEE WEE, 103

S

SAHARA-RENO HOTEL, 147
SAHARA TAHOE HOTEL, 147
SANDLER & YOUNG, 22, 23
SANDS HOTEL (Vegas), 147
SCOBY, BOB (Dixieland), 103
SCRIBNER, RON (I.T.A.A.), 261
SEALS & CROFTS, 100
SEDAKA, NEIL, 63, 210, 216, 227, 230
SEMI-NAME ARTISTS, 182
SHELTON, DICK, 87, 257
SHORE, DINAH, 11, 68, 143
SHERATON HOTELS INC., 90
SHOW & BUSINESS, TWO WORDS, 26, 27
SHOW, LOUNGE GROUPS
    format, 30, 32, 52-56; outside direction, 37
SHY CLOWN, THE (Reno), 147
SIDROS ARMADA, with BEVERLY BROWN, 88
SILVER SLIPPER (Vegas), 147
SIMON AND GARFUNKLE, 88, 100
SINATRA, FRANK SR.,
    special appeal, 25, 46; seasoned
    performer, 143; "fun" in the casino
    lounges, 142; big band singer, 215; Frank
    Sinatra Jr., 266
SINATRA, FRANK JR., 88, 148, 266
SINGERS SUMMER WORKSHOP (Davidson), 43-46
SKELTON, RED, 143, 216
SKILLS, ADVANCE PREPARATION, 30, 31
SMITH, D.D., 88
SMITH, GLEN, 88
SMITH, KEELY, 87, 141, 147
SMOTHERS BROTHERS, 88, 100
SNYDER, TOM, 68
SONGS, PROPER KEYS, 37, 38
SOUL, DAVID (Starsky & Hutch), 66
SOUND, CONTROLLABLE AND UNCONTROLLABLE, 200
SOUND EQUIPMENT, 204
SPARKS NUGGET (Reno), 270
SPINNERS, THE, 88

SPOTLIGHTING, 205
STACEY, E.O. (I.C.M.), 144
STAGE, SIZE & TYPE, 203, 223-226
STAGE SOUND SCHEMATICS, 207, 208, 222-227
STATLER BROTHERS, 89
STELT, MILO, 87, 278
STEVENS, DICK, 87
STEVENS, RAY, 228
STEWART, GREG (C.W.S.F.), 230
STEWART, ROD, 112
STOKES, TERRY, 88
STREISAND-LIBERACE, 46, 49
SUBCONSCIOUS DELIVERY, 34
SULLIVAN, ED, 71
SULLIVAN, ED-SINATRA, FRANK JR., 266
SUN, JERRY, SHOW (Group), 88
SUPER-STARS, DIMINISHING, 142, 143
SWARTZ, HERB (Harrahs), 206

T

TAFT-HARTLEY ACT, 241, 249
TALK SHOWS, IMPORTANCE OF, 68
TATUM, ART, 100
TAYLOR, JAMES, 63, 100
TEAGARDEN, JACK, 103
TELEVISION, DEVELOPMENT OF STARS, 143
TEMPTATIONS, THE, 88
TEN COMMANDMENTS OF SHOW-BUSINESS, 24-27
THALER, HOWARD, (Attorney), 27
THOMAS, DANNY, 11, 57, 143
THOMAS, ROSEMARIE (Mrs. Danny Thomas), 57
THOMPSON, HANK, 240
THUNDERBIRD HOTEL (Vegas), 147
TILLUS, MEL, 88, 144, 219, 227, 230
TOPICAL MATERIAL, 34-36
TORRES, EDDIE, 281
TRACE, AL (Big Band), 277
TRENDS, ANTICIPATE, 26
TRENIERS, THE, 88
TUCKER, TANYA, 144, 228
TUNESMEN, THE, 88
TWITTY, CONWAY, 89
TYRALA, ROBERT (I.T.A.A.), 261

V

VAGABONDS, THE, 88
VALLEE, RUDY, 215
VAN DAMME, ART (Quintette), 277
VAN DYKE, DICK, 86
VAN DYKE, JERRY, 86, 88
VAN, BOBBY, 15

"SHOW-BUSINESS"

VAN ZEELAND, GARY (I.T.A.A.), 254, 255
VARIETY MAGAZINE, 130
VAUDEVILLE CIRCUITS, 62
VILLA HARRAH (Lake Tahoe), 82
VINCENT, BOB, 58, 237, 255
VINCENT, CINDY, 219
VINTON, BOBBY, 143, 146, 221, 228
VOGT, JACK (Harrahs), 206
VOICE, PROPER CONDITIONING, 37, 38

WARWICK, DION, 228
WEBB, CHICK (Big Band), 236
WEBB, JIM, 63
WELK, LAWRENCE, 56-59
WESTERN WASHINGTON FAIR, 220
WHITE, ROSS (I.T.A.A.), 257, 261
WIENER, FRANK (I.T.A.A.), 261
WILLIAMS, ANDY, 46, 143
WILLIAM MORRIS AGENCY, 153
WILIAMS, PAUL, 63

W

WAGNER, BILL (Architect), 274
WAKELY, JIMMY, 148
WALTERS, LOU, 62
WAR (Rock Group), 88
WARREN, RUSTY, 147

Z

ZANY-ACKS, THE (Group), 87, 277
ZARAS, THE (Group), 88
ZENTNER, SY (Big Band), 240
ZIEGFIELD, FLO, 62
ZUCKER, STAN, 87